DATE DUE

Demco, Inc. 38-293

The One God

To Angie

The One God

*A Critically Developed Evangelical
Doctrine of Trinitarian Unity*

Michael L. Chiavone

©

James Clarke & Co

James Clarke & Co
P.O. Box 60
Cambridge
CB1 2NT
United Kingdom

www.jamesclarke.co

publishing@jamesclarke.co

ISBN: 978 0 227 17362 6

British Library Cataloguing in Publication Data
A record is available from the British Library

Published by arrangement with Pickwick Publications,
a division of Wipf and Stock Publishers.
First published by James Clarke & Co, 2011.

Contents

Acknowledgments

SPECIAL THANKS ARE OWED to Frank Sirianni, Bob Cole, and Josh Williams, who served as sounding boards for ideas throughout my doctoral work, to Steven McKinion, whose interest in Patristic work on the Trinity and Christology was contagious, to John Sailhamer, who taught me how to read again, and to Sam Williams, who provided wise counsel about the relationship between God's gifts and God's call.

Abbreviations

ANF   *The Ante-Nicene Fathers*. Edited by Alexander Roberts and
       James Donaldson. 10 vols. Buffalo: Christian Literature,
       1885–1887. Reprint, Peabody, MA: Hendrickson, 1994.

BE   Albright, Carol Rausch and Joel Haugen, ed. *Beginning with*
       the End: God, Science, and Wolfhart Pannenberg. Chicago:
       Open Court, 1997.

BF   Aquinas, Thomas. *Summa Theologiae*. 60 vols. Blackfriars.
       New York: McGraw Hill, 1964–66.

NPNF[1] *The Nicene and Post-Nicene Fathers*, Series 1. Edited by
       Philip Schaff. 14 vols. New York: Christian Literature,
       1886–1889. Reprint, Peabody, MA: Hendrickson, 1994.

NPNF[2] *The Nicene and Post-Nicene Fathers*, Series 2. Edited by
       Philip Schaff and Henry Wace. 14 vols. New York: Christian
       Literature, 1890–1898. Reprint, Peabody, MA: Hendrickson,
       1999.

PG   *Patrologia Graecae*. Edited by J. P. Migne. 162 vols. Paris,
       1857–1886.

1

Introduction to the Doctrine of Trinitarian Unity

THE DOCTRINE OF THE Trinity, the belief that there is one God who is in some sense three, is perhaps the most distinctive doctrine of Christianity. This belief quickly found doxological expression in the worship of the early church and theological expression in the summary that God was one essence (*ousia/substantia/natura/essentia*) and three persons (*hypostaseis/persona*), a formula which grounded both the unity and diversity of God throughout the Middle Ages.[1] While interest in the doctrine of the Trinity waned during the Enlightenment, recent theology, beginning with the work of Karl Barth, has experienced renewed interest in this doctrine, as several authors have noted.[2]

This renewed interest has caused numerous authors to criticize the classical form of the doctrine, in large part because the Christian metaphysical consensus which gave support to the ancient trinitarian formula no longer exists.[3] This leads to a difficulty for contemporary Christians which Millard Erickson characterizes aptly:

> The formula was worked out quite definitely in the fourth century. God is one substance or essence, existing in three persons. The difficulty is that we do not know exactly what these terms mean. We know that the doctrine states that God is three in some respect

1. Such language is seen as early as Tertullian, *Adversus Praxean* 2, 25 (*ANF* 3:598, 621). On the Greek side, the Cappadocians are usually credited with first consistently distinguishing three *hypostaseis* and one *ousia*. See Gregory Nazianzen, *Orations* 21 (*NPNF2* 7:279), where he equates *hypostasis* with the Latin *persona*.

2. Barth, *Church Dogmatics*, vol. 1/1, *The Doctrine of the Word of God*. This trend is noted in Erickson, *God in Three Persons*, 13; Fox, *God as Communion*, 25–26; Schwöbel, *Persons, Divine and Human*, 10–11.

3. Peters, "Trinity Talk: Part 1," 44; Peters, *God as Trinity*, 30–33; Wilks, "The Trinitarian Ontology of John Zizioulas," 83; Badcock, *Light of Truth and Fire of Love*, 1997, 175–77; Erickson, *God in Three Persons*, 211.

and one in some other respect, but we do not know precisely what those two different respects are.[4]

Recent theologians have therefore attempted to gain an understanding of the respects in which God is one and three.

Such efforts have two related sides. They must develop an understanding of what is three about God to provide a meaning, or an alternative, for the term "person" in trinitarian discourse, and must also do the same thing for what is one about God and the term "essence." This text will examine the work of four selected theologians in regard to the latter task, that of defining the unity of the trinitarian God, and will attempt to draw from them elements for a successful evangelical doctrine of trinitarian unity.[5] Then, it will offer a proposal for how evangelical Christians ought to understand the Triune God to be one.

Each of the four theologians selected, Karl Rahner, Millard Erickson, John Zizioulas, and Wolfhart Pannenberg, represents a distinct tradition within contemporary Christendom and has contributed to the doctrine of the Trinity.[6] Rahner's rule for contemplating the Trinity, "*The 'economic' Trinity is the 'immanent' Trinity and the 'immanent' Trinity is the 'economic' Trinity*,"[7] has influenced the discussion of the Trinity since its publication. Gregory Havrilak notes Rahner's contribution to Roman Catholic theology in general and the doctrine of the Trinity in particular, stating "Karl Rahner is without question one of the most important and influential Roman Catholic theologians of the twentieth century. . . . Following Barth,

4. Erickson, *God in Three Persons*, 19; cf. 132. Note that Erickson recognizes the relationship between language and reality. The question of the meaning of essence is not a different question than the question of how God is one.

5. Obviously, these two aspects cannot be severed. However, the primary focus of this text is on trinitarian unity, and the question of persons will be touched on only as it relates to unity.

6. Veli-Matti Kärkkäinen, for example, notes that all four of these theologians have contributed to the doctrine of the Trinity in his *Doctrine of God*. Major contributions by these authors include Rahner, *Trinity*; Rahner, "Remarks on the Dogmatic Treatise 'De Trinitate'" in *Theological Investigations*, vol. 4; Erickson, *God in Three Persons*; Zizioulas, *Being as Communion*; Zizioulas, "On Being a Person"; Zizioulas, "Communion and Otherness," 347–61; Zizioulas, "Human Capacity and Human Incapacity," 401–48; and Pannenberg, *Metaphysics and the Idea of God*; Pannenberg, *Systematic Theology*.

7. Rahner, *Trinity*, 22.

Rahner's classic work *The Trinity* appeared as the most innovative contribution to trinitarian theology until the advent of Moltmann."[8]

Erickson, a former student of Pannenberg's, has written extensively about theology proper and the doctrine of the Trinity from the evangelical perspective. In addition to a well-used text on systematic theology, Erickson has recently written three volumes presenting contemporary interpretations of the Trinity, Christology, and the divine attributes.[9]

Zizioulas is concerned in his writings primarily with ecclesiology. However, he sees the basis for ecclesiology, and indeed all of Christian life, in the Trinity. As he puts it, "Orthodoxy concerning the being of God is not a luxury for the Church and for man: it is an existential necessity."[10] As a Greek Orthodox, he seeks to draw heavily from the Eastern tradition, and his work on the Trinity is seen by some to epitomize the contemporary form of that tradition.[11]

Pannenberg has sought to restore a strong metaphysical basis for theology, and has both criticized the classical metaphysics of the Fathers and developed one of his own.[12] He interacts critically with a wide variety of theologians, both ancient and contemporary. He makes a unique contribution to the doctrine of the Trinity by drawing on modern physics and the concept of a field in discussing the one essence of the Triune God.[13]

There is much to be commended in the work of these authors, and indeed, in the work of the many authors who have furthered trinitarian studies in the recent past. However, these four authors, along with all of the scholarship they represent, present a problem to the Christian believer, because they show considerable disagreement as to how the God of the Bible, while Triune, is, in fact, one. This text attempts to help settle that disagreement by determining which, if any, of the four positions presented within are acceptable and, if none are,

8. Havrilak, "Karl Rahner and the Greek Trinity," 61.

9. Erickson, *God in Three Persons*; Erickson, *Word Became Flesh*; Erickson, *God the Father Almighty*.

10. Zizioulas, *Being as Communion*, 15.

11. See, for example, Collins, *Trinitarian Theology: West and East*; Thompson, *Modern Trinitarian Perspectives*, 143.

12. Pannenberg, *Metaphysics*, 3–6; Pannenberg, *Systematic Theology*, 1:128; Schwöbel, "Rational Theology in Trinitarian Perspective," 526.

13. Pannenberg, *Systematic Theology*, 1:382–83.

what positive elements can be taken from them to help construct an evangelical doctrine of the Trinity.

The position of each of these theologians will be examined in two stages. First, each author's understanding of divine unity will be presented. Where it is relevant, information regarding methodology and presuppositions will also be included. Then, that understanding of divine unity will be subjected to several critiques, some original to this text and some from other sources.

Historical critiques will be offered in light of the historical development of the doctrine of the Trinity, particularly when the author in question claims to draw upon a particular author or tradition for support. For example, Zizioulas consistently associates his position with that of the Cappadocians.[14] Thus, the question of whether he accurately portrays and develops the Cappadocian understanding of divine unity is a valid one. While no historical position will be afforded normativity, positions at variance with such historical milestones as the Council of Nicaea, the writings of Athanasius, and the work of the Cappadocians will be seen as having the burden of proof.[15]

Philosophical critiques will consider the coherence and consistency of each position. As much as is possible, these critiques will be made from within the system in question. Therefore Pannenberg's futurist ontology will not be critiqued from the perspective of a Platonic idealism.

Theological critiques will question whether a position is biblically adequate and whether it can be integrated into a full doctrine of God. The first aspect is warranted because biblical faithfulness is the *sine qua non* of an evangelical theology. The second aspect is necessary because, as Gerald Bray has noted, many contemporary theologies, in breaking with classical

---

14. For example, Zizoulas, *Being as Communion*, 17–18, 35–40, 88; Zizioulas, "Church as Communion," 7–8; Zizioulas, "On Being a Person," 40.

15. These writings, and the Nicene Creed in particular, are generally viewed as authentic expressions of the Christian teaching about God. Timothy Bartel, who believes he breaks with Augustine and Aquinas, believes agreement with Nicaea is sufficient historical validation of a doctrine of the Trinity. Bartel, "Plight of the Relative Trinitarian," 151–53. Thompson cites the British Council of Churches, which stated, "There was remarkable unanimity in the Study Commission in looking for resources to the three Cappadocian Fathers." British Council of Churches, *The Forgotten Trinity*, vol. 1, Report of the BCC Study Commission on Trinitarian Doctrine Today, 21; quoted in Thompson, *Modern Trinitarian Perspectives*, 126.

trinitarian metaphysics, have failed to consider the implications of this breach for the rest of their theology.[16]

The final potential area of critique will be Christological. The trinitarian and Christological questions are intimately related.[17] The church Fathers, beginning with Tertullian, have used similar language and reasoning to settle the trinitarian and Christological difficulties of unity and diversity, so Christological critiques will examine whether an understanding of divine unity can coherently be translated into Christological diversity.[18] The Christology officially sanctioned by the Council of Chalcedon will serve as a generally recognized benchmark in this regard.[19] As Erickson states, "The council affirmed the Nicene Creed, and issued a statement that was to become the standard for all of Christendom."[20]

This process, executed upon the position of each of the four selected authors, will attempt to winnow the wheat from the chaff. It will be found that none of the understandings of trinitarian unity presented here can be accepted as-is, but that positive elements found in each system, which survive the critical process, can serve as a foundation for developing an evangelical understanding of trinitarian unity which is historically based, biblically and theologically adequate, philosophically coherent, and Christologically orthodox. The final chapter will set forth such an understanding.

CRITICAL BACKGROUND

This text is a critical study, and as such requires criteria against which positions can be evaluated. This section will serve to set forth those criteria. It will begin with an historical survey of the doctrine of trinitarian unity. Special attention will be given to teachings of the Council of Nicaea and

16.. Bray, *Doctrine of God*, 61.

17. Welch, *In This Name*, 240–41.

18. Tertullian, *Prax.* 25 (*ANF* 3:624); Porter, "On Keeping 'Persons' in the Trinity," 532n4; van Inwagen, "And Yet They Are Not Three Gods But One God," 248; Hill, *Three-Personed God*, 271; Hopko, "Trinity in the Cappadocians," 267.

19. For an excellent brief presentation of both the key documents behind and the text of the Definition of Chalcedon, see Bettenson, *Documents of the Christian Church*, 46–48.

20. Erickson, *Christian Theology*, 746. See also Erickson, "Evangelical Christology and Soteriology Today," 256. The definition carries particular authority among Catholics. See Doud, "Rahner's Christology," 144.

the Nicene Creed. Next, it will present background for the theological critique by examining the biblical teaching on the unity of God and the traditional connection between the nature of God and the divine attributes. Finally, it will present the Christological teaching of the Council of Chalcedon, so that the Christological implications of the views of trinitarian unity presented may be compared against this standard. Because no external philosophical standard will be imposed upon the positions, aside from standard considerations of coherence and consistency, no background information for the philosophical critiques will be presented.[21]

Historical Background

Key figures in the historical development of the doctrine of the unity of God will now be surveyed.[22] Several conclusions will arise from this study. First, the doctrine of divine unity was believed to be one of biblical necessity and not a conclusion of external philosophy. Second, Christian tradition generally trended towards stronger expressions of divine unity over time. Third, theologians generally sought to express the unity of God in several ways; the true unity of God was not an isolated aspect of the deity. Fourth, authors were not always consistent, either with themselves or with one another, in their referent for the phrase "The One God." The final conclusion will be that the dominant historical view, seen in Tertullian and traced through Nicaea and into the Cappadocians, Augustine, Aquinas, and Barth, is that the one essence of God is a genuine *res*, an actuality of which there is only one for the three persons of the Godhead.

Before Nicaea

The Apostolic Fathers are generally content to express their understanding of divine unity with biblical trinitarian formulae.[23] Geoffrey Bromiley notes that, "Only at isolated points do these authors engage in anything approaching technical theology."[24] Without giving much in the way of explanation, they insist that God is one, and that it is appropri-

---

21. For arguments for the need for theology to be rationally consistent, see Clark, *Trinity*, 88–89; Erickson, *Making Sense of the Trinity*, 43–44.

22. For other recent surveys, see Olson and Hall, *Trinity*; Hill, *Three-Personed God*.

23. For example, *1 Clement* 42 (*ANF* 1:16); Polycarp, *To the Philippians* 12 (*ANF* 1:35); Ignatius, *To the Magnesians* 13 (*ANF* 1:65).

24. Bromiley, *Historical Theology*, 3.

ate to worship Christ.[25] It is clear that they generally think of "God" as referring to the Father, as *2 Clement* illustrates well, praising, "the only God invisible, the Father of truth, who sent forth to us the Saviour and Prince of incorruption."[26] Yet, like the rest of the Apostolic Fathers, he can juxtapose against this that "it is fitting that you should think of Jesus Christ as of God."[27]

It is in the Apologists that reasonable explanations for monotheists worshiping Christ begin to emerge. Justin's *Dialogue with Trypho* is an example. Justin begins with wholehearted agreement with Old Testament monotheism, stating, "There will be no other God, O Trypho, nor was there from eternity any other existing . . . but He who made and disposed all this universe."[28] However, he goes on to demonstrate, still relying on the Old Testament, that "He who is said to have appeared to Abraham, and to Jacob, and to Moses, and who is called God, is distinct from Him who made all things,—numerically, I mean, not [distinct] in will."[29] For Justin, then, God is one because the Son only does what the Father wills, even though he is "another God."[30] Justin also introduces analogies for the begetting of the Son. As a word spoken does not deprive the mind of thought, or fire kindled deprive its source of fire, so the Son is begotten without diminution of the Father.[31] While Justin is not successful in developing a clear doctrine of the unity of God, he fervently attempts to do so from the Bible.[32]

Like Justin, Irenaeus approaches the trinitarian question believing "in one God, the Father Almighty, Maker of heaven, and earth, and the sea, and all things that are in them; and in one Christ Jesus, the Son of God, who became incarnate for our salvation; and in the Holy Spirit, who proclaimed through the prophets the dispensations of God."[33] There is one God because there is the Father. Irenaeus sees several elements,

25. Olson and Hall, *Trinity*, 20; Kärkkäinen, *Doctrine of God*, 70.

26. *2 Clement* 20 (*ANF* 7:523).

27. *2 Clement* 1 (*ANF* 7:517).

28. Justin, *Dialogus cum Tryphone* 11 (*ANF* 1:199).

29. Ibid., 56 (*ANF* 1:223). Unity of will here means obedience.

30. Ibid.

31. Ibid., 61 (*ANF* 1:227). This is also used and explained in Tatian, *Oratio ad Graecos* 5 (*ANF* 2:67).

32. This is also the conclusion of Bromiley. Bromiley, *Historical Theology*, 16–17.

33. Irenaeus, *Adversus haereses* 1.10.1 (*ANF* 1:330).

however, that assure the unity of the Son and Spirit with the Father, and therefore of God. He notes the extensive Old Testament references by the Holy Spirit to the One God.[34] Like Justin, he believes that, because the Son is the instrument of the Father's will and God does not need tools, there is unity.[35] Irenaeus also argues that, because of God's simplicity, which means he is entirely thinking, and his immensity, which means he contains all things, God's expressed Word cannot go otherwhere than God, so that the Word remains in the Father, and therefore one with God.[36] He expresses the same thought elsewhere, stating that "God being all Mind, and all Logos, both speaks exactly what He thinks, and thinks exactly what He speaks. For His thought is Logos, and Logos is Mind, and Mind comprehending all things is the Father Himself."[37] Thus, while Justin had difficulty maintaining unity in light of diversity, Irenaeus seems in danger of uniting the Son with the Father by reducing the Son to a faculty or property of the Father.

Clement of Alexandria seems to present a more balanced view of the divine unity, though it may not be coherent. He remains grounded in the Bible; his works in the *Ante-Nicene Fathers* cite 31 books of the Old Testament and every book of the New Testament save Philemon, 2 John, and 3 John.[38] He makes clear that the unity of God is not a bare philosophical solitude, writing, "God is one, and beyond the one and above the Monad itself."[39] At times, he refers to the Father as the one God, writing about the ascending nature of beings that "the nature of the Son, which is nearest to Him who is alone the Almighty One, is the most perfect."[40] At other times he calls the Son God, referring to him as "the holy God Jesus" and "the God who, before the foundation of the world, was the counsellor of the Father."[41] Yet he also occasionally seems to suggest that it is not either one alone who is God, but the two of them together. He writes, "So that it is veritably clear that the God of all is only one good, just Creator,

---

34. Ibid., 3.6 (*ANF* 1:418–20); Robert Letham also notes Irenaeus's biblical emphasis on unity in *Holy Trinity*.

35. Irenaeus, *Haer.* 2.2.3–5 (*ANF* 1:361).

36. Ibid., 2.13.3–6 (*ANF* 1:374).

37. Ibid., 2.28.5 (*ANF* 1:400).

38. From the index, *ANF* 2:623–29.

39. Clement of Alexandria, *Paedagogus* 1.8 (*ANF* 2:227).

40. Clement of Alexandria, *Stromata* 7.2 (*ANF* 2:524).

41. Clement of Alexandria, *Paed.* 1.7 (*ANF* 2:223); *Strom.* 7.2 (*ANF* 2:524).

and the Son in the Father," and "the Father of all alone is perfect, for the Son is in Him, and the Father is in the Son."[42] Clement also notes the united work of the three.[43] Thus, he sees a unity of interpenetration and cooperation, and hints that the presence of the Son is as important to the Father's deity as the Father is to the Son's.

Clement is also important because he provides an early instance of a term that will later become important, *homoousios*, when he writes, "But God has no natural relation to us, as the authors of the heresies will have it . . . unless we shall dare to say that we are a part of Him, and of the same essence as God."[44] While Stead groups this usage with that of Irenaeus, and suggests that it carries the meaning "belonging to the same order of being,"[45] the context, in which Clement argues this would mean that part of God sinned, suggests the last two phrases are in apposition; to be *homoousios* with something means to be part of it.

Clement does not use *homoousios* to describe God, and therefore does not make the Son and Spirit parts of God. Tertullian, however, does exactly that. With language which will become definitive in the future, he confesses belief in "three *Persons* . . . three, however, not in condition, but in degree; not in substance, but in form; not in power, but in aspect; yet of one substance, and of one condition, and of one power, inasmuch as He is one God, from whom these degrees and forms and aspects are reckoned, under the name of the Father, and of the Son, and of the Holy Ghost."[46]

Tertullian sees the distinction between the three persons and the *una substantia* reflected in John 10:30, in which John uses the neuter, *unum*, rather than *unus*. What is one is not personal, but impersonal substance.[47] This substance, which is spirit, is the material of which God is made, and is, in the words of R. P. C. Hanson, "a kind of thinking gas."[48] Thus there is a substance, spirit, which God is, of which "the Father is the entire substance, but the Son is a derivation and portion of the whole."[49]

42. Clement of Alexandria, *Paed.* 1.8, 1.7 (*ANF* 2:228, 222).

43. Ibid., 1.6 (*ANF* 2:220).

44. Clement of Alexandria, *Strom.* 2.16 (*ANF* 2:364).

45. Stead, *Divine Substance*), 206–9.

46. Tertullian, *Prax.* 2 (*ANF* 3:598), emphasis original, as it will be in all quota-tions.

47. Ibid., 22 (*ANF* 3:618).

48. Ibid., 7 (*ANF* 3:602); Hanson, *Search*, 184.

49. Tertullian, *Prax.* 9 (*ANF* 3:603–4). Immediately after this, the editors add a note pointing out the imprecision, but orthodoxy, of this passage in light of later orthodoxy.

Tertullian is not opposed to the gnostic concept of prolation in the generation of the Son; it is the separation the gnostics taught which he rejects. To counter this implication, he illustrates the generation of the Son with several natural analogies. The Father puts forth the Son as root puts forth tree, fountain produces river, and sun emits ray. In these analogies, as in God, there is source without separation.[50]

In addition to asserting the *una substantia* of God, Tertullian seeks to secure unity with the concept of monarchy. Just as a monarch can have a son without endangering his rule, so the Son of God serves to bolster and support the one rule of God the Father.[51] He also develops the linguistic argument that the Son is essential to the Father, for a Son makes a Father as much as a Father makes a Son.[52] There is therefore interdependence in God. Tertullian provides terminology for the oneness and threeness of God and adds to the previous unity of operation and interpenetration a clear belief that there is *unum res* that is God, the substance spirit.

No survey of pre-Nicene theology could be complete without an examination of the ideas of Origen. Much that Origen believes about the unity of God has been mentioned before. He shows a clear subordination of the Son and the Spirit to their source, the Father, though the Son and Spirit retain the Father's nature.[53] He stresses the coordinated operation of the three, and the fact that the Son, as the Father's wisdom and power, is eternally in the Father.[54] He also advances the argument that the Father, to be ever Father, must have ever had a Son.[55]

Origen's greatest contribution to the doctrine of God's unity, however, is his emphasis on the radical consequences of the incorporeal nature of God. Far from Tertullian, who granted God a body, Origen hints at, but does not fully accept, the consequences of belief in a God with

---

50. Ibid., 8 (*ANF* 3:602–3).

51. Ibid., 3–4 (*ANF* 3:599–600).

52. Ibid., 10 (*ANF* 3:604–5).

53. Origen, *De principiis* 1.2.13 (*ANF* 4:251), *Fragmenta in evangelium Joannis* 2.2 (*ANF* 9:323). Henri Crouzel denies that Origen is inappropriately subordinationist in *Origen*, 181–204, 268.

54. Origen, *Princ.* 1.2.2, 1.2.10 (*ANF* 4:246, 250) Wolfson sees Origen teaching unity of genus and of rule. Wolfson, *The Philosophy of the Church Fathers*, 1:322.

55. Origen, *Princ.* 1.2.3 (*ANF* 4:246). Behr places great emphasis on this point in Origen. Behr, *The Way to Nicaea*, 185.

simple mental existence.[56] He does suggest the conclusion later trinitarians will draw, however, when he writes, "God is not a part, so neither is He properly the whole, since the whole is composed of parts; and reason will not allow us to believe that the God who is over all is composed of parts, each one of which cannot do what all the other parts can."[57] Origen also anticipates further trinitarian thought by his use of *homoousios*, a key term of the Nicene Creed, to which this discussion now turns.[58]

The Nicene Creed

If there is a universally recognized standard for Christian orthodoxy, it is the Nicene Creed, which is "the most universally accepted Christian creed."[59] The Council of Nicaea was convened in 325 in response to the Arian controversy, and produced the Nicene Creed:

> We believe in one God the Father All-sovereign, maker of all things visible and invisible;
>
> And in one Lord Jesus Christ, the Son of God, *begotten of the Father*, only-begotten, *that is, of the substance of the Father*, God of God, Light of Light, *true God of true God*, *begotten not made, of one substance with the Father*, through whom all things were made, *things in heaven and things on the earth*; who for us men and for our salvation *came down* and was made flesh, *and became man*, suffered, and rose on the third day, ascended into the heavens, is coming to judge the living and dead.
>
> And in the Holy Spirit.
>
> And those that say 'There was when he was not,'
>> and, 'Before he was begotten he was not,'
>> and that, 'He came into being from what-is-not,'
> or those that allege, that the son of God is
>> 'Of another substance or essence'
>> or 'created'
>> or 'changeable'
>> or 'alterable,'
> these the Catholic and Apostolic Church anathematizes.[60]

56. Origen, *Princ.* 1.1.4–9 (*ANF* 4:243–45).

57. Origen, *Contra Celsum* 1.23 (*ANF* 4:406). See also *Princ.* 4.1.32, 4.1.28 (*ANF* 4:379, 376).

58. For a defense of Origen's use of the term, see Stead, *Divine Substance*, 211.

59. González, *The Story of Christianity*, 1:165. See also Schaff, *The Creeds of Christendom*, 1:24.

60. Translation and format from Bettenson, *Documents of the Christian Church*, 25. Italics original, indicating alterations from Eusebius's proposed creed. For thor-

This creed, though it has been slightly revised, has been consistently respected and affirmed by later ecumenical councils.[61]

For centuries, the Nicene Creed, and especially the term *homoousios*, translated "of one substance" above, was viewed by the majority of scholars as asserting a numerical identity of the essence of Father and Son.[62] Archibald Robertson represents this position when he writes, "The conclusion is that in their original sense the definitions of Nicaea assert not merely the *specific* identity of the Son with the Father . . . but the full unbroken continuation of the Being of the Father in the Son, the inseparable unity of the Son with the Father in the Oneness of the Godhead. . . . The Nicene definition in this sense emphasized the *unity* of the Godhead in Three Persons, against the Arian *division* of the Son from the Father."[63] According to this view, the Nicene Creed, and the term *homoousios* in particular, affirm that there is one object, God, which the Father and Son, and by extension, the Holy Spirit, are.

Despite the prevalence of this view, many contemporary scholars oppose it, effectively denying that Nicaea dealt with the unity of God. J. N. D. Kelly, for example, while acknowledging that *homoousios* in the end requires an interpretation in terms of divine unity, states that "there are the strongest possible reasons for doubting" that this is the meaning in the Nicene Creed.[64] Stead agrees that it is wrong to impose the received understanding of Nicaea on the creed itself.[65] Nicaea meant to assert the full equality of the Son with the Father, not their unity.[66]

---

ough discussions of the Arian controversy, see Williams, *Arius: Heresy and Tradition*; Kannengiesser, *Arius and Athanasius*.

61. For example, *The Council of Ephesus: Extracts from the Acts*, Session 1 (*NPNF2* 14:199); *The Definition of Faith of the Council of Chalcedon*, (*NPNF2* 14:262–63); For the revised form of the creed, the Niceno-Constantinopolitan, see Bettenson, *Documents of the Christian Church*, 26; Schaff, *Creeds of Christendom*, 28–29.

62. Kelly, *Early Christian Doctrines*, 234.

63. Robertson, introduction to *Athanasius* (*NPNF2* xxxii), emphasis original. See also Wolfson, *Philosophy of the Church Fathers*, 335, 352; *Augsburg Confession*, Art. 1; Clark, *Trinity*, 113; Hill, *Three-Personed God*, 220.

64. Kelly, *Early Christian Doctrines*, 234.

65. Stead, *Divine Substance*, 251.

66. Bartel, "Relative Trinitarian," 152; Stead, *Philosophy in Christian Antiquity*; Wiles, *Making of Christian Doctrine*, 130–31.

It does seem true that the unity of God was not an explicit issue at Nicaea.[67] The council was dealing with Arianism, and the Creed was meant to deal with that specific issue. Yet the reason that unity was not an explicit issue is that it was assumed by all parties; no one at the council believed there could be more than one God,[68] especially Arius.[69] Four lines of evidence indicate that the authors of the Creed intended it to teach both the unity and equality of the Son with the Father. The prior ecclesiastical usage of *homoousios*, Arius's use of the term, Athanasius's teachings, and the reaction of the *homoiousians* all suggest that the term included, in the minds of those at the council, the concept of unity.[70] These four lines of evidence will now be presented.

The term *homoousios* did not first appear at the council, but had been used with a variety of meanings in prior writings.[71] Kelly's first evidence for refuting the traditional understanding of the creed is that *homoousios* "in both its secular and its theological usage prior to Nicaea . . . always conveyed, primarily at any rate, the 'generic' sense."[72] There are certainly cases where that is its meaning, as in Irenaeus.[73] Yet it has already been shown that Clement of Alexandria did not use such a generic definition, but that of the relation of parts to a whole.[74] Similarly, its use by the two Dionysiuses in the middle of the third century suggests that it should be understood in terms of unity and derivation.[75] Dionysius of Rome writes against those who "divide the holy unity into three different substances, absolutely separated from one another. For it is essential that the Divine Trinity should be reduced and gathered into one, as if into a certain

---

67. Weinandy, *Father's Spirit of Sonship*, 11.

68. Ibid., 57; Wiles, *Making of Christian Doctrine*, 144–45.

69. Kelly, *Early Christian Doctrines*, 57; Williams, *Arius*, 97.

70. The vagueness of Constantine is sometimes pointed to as countervailing evidence. See Kelly, *Early Christian Doctrines*, 237. However, it was the council, after debate and consideration, that approved the *homoousios*, and therefore their intent that is definitive. See Williams, *Arius*, 69; Hanson, *Search*, 162.

71. Hanson, *Search*, 190–97; Stead, *Divine Substance*, 190–214; Hill, *Three-Personed God*, 46.

72. Kelly, *Early Christian Doctrines*, 235.

73. Irenaeus, *Haer.* 1.5.1, 1.5.5, 1.5.6 (*ANF* 1:322, 323). This is also Stead's interpretation, *Divine Substance*, 193.

74. Clement of Alexandria, *Strom.* 2.16 (*ANF* 2:364). For analysis, see p. 8–9 above.

75. Robertson, introduction to *Athanasius* (*NPNF2* 4:xxxii).

head—that is, into the omnipotent God of all."[76] Dionysius of Alexander denies that he does "not maintain that Christ is consubstantial with God," and proves his agreement with *homoousios* with the analogies of the seed and the plant and the spring and the river.[77] The similarity of these analogies to those of Tertullian, who clearly affirmed a singular divine essence, cannot be ignored.[78] The Council of Antioch in 270 condemned the term *homoousios* as it was used by Paul of Samosata, who apparently had used "this term to make the *Logos* a mere attribute of God at work in Christ."[79] If this is true, the term carries the meaning of unity rather than of equality. Thus, it seems that in the sixty years prior to the Council of Nicaea, *homoousios* was understood in East and West as meaning united in nature, and an exaggerated form of that definition had been condemned.

Athanasius states that *homoousios* was included in the Nicene Creed to detect the Arians, who could agree to any other language, and "as a bulwark against their irreligious notions one and all."[80] This was possible because it was a term with which Arius had specifically disagreed in the *Thalia*, stating of the Son, "For he is not equal, no, nor one in essence with Him."[81] If the Nicene *homoousios* was meant to specifically reject Arius, then the Fathers at Nicaea had to mean by *homoousios* what Arius had meant.

What Arius meant by it seems rather clear. In his confession to Alexander, Arius asserts that the Son is an offspring, but not a Valentinian prolation, "nor as Manichaeus taught that the offspring was a portion of the Father, one in essence."[82] Arius both denies the concept of prolation, which Tertullian affirmed, as long as it was understood to be without separation, and places belief in the Son as a portion of the Father in apposition to *homoousios*. Arius had originated the controversy by accusing Alexander

76. Dionysius of Rome, *Against the Sabellians* 1 (*ANF* 7:365).

77. Dionysius of Alexandria, *Fragment* 1.6 (*ANF* 6:92). Kelly calls his judgment into question here, stating that Dionysius equated *homoousios* with homogenous.

78. Cf. pp. 9–10 above; Tertullian, *Prax.* 8 (*ANF* 3:602–3).

79. Hill, *Three-Personed God*, 45. See also O'Carroll, *Trinitas*, 78.

80. Athanasius, *De synodis* 45 (*NPNF2* 4:474); Williams notes Eusebius of Nicomedia's opposition to the term, *Arius*, 68–69.

81. Athanasius, *Syn.* 15 (*NPNF2* 4:457). Hanson believes that Athanasius is accurate in his representation of Arius. See Hanson, *Search*, 15.

82. Athanasius, *Syn.* 16 (*NPNF2* 4:458).

"of Sabellianism because he insisted on the unity of the Triad."[83] The Arian party at the council saw the *homoousios* as a "blasphemously materialistic" assertion of the Son's unity with the Father.[84] Arius rejected unity, so the Nicene Creed, to refute Arius, could be expected to affirm unity.

Arius and the like-minded saw the *homoousios* as an assertion of the Son's unity with the Father because of the clear distinction all parties drew between the created and the uncreated. If the Son is not created, he is uncreated. Yet there is only one unoriginated principle in the universe.[85] Thus if the Son has an uncreated nature like the Father, he has the uncreated nature of the Father. Equality entails unity, so Arius denied both, and the council affirmed both, by their respective positions towards *homoousios*.

Athanasius shares this line of reasoning, and states that it was the intention of the Council of Nicaea to assert the unity of Father and Son with the term *homoousios*:

> For bodies which are like each other may be separated and become at distances from each other, as are human sons relatively to their parents . . . but since the generation of the Son from the Father is not according to the nature of men, and not only like, but inseparable from the essence of the Father, and He and the Father are one, as He has said Himself, and the Word is ever in the Father and the Father in the Word, as the radiance stands towards the light . . . therefore the Council, as understanding this, suitably wrote "one in essence," that they might both defeat the perverseness of the heretics, and shew that the Word was other than originated things.[86]

The Son is not an originated thing, and therefore must be generated from the Father. Yet because the Father is God, the generation of the Son cannot result in separation. Athanasius maintains the same argument in *De synodis* 48, claiming that the Son must either be the work of or the essence of the Father; there is no other type of reality.[87]

Kelly acknowledges that Athanasius asserts that the Nicene Creed intended to establish the unity of God. "But this was a politically mislead-

83. Kelly, *Early Christian Doctrines*, 224.

84. Williams, *Arius*, 68.

85. Athanasius, *Syn.* 16 (*NPNF2* 4:458); Kelly, *Early Christian Doctrines*, 227; Williams, *Arius*, 97.

86. Athanasius, *De decretis* 20 (*NPNF2* 4:164).

87. Athanasius, *Syn.* 48 (*NPNF2* 4:475–76).

ing reconstruction of events."[88] Yet this accusation seems unfounded. It is clear that *homoousios* had carried at least implications of unity in prior ecclesiastical use and the use of Arius, especially if the term is connected with Tertullian's *una substantia*, as Stead argues.[89] More importantly, the politics of Athanasius were Nicene; he had no reason to misrepresent the council because his concern was for the council's teaching. Robertson points out that Athanasius was not obsessed with the term *homoousios*, but accepted it because of the council.[90] The term did not appear prominently in his sermons, but "he communicates the *substance* of the Nicene Creed in the language proper to *his* church."[91] It therefore makes no sense for Athanasius to misrepresent the meaning of a word he only uses because it was used by the council.

The final reason *homoousios* should be understood to mean the unity of Father and Son is the reaction of its opponents who favored *homoiousias*. Many of these suspected the Nicene Creed of endorsing a Sabellian view of God, of compromising the clear personal distinction favored by Eusebius and Origen.[92] Yet they would only fear this if *homoousios* meant unity rather than equality. Kelly himself writes that "we may be sure that, if Eusebius and his allies had had the slightest suspicion that numerical identity of substance was being foisted on them in ὁμοουσιος, they would have loudly objected to it as Sabellian."[93] Thomas Weinandy makes the point well:

> Much is made of the fact that seemingly most of the Fathers at Nicaea only understood *homoousios* in the generic sense. . . . However, since there was the fear, and later the accusation, that the *homoousios* was Sabellian, more of the Fathers must have un-

88. Kelly, *Early Christian Doctrines*, 237. Hanson similarly is skeptical about "Athanasius, a fierce opponent of Arius who certainly would not have stopped short of misrepresenting what he said." Hanson then goes on to accept his reconstruction of Arius's teaching. Hanson, *Search*, 10, 15.

89. Stead, *Divine Substance*, 204. Certainly Arius read corporeal implications in *homoousios*. Athanasius, *Syn.* 16 (*NPNF2* 4:458).

90. Robertson, introduction to *Athanasius* (*NPNF2* 4:xviii).

91. Kannengiesser, *Arius and Athanasius*, 97. Emphasis original.

92. Hill, *Three-Personed God*, 42, 45; Kelly, *Early Christian Doctrines*, 239; Hanson, *Search*, 437.

93. Kelly, *Early Christian Doctrines*, 236. In fairness, Kelly may be implying that the objections to Nicaea were not intense enough or immediate enough, to read the feared unity into *homoousios*.

derstood the *homoousios* in the latter sense of "one being" than is customarily supposed. Only if one conceives the *homoousios* as meaning the Father and the Son are one and the same being, and not just generically composed of the same common divine "stuff," could there be any fear or accusation of Sabellianism.[94]

Only if *homoousios* was understood to mean unity could it be suspected of Sabellianism. It was suspected of Sabellianism, therefore it was understood to mean unity.

The Nicene Creed, the most universal creed of Christendom, asserted that God's unity was found in the derivation of the Son and Holy Spirit from the Father and in the single divine being which they have in common. Like Tertullian, Dionysius associated physical analogies which indicate source without separation with the term *homoousios*. Arius rejected the term because it implied that the Son was a part of God rather than a creature. Athanasius affirms that, while physical partition is excluded, the Nicene Creed was meant to be read as asserting the unity of Father and Son. Finally, many opposed the term *homoousios* because they believed it endangered the distinction of Father and Son, a danger only present if the term asserts unity. As such, it is best to understand *homoousios*, and therefore the Nicene Creed, as asserting the unity of Father, Son, and Holy Spirit in one single divine reality.

Cappadocians

There is an amusing amount of variety in contemporary opinions of the Cappadocian Fathers (Gregory of Nazianzus, Gregory of Nyssa, and Basil). There is no doubt that they brought about the settlement of the trinitarian controversy. As Hanson writes, "They were together decisively influential in bringing about the final form of the doctrine of the Trinity and thereby resolving the conflict about the Christian doctrine of God which had vexed the Church for fifty years before their day."[95] Yet what they taught, and how it relates to what came before, is still widely disputed. It is asserted that they failed to capture the metaphysical insight of Nicaea and Athanasius[96] and that they faithfully developed the teachings of Nicaea and Athanasius,[97] that they understood God's unity in terms

94. Weinandy, *Father's Spirit of Sonship*, 11, n. 19.

95. Hanson, *Search*, 676.

96. Weinandy, *Father's Spirit of Sonship*, 13.

97. Stead, *Philosophy*, 183; David Coffey, "Proper Mission of the Holy Spirit," *Theological Studies* 47.2 (1992) 235.

of perichoresis rather than unity of rule or substance[98] and that they continued to teach that God was one in operation and substance,[99] that they moved away from the pluralistic impulses of Origen and Eusebius to embrace the position of Athanasius[100] and that they reverted from the teachings of Athanasius to the pluralism of Origen.[101] In fact, Pannenberg denies that they succeeded in finding a basis for trinitarian unity at all.[102]

Clearly, the secondary literature is of limited value in determining the total teaching of the Cappadocians. Yet the teaching of the Cappadocians concerning the unity of God specifically does not appear to be difficult to discern from their own writings. First, they see unity of operation as a key element in the unity of God, because it reveals a unity of nature.[103] As Gregory of Nyssa writes, "Thus the identity of operation in Father, Son, and Holy Spirit shows plainly the undistinguishable character of their substance."[104] Second, they believe that God is one because the Father is the sole first principle, who generates the Son and Spirit without separation or inferiority, because no inferiority is possible in the infinite essence of God.[105] Thus it is belief in the unity of essence of Father, Son, and Holy Spirit which sits at the core of the Cappadocian belief, and to which they make repeated reference.[106]

It is sometimes suggested, however, that, contrary to the explication of Nicaea above, the Cappadocians understood there to be a generic unity of essence in God.[107] Pannenberg notes that Basil's conception of

---

98. Erickson, *God in Three Persons*, 230; cf. Christoph Schwöbel, *Persons, Divine and Human*, 12.

99. Bromiley, *Historical Theology*, 88; cf. Richardson, *Doctrine of the Trinity*, 65 .

100. Wiles, *The Making of Christian Doctrine*, 138.

101. Robertson, introduction to *Athanasius* (*NPNF2* 4:xxxii).

102. Pannenberg, *Systematic Theology*, 1:280.

103. Gregory of Nyssa, *Contra Eunomius* 1.31 (*NPNF2* 5:76); *On "Not Three Gods"* (*NPNF2* 5:334); Gregory Nazianzen, *Or.* 3.2 (*NPNF2* 7:301).

104. Gregory of Nyssa, *On the Holy Trinity* (*NPNF2* 5:329).

105. Gregory of Nyssa, *C. Eun.* 1.15, 1.34, 1.39 (*NPNF2* 5:51–52, 79–81, 93–95); Gregory Nazianzen, *Or.* 3.3 (*NPNF2* 7:302); Basil, *Epistulae* 38.3–4, 52.3 (*NPNF2* 8:138–39, 156).

106. For example, Gregory of Nyssa, *C. Eun.* 2.1, 2.2, 2.9, 4.1 (*NPNF2* 5:101, 102, 114, 153–54); Gregory Nazianzen, *Or.* 4.20 (*NPNF2* 7:320); Basil, *Ep.* 8.2 (*NPNF2* 8:116).

107. Wolfson, *Philosophy of the Church Fathers*, 342; Pannenberg, *Systematic Theology*, 1:336.

the three as realizations of a single concept threatens monotheism.[108] The Cappadocians do open themselves to such a charge when they compare the three in God to three men,[109] or when Basil writes, "I shall state that ousia has the same relation to hypostasis as the common has to the particular."[110]

However, many today recognize that the Cappadocians did not believe such a generic likeness was possible with God.[111] Basil, after presenting *ousia* as a class susceptible to subdivision, states, "But I hesitate to believe they have reached such a pitch of infatuation as to assert that the God of the universe, like some common quality conceivable only by reason and without actual existence in any hypostasis, is divided into subordinate divisions."[112] Language about God must be connected to this world to be intelligible, but it must always be remembered that God is unlike creation.[113] Thus, while the one *ousia* and the three *hypostases* may be related like the common to the specific, that does not mean that is all they are in God; they are both concrete realities.[114] The Cappadocians can be seen to sum up the points of divine unity which have been seen so far, recognizing a unity of operation, mutual indwelling, singular shared essence, and perfect, eternal derivation from the single source of the Father.

Augustine

Augustine provides two new developments in the doctrine of the unity of God. However, his contribution, or corruption, does not lie in beginning his doctrine of the Trinity with the unity of God, as many claim.[115] The Fathers before Augustine, including the Cappadocians, also begin their

---

108. Pannenberg, *Systematic Theology*, 1:274.

109. Basil, *Ep.* 38.2 (*NPNF2* 8:137); Gregory of Nyssa, *On "Not Three Gods,"* (*NPNF2* 5:332).

110. Basil, *Ep.* 214.4 (*NPNF2* 8:254); also *Ep.* 236.6 (*NPNF2* 8:278).

111. Hill, *Three-Personed God*, 48; Richardson, *Doctrine of the Trinity*, 65.

112. Basil, *De Spiritu Sancto* 17.41 (*NPNF2* 8:26); cf. Gregory of Nyssa, *C. Eun.* 19, 21 (*NPNF2* 5:57, 61); Gregory Nazianzen, *Or.* 4.20 (*NPNF2* 7:317).

113. Basil, *Ep.* 38.5 (*NPNF2* 8:139).

114. Wilks, "Trinitarian Ontology of John Zizioulas," 69–70.

115. Olson and Hall, *The Trinity*, 44; Thompson, *Modern Trinitarian Perspectives*, 5; Coffey, "Proper Mission," 233; LaCugna, "Philosophers and Theologians on the Trinity," 173; O'Carroll, *Trinitas*, 42.

trinitarian contemplation certain that God is one.[116] As Henri Blocher notes, throughout the trinitarian controversies, "The most powerful constraint was, simply, *biblical* monotheism!"[117] Nor is Augustine's contribution to the doctrine of God's unity found in his belief in the unity of divine actions; it was already present in the Cappadocians.[118] Augustine's new ideas are two: he explicitly states that it is the Trinity as such that is the One God,[119] and he thinks of the Holy Spirit in the Trinity as the bond of the Father and Son.[120]

The first point, that it is the Trinity, and not the Father, who is the One God had been hinted at in Clement and Tertullian.[121] However, the language of Augustine is strikingly clear. He writes "concerning the Trinity, Who is God," concerning "the One and only God, which is the Trinity itself."[122] This God is the one God who spoke, as Trinity, to Adam, to Moses, and on Pentecost.[123] By identifying the Trinity, and not the Father, as the one God, Augustine moves away from a model in which the one divine essence is given eternally to the Son and Spirit from the Father towards a model in which there is no such priority. This is a new development, for even Clement and Tertullian saw the Father as the first in God.

The second new development in Augustine is that he sees the Holy Spirit serving as the bond of unity between the Father and Son.[124] Augustine writes that "the Holy Spirit, according to the Holy Scriptures,

116. Cary, "On Behalf of Classical Trinitarianism," 392.

117. Blocher, "Immanence and Transcendence in Trinitarian Theology," 107; emphasis original.

118. Pannenberg, *Systematic Theology*, 2:3–4; Gregory of Nyssa, *On the Holy Trinity* (*NPNF2* 5:329). See also pp. 17–19 above.

119. Wolfson, *Philsophy of the Church Fathers*, 353; O'Carroll, *Trinitas*, 42; Zizioulas, "On Being a Person," 40.

120. Olson and Hall, *Trinity*, 56; Blocher, "Nature of Biblical Unity," 394; Richardson, *Doctrine of the Trinity*, 44. While Hill asserts Augustine also made God one person, *Three-Personed God*, 61, that is not clear in Augustine.

121. See pp. 8–10 above.

122. Augustine, *De Trinitate* 4.7, 6.9 (*NPNF1* 3:20, 22). Olson and Hall write that Augustine places the unity in the Father in *On Christian Teaching* (*The Trinity*, 46), but the full quote, "In the Father is unity, in the Son equality, in the Holy Spirit the harmony of unity and equality," and the context suggest thought in line with that below. Augustine, *De doctrina christiana*, 1.5 (*NPNF1* 2:524).

123. Augustine, *Trin.* 10.18, 10.19, 15.25 (*NPNF1* 3:46, 49–50).

124. For a full discussion of this aspect of Augustine's theology, see Bray, *Doctrine of God*, 165–177.

is neither of the Father alone, nor of the Son alone, but of both; and so intimates to us a mutual love, wherewith the Father and the Son reciprocally love one another."[125] He goes on to correlate the assertions, "God is love," and, "God is spirit," and concludes that the Holy Spirit is especially worthy of the title "love" in the Trinity, though all are love.[126] He argues that the Spirit, who is the Spirit of both Father and Son, the love of both, proceeding from both, and himself spirit, the substance of both, is the bond of unity within the Trinity.[127] In Augustine the Holy Spirit, who receives little attention in the Nicene Creed, becomes a personal bond between the Father and Son.

Medieval Sources

The medieval period can be treated relatively briefly. Olson and Hall point out that the medieval period showed little advancement in expressing the doctrine of the Trinity.[128] However, there are two theologians whose work on the doctrine of trinitarian unity deserve comment, Anselm and Aquinas.

Anselm, as a western theologian, continues in line with Augustine, thinking of the One God as the Trinity.[129] Anselm begins his *Monologion* with the disclaimer that he was asked not to refer to Scripture, and thus he records only his meditations on the divine essence.[130] This supreme substance has property simplicity. It is its properties, and has no accidents.[131] He then speaks of the supreme essence producing a word, which is equal to itself, and mutual love between these two, which is also the supreme essence.[132] In between these accounts of the processions, he discusses the presence of unity and plurality in God:

> There are two upshots of this, namely unity and plurality: first, there is always one single unity with respect to the signs that signify what they are substantially and what they are in relation to cre-

125. Augustine, *Trin.* 15.17.27 (*NPNF*1 3:215).

126. Ibid., 15.17.27–28 (*NPNF*1 3:215–16). 1 John 4:16. John 4:24.

127. Ibid., 15.17–20 (*NPNF*1 3:216–220).

128. Olson and Hall, *Trinity*, 66.

129. Thompson, *Modern Trinitarian Perspectives*, 5; Coffey, "Proper Mission," 233.

130. Anselm, *Monologion* prologue (5). All Anselm citations and page numbers from *Anselm of Canterbury: The Major Works*.

131. Ibid., 16, 17, 25 (28–30, 41–42).

132. Ibid., 29–38, 51–57 (45–52, 61–64).

ation. Secondly, insofar as the Word is derived from the supreme spirit, while the supreme spirit is not derived from the Word, there is an ineffable plurality.

And I do mean ineffable. For although there must be two of them, one just cannot express what they are ... It is not like talking about two equal lines or two similar men ... I reach the conclusion, then, that what these two things—the supreme spirit and its Word—are, is inexpressible, although they are distinguished from each other in thought by what is proper to each.[133]

Anselm's view of divine unity, shaped as it is by his meditation on the supreme substance, leaves him no room for comprehensible plurality within the Godhead. It is so clear that everything in them is one, it makes it unclear what could be plural.[134]

In *On the Procession of the Holy Spirit*, Anselm asserts that the three are differentiated by relations of opposition of origin; that is, the Son is defined as that which is begotten by the Father, the Father as that which begets the Son. That is the only way in which the three are differentiated. As Anselm writes, "The unity should never lose its consequences except when a relational opposition stands in the way, nor should the relations lose what belongs to them except when the indivisible unity stands in the way."[135] This allows Anselm to argue for the procession of the Holy Spirit from both Father and Son; there is nothing about being Son to the Father that prevents the Son from breathing the Holy Spirit.[136] Despite the second half of Anselm's sentence quoted above, it appears that Anselm has so emphasized the unity of God that he has little room for the persons.

Aquinas's view of the divine unity is similar to that of Augustine and Anselm, though he does establish a clearer distinction between the generation of the Son and the procession of the Spirit.[137] Carrying the position of his predecessors to its logical end, Aquinas reduces each of the three to the relation which defines him, which is, as a relation, identical

133. Ibid., 38 (52).

134. Ibid., 43 (56).

135. Anselm, *On the Procession of the Holy Spirit*, 1 (393). Part of this is incorporated into the Council of Florence, which states, "*Hae tres personae sunt unus Deus ... omniaque sunt unum, ubi non obviat relationis oppositio.*" Denzinger, *Enchiridion Symbolorum Definitionum*, 461.

136. Anselm, *On the Procession*, 1–10 (393–419).

137. Hill, *Three-Personed God*, 77; Bray, *Doctrine of God*, 182; Aquinas, *Summa Theologiae* 1a.27 (BF 6:5–24).

with the divine nature. Aquinas writes that "a relation is in God not as an accidental entity in a subject, but it is the divine nature itself; therefore it is something subsisting just as the divine nature is. Consequently just as Godhead is God, so God's fatherhood is God the Father who is a divine person" and that "subsisting fatherhood is the person of the Father, and subsisting sonship is the person of the Son."[138] Aquinas conceives of the generation of the Son and Spirit as the two intrinsic processes of a spiritual, or mental, nature: knowledge and will.[139] Since the Son and Spirit are these relations, they clearly seem to be reduced to aspects of a single divine mind, as Olson and Hall conclude.[140] Aquinas seems unable to give any more support than bare assertions for the reality of the three in God. He writes, "Characteristics are signified in God, not as realities, but as concepts whereby the persons are known, although they and relations are really in God."[141] Aquinas, like Anselm, seems to see only unity in God, to the point that assertions of plurality appear to be hollow linguistics.

Barth

It may seem odd to jump from Aquinas to Barth in an historical survey, but there is little development in the doctrine of trinitarian unity in the intervening years.[142] Barth, however, marks a new dawn of trinitarian studies, as was noted at the beginning of this study. Barth's understanding of the unity of the Trinity now will be considered to conclude this historical survey.

Barth's significance for trinitarian studies is not found in the fact that he adds anything to the medieval understanding of God's unity. Barth asserts that the three in God are one essence, and that "the truth we are emphasizing is that of the numerical unity of the essence of the 'persons.'"[143] This one essence is the seat of the divine personality, so that God has one personality. The three in God are not distinguished by any act or attribute, so there is unity of operation amongst them.[144] They are the One God in

138. Aquinas, *Summ. Theol.* 1a.29.4, 30.2 (BF 6:61, 69–71).

139. Ibid., 1a.27.3 (BF 6:13).

140. Olson and Hall, *Trinity*, 46; Also Pannenberg, "Christian Vision of God," 56.

141. Aquinas, *Summ. Theol.* 1a.32.2 (BF 6:115).

142. Cf., Olson and Hall, *Trinity*, 80. Bray does give attention to the work of the Reformers on the Trinity. *Doctrine of God*, 197–212.

143. Barth, *Church Dogmatics*, vol. 1/1, 350.

144. Ibid., 350–51, 362.

threefold repetition, and that threefold repetition is essential to the One God; he could not be other than the thrice repeated God that he is.[145] Barth points out this is only true because the Triune God is the God of the Bible; only as he is revealed can his unity and triunity be successfully juxtaposed.[146] There is little, if any, difference between the elements that Aquinas and Barth understand to be one in God.

Conclusion

As suggested, this historical survey has led to several conclusions. First, from Justin to Barth, the drive to see One God in the persons of Father, Son, and Holy Spirit has been based upon the Bible.[147] Second, while Justin had difficulty asserting the unity of the three, and Tertullian cast suspicion on their equality, the historical movement has consistently strengthened the way in which the Triune God is understood to be one, to the point where, as Anselm states, what is distinct in them is ineffable. Third, theologians throughout history have established God's unity via multiple avenues. It has been argued that God's unity resides in his singular operation, singular essence, singular originating principle, singular personality, and even in the binding love which is the Holy Spirit. Fourth, while later Trinitarian thought, since Augustine, clearly identifies the One God as the Trinity, earlier theologians used the term variably for the Father and the Trinity. Finally, that there is one divine essence, a single concrete, though incorporeal, reality which unites Father, Son, and Holy Spirit, has been a dominant position in the Christian understanding of the unity of God.

Theological Background

The doctrine of the Trinity lies at the heart of theology, for the doctrine of the Trinity is not something other than the doctrine of God. The key resource in evangelical theology is the Bible, so an evangelical doctrine of the Trinity must be compatible with the biblical teaching about God's unity. In addition, any doctrine of the Trinity must be compatible with a fully developed doctrine of God. Traditionally, theologians have located the divine attributes in the one essence of God, which allowed the three in God to share the same omnipotence, the same omniscience, etc. Biblical

145. Ibid., 350.
146. Ibid., 352–54.
147. Hanson, *Search*, 825–26.

statements about the unity of God, and theological teachings about the relationship between God's unity and his attributes, will now be examined. Specific theological issues pertinent to individual critiques will be presented in the appropriate chapters.

The Biblical Statements

Carl E. Braaten contrasts the new movement in trinitarian studies, in which most believe starting with the Bible means starting with the three persons of the Trinity, with earlier trinitarian theologians, who "start with a philosophical principle of absolute unity before trying to understand the biblical history of the relations between three personal identities."[148] This assertion, however, seems to ignore the vast amount of scholarship which recognizes that the biblical picture of God begins with unity.[149] As Veli-Matti Kärkkäinen points out, "The term *monotheism* . . . characterizes Old Testament belief."[150] This Old Testament monotheism is not only assumed in the New Testament, but is asserted by its authors. As Stead writes, "Christians of course discovered the notion of unity in the Bible; the Old Testament claims that God is one; the New Testament endorses this claim."[151] Both the Old and New Testaments teach that God is one.

But one in what sense? Theologians through history have suggested various elements of divine unity, and Rahner, Erickson, Zizioulas, and Pannenberg will be shown to do the same. What type of unity does the Bible ascribe to God?

It is common to begin consideration of God's unity with the *Shema*, Deut 6:4, "Hear, O Israel! The LORD is our God, the LORD is one!"[152] John Sailhamer writes that, while the meaning of the phrase is sometimes debated, "The sense of the phrase becomes quite clear if read in the light of the strict prohibition of idolatry and polytheism in the present text of Deuteronomy. The intent of the phrase is to give a clear statement of the

---

148. Braaten, "Triune God," 422.

149. For example, Welch, *In This Name*, 156; Hill, *Three-Personed God*, 5; Wiles, *Making of Christian Doctrine*, 144–45; O'Carroll, *Trinitas*, 179. For a recent treatment of the biblical doctrine of the Trinity, see Toon, *Our Triune God*.

150. Kärkkäinen, *Doctrine of God*, 17.

151. Stead, *Divine Substance*, 180; cf. Cobb, "Reply to Jürgen Moltmann's 'The Unity of the Triune God,'" 175; Erickson, *Making Sense of the Trinity*, 18.

152. Quoted from White, *Forgotten Trinity*, 35, where White uses it to begin his presentation of monotheism.

principle of monotheism, that is, that there is one God and only one God who exists."[153] Clark similarly connects the *Shema* to the commandments against idolatry and polytheism, and believes it intends to teach that there is only one God.[154] It is not, therefore, an argument for henotheism, but monotheism.[155] Agreement with this verse is seen as a key test for the doctrine of the Trinity. Morris writes, "In understanding the doctrine of the Trinity, the challenge is to balance the distinctness of the persons with the real unity of the divine nature, a unity sufficient to justify the Christian insistence that monotheism has not been utterly abandoned, that, in the words of Deuteronomy, 'The LORD our God is one God' (Deut 6:4)."[156]

Fortunately for Christians, the unity ascribed to the one God here is a unity open to diversity. The Hebrew word chosen for "one" allows some multiplicity, as Erickson explains, "There is a Hebrew word for one, *yahid*, which means simply uniqueness. It is the word used of Isaac in Jehovah's command to Abraham to offer Isaac as a sacrifice. The word here, *ehad*, however, while it may also bear the meaning of the only one, can be used to speak of a unity that is actually a union or composite of several factors."[157] A key example of this use of *ehad* is in Gen 2:24, where Adam and Eve are said to become "one flesh."[158] God's oneness is such that it allows some sort of multiplicity.[159]

There are clear constraints on that multiplicity, however, throughout the Old Testament. Perhaps the most important is that drawn from the Bible's earliest identification of God in Gen 1:1, that he is creator of all things.[160] It has already been shown what a key role the distinction between creator and creation played in the Arian controversy; if the Son

153. Sailhamer, *Pentateuch as Narrative*, 439. See also Erickson, *Making Sense of the Trinity*, 18.

154. Clark, *Trinity*, 1.

155. Toon, *Our Triune God*, 73.

156. Morris, *Our Idea of God*, 175.

157. Erickson, *Making Sense of the Trinity*, 33. Sailhamer makes the same observation, *Pentateuch as Narrative*, 439.

158. Erickson, *Making Sense of the Trinity*, 33; Sailhamer, *Pentateuch as Narrative*, 439.

159. There are other hints of divine multiplicity in the Old Testament. See Thompson, *Modern Trinitarian Perspectives*, 10; Toon, *Our Triune God*, 90–111; Clark, *Trinity*, 3–7; Kärkkäinen, *The Doctrine of God*, 45.

160. White, *Forgotten Trinity*, 35.

is creator, the only thing he can be is God.[161] God alludes to the clear distinction between creator and all else in his derision of idols in Isaiah. He says, "Before Me there was no God formed, and there will be none after Me" (Isa 43:10).[162] No God could have come into being before the God who brought all else into being, nor could one brought into being after be properly God. There can be no temporal priority amongst the multiplicity in God, nor can any "part" be created.

The New Testament continues the Old Testament teaching about the oneness of God. It denies that other gods, whom idols are thought to represent, are gods at all.[163] It continues to assert the unity and uniqueness of the One God.[164] However, the New Testament clearly fleshes out the Old Testament teaching about the multiplicity in God, ascribing to Jesus and the Holy Spirit divine functions and titles, and associating them with God the Father.[165] Both John (John 1:1–18) and Paul (Col 1:16, Eph 3:9) attribute to Christ the role of creator, a key sign of deity in the Old Testament. The New Testament indicates that Jesus Christ and the Holy Spirit are God, without showing any discomfort with the monotheism of the Old Testament. Hill notes that, in spite of the New Testament teaching about Jesus and the Holy Spirit, "Yet in all this the unity of God is never so much as broached as a question; it is the one sole Godhead who is worshipped [*sic*], not simply in a threefold manner but as somehow threefold in himself."[166]

A biblical view of the Trinity must therefore unashamedly allow for the incorporation of the Son and Spirit into God. In addition, it must allow for the biblical interaction amongst them. In the New Testament, Jesus prays to the Father (for example, Matt 14:23, 26:36–44, Mark 1:35, 6:46, John 17), and hears from the Father (Matt 17:5, Luke 9:35). The Spirit is sent from the Father (John 14:26), bears witness to and glorifies the Son

161. See p. 15 above. For the importance of the creator/created distinction in Christian and Jewish monotheism, see Bauckham, *God Crucified*, 10–22.

162. See also Isa 40:26, 42:5, 45:5–18.

163. Gal 4:8. See Pannenberg, *Basic Questions in Theology*, 2:136.

164. Rahner lists numerous instances: Mark 12:29, John 5:44, 17:3, Rom 3:30, 16:27, 1 Cor 8:6, Gal 3:20, Eph 4:6, 1 Tim 1:17, 2:5, 6:15, Jas 2:19, Jude 25, Rev 15:4. Rahner, *Theological Investigations*, 1:100. See also Welch, *In This Name*, 252.

165. Erickson, *Making Sense of the Trinity*, 34–41; Hill, *Three-Personed God*, 11–14, 23; For a full discussion, see Erickson, *Christian Theology*, 350–52, 700–10, 873–75; Behr, *Way to Nicaea*, 52–60.

166. Hill, *Three-Personed God*, 252.

(John 15:26, 16:14), and intercedes for believers (Rom 8:26). A biblical understanding of the unity of God must allow for such activities amongst the three in God.

It should be noted that Tertullian sees one other New Testament suggestion about the nature of God's unity. He looks to John 10:30, "I and the Father are one," in which "one" is a grammatical neuter.[167] He sees this as a foundation for his assertion that what is one in God is the essence, rather than the person. This exegesis, which reveals total confidence in the written Scriptures as authoritative revelation, is perhaps suspect today, but it does lend itself well to Tertullian's position, and that decided upon at Nicaea.

To summarize, a biblical doctrine of the unity of God must allow the unashamed unity of Father, Son, and Spirit without interfering with their interactions. It must see all three as the single uncreated creator of the universe. It must be a unity which does not involve a temporal addition to God. Finally, a unity in terms of an impersonal reality would fit Tertullian's exegesis well.

The Divine Attributes

The term *ousia*, like its Latin equivalents *essentia*, *substantia*, and *natura*, was not coined to discuss the unity of God. It is a word with a rich philosophical history which enjoyed a variety of uses.[168] Plato contrasts *ousia* as permanence with words that suggest change or flux, and he primarily uses the term to mean either existence or those properties which an item normally has.[169] Aristotle similarly views *ousia* as either existence or the manner in which something exists. By manner he means that aspect of a thing which is unqualified by degree, which lacks an opposite, and which can, over time, obtain contrary qualifications.[170] A man, for example, is either a man or not, has no opposite, and may be short at one time and tall at another. *Ousia* carries the sense of what is permanent about a thing, the underlying basis to which properties attach. It is not simply a list of

167. Tertullian, *Prax.* 22 (*ANF* 3:618).

168. For a thorough discussion of the history of the word, see Stead, *Divine Substance*. The three terms are generally used as synonyms, at least in Roman Catholic theology. See Denzinger, *Enchridion Symbolorum*, 261; Rahner, *Trinity*, 51.

169. Ibid., 25–28; Plato, *Republic* 525b (1142), *Sophist* 246c (268), *Euthyphro* 11a (10–11). Citations from Plato, *Plato: Complete Works*.

170. Stead, *Divine Substance*, 59; Aristotle, *Categoriae* 5 (1:7).

properties essential to a thing, or even a complex of those properties, but an underlying reality.[171]

Therefore, when the Fathers spoke of the *ousia* of God being one, they had in mind the underlying reality of God in which the attributes inhered.[172] Many suggest some form of property simplicity, in which the nature of God is identified with his attributes.[173] When the Fathers speak of the one nature of God, then, they include the notion that the Father, Son, and Spirit all share the one goodness, justice, wisdom, love, omnipotence, etc., which are or are in that nature. Origen writes that "the omnipotence of Father and Son is one and the same."[174] Gregory of Nyssa states that those who believe that the One God is only the Father "see in the One Him Who is completely united with Him in truth, and deity, and essence, and life, and wisdom, and in all attributes whatsoever," and he writes of "all the attributes ascribed to the Divine nature."[175] For the Fathers, God's unity is "where" his attributes are located.

This idea continues in contemporary treatments of the divine attributes. After discussing the modern assault of process theism on the classical attributes of God, Bray writes of the possible "injury to the biblical concept of God's essence."[176] Kärkkäinen writes of "attributes deemed essential to the Godhead."[177] It is possible to read these contemporary expressions of the relation between nature and attributes differently. Gordon H. Clark writes that to say God's essence is his attributes means, "The attributes constitute the definition of God."[178] Yet this leads to the question of what is being defined, which seems to require the answer,

---

171. Stead, *Divine Substance*, 20–23.

172. The Fathers were not always comfortable using *ousia* to speak of God, because it might carry inappropriate implications. See, for example, Origen, *Cels.* 6.64 (*ANF* 4:602–3). Stead gives more examples, *Divine Substance*, 161–64.

173. For example, Irenaeus, *Haer.* 2.13.3 (*ANF* 1:374); Athanasius, *Decr.* 22 (*NPNF2* 4:164–65); Augustine, *Trin.* 2.2.4 (*NPNF1* 3:39); Anselm, *Mon.* 16–17 (28–30); Aquinas, *Summ. Theol.* 1a.30.1 (BF 6:67). For a discussion of the logic of property simplicity, see Plantinga, *Does God Have a Nature?*

174. Origen, *Princ.* 1.2.10 (*ANF* 4:250).

175. Gregory of Nyssa, *C. Eun.* 2.4 (*NPNF2* 5:104); Gregory of Nyssa, *On the Holy Trinity* (*NPNF2* 5:327). See also Jenson, *Triune Identity*, 111.

176. Bray, *Doctrine of God*, 106.

177. Kärkkäinen, *Doctrine of God*, 57.

178. Clark, *Trinity*, 77.

"God's essence." Thus, God's attributes are intimately connected with God's unity.

This will become important to any understanding of God's unity which moves away from a unity of essence. Such a doctrine will be faced with either "relocating" the divine attributes or attributing to Father, Son, and Spirit separate attributes. If this seems rather abstract, perhaps an example will serve. Something about God made him able to, and was used by him to, create the universe. Because that potency has been traditionally located in the one divine essence, creation can reasonably be credited to Father, Son, and/or Spirit. Changing the "location" of that potency, however, would obviously change how the Trinity is related to creation.

The positions of Rahner, Erickson, Zizioulas, and Pannenberg will be considered in light of these theological criteria. To be biblical, a position must assert a unity which allows the diversity seen in the New Testament and the unity seen in the Old without equivocation or contradiction. To be theologically sound, a position which severs the one divine essence must credibly account for the attributes of God.

Christological Background

As was previously stated, this text will evaluate the Christological adequacy of the positions of these authors according to the definition of the Council of Chalcedon:

> Following the holy Fathers we teach with one voice that the Son [of God] and our Lord Jesus Christ is to be confessed as one and the same [Person], that he is perfect in Godhead and perfect in manhood, very God and very man, of a reasonable soul and [human] body consisting, consubstantial with the Father as touching his Godhead, and consubstantial with us as touching his manhood; made in all things like unto us, sin only excepted; begotten of his Father before the worlds according to his Godhead; but in these last days for us men and for our salvation born [into the world] of the Virgin Mary, the Mother of God according to his manhood. This one and the same Jesus Christ, the only-begotten Son [of God] must be confessed to be in two natures, unconfusedly, immutably, indivisibly, inseparably [united], and that without the distinction of natures being taken away by such union, but rather the peculiar property of each nature being preserved and being united in one Person and subsistence, not separated or divided into two persons,

but one and the same Son and only-begotten, God the Word, our Lord Jesus Christ, as the Prophets of old time have spoken concerning him, and as the Lord Jesus Christ hath taught us, and as the Creed of the Fathers hath delivered to us.[179]

It is a lengthy and complex definition. It begins by asserting, at length and in various ways, that the one Jesus Christ is fully divine and fully human, and that these two natures[180] enjoy disparate origins, implying they may enjoy diverse relations to the rest of reality. It then asserts that these two natures do not change one another; what it is to be God and what it is to be man, are not altered by the union of God and man in Jesus Christ. Finally, it asserts that the one person present in these two natures, the only person present, is the person God the Word.[181] As Porter asserts, "[T]he ancients would have insisted that the person born of the Father before all ages (Trinitarian sense of the word) is born of Mary in time (Christological sense of the word)."[182]

This definition was not meant to stand alone, however. The Council of Chalcedon was called in response to three contemporary heresies, Apollinarianism, Nestorianism, and Eutychianism,[183] and appended its definition to three other approved documents upon which the definition was based. Richard Norris characterizes the council's response to these threats when he writes, "As correctives to these heretical views, it proposes three documents: the *Tome* of Pope Leo, the second letter of Cyril to Nestorius, and Cyril's letter to John of Antioch accepting the Formula of Reunion of 433. These standards of orthodoxy are supplemented, finally, by a statement composed by the council itself in obedience to the wishes of the emperor."[184] The analysis of the definition proposed above will be borne out by an examination of these foundational documents.

---

179. *NPNF2* 14:264–65. For alternative renderings, see Bettenson, *Documents of the Christian Church*, 51–52; Grillmeier, *Christ in Christian Tradition*, 1:544.

180. Here nature is a form of *phusis* rather than *ousia*.

181. Here the trinitarian term *hypostasis* is used. Grillmeier gives roughly the same analysis of the definition in *Christ in Christian Tradition*, 545–50.

182. Porter, "Keeping 'Persons' in the Trinity," 532.

183. For a full treatment of these heresies, see Grillmeier, *Christ in Christian Tradition*, 329–40; 447–72; 520–56.

184. Norris, *Christological Controversy*, 30. For confirmation, see Labbe and Cossart, *Concilia*, vol. 4, col. 343, 368 (*NPNF2* 14:253, 259).

In Cyril's second letter to Nestorius, he simultaneously affirms the full deity and full humanity of Christ and the personal union, writing "that the Word having personally united to himself flesh animated by a rational soul, did in an ineffable and inconceivable manner become man . . . the two natures being brought together in a true union."[185] Explaining what "two natures" means, he points out that events in the life of Christ happened to the Word because he took on human nature. Because Christ has a human nature, he is born from Mary, suffers, and dies. Affirming a personal union, Cyril points out that the only other alternative is for God to have two Sons. Throughout his letter, Cyril emphasizes that the Word is the sole subject in Christ "for the Scripture has not said that the Word united to himself the person of man, but that he was made flesh. This expression, however, 'the Word was made flesh,' can mean nothing else but that he partook of flesh and blood like to us; he made our body his own, and came forth man from a woman, not casting off his existence as God, or his generation of God the Father, but even in taking to himself flesh remaining what he was."[186] Note the consistent use of "he," and its association with the divine and dissociation from the human. It is "his generation of God the Father," but "our body." The one subject, God the Word, united to himself humanity without changing what it means to be God or man, but being both. For Cyril, personal unity means unity of subject.[187]

The language in Cyril's letter to John of Antioch is similar to that of his letter to Nestorius and to the Definition of Chalcedon. He writes of "our Lord Jesus Christ," who was begotten "in the last days, for us and for our salvation, of Mary the Virgin according to his humanity."[188] He speaks of Christ as consubstantial "with his Father" and "with us," and continues to demonstrate his belief that Christ is first of all God the Word, who then adds to himself human nature.[189]

Leo's thought regarding the person and natures of Christ differs little from that of Cyril. Like Cyril's writings, the Tome of Leo emphasizes the two intact natures and their union in one person:

185. Cyril, *Epistulae* 4 (*NPNF2* 14:198).
186. Ibid.
187. Grillmeier, *Christ in Christian Tradition*, 460.
188. Cyril, *Ep.* 39 (*NPNF2* 14:251).
189. Ibid. (*NPNF2* 14:252).

For although in the Lord Jesus Christ there is one Person of God and man, yet that whereby contumely attaches to both is one thing, and that whereby glory attaches to both is another; for from what belongs to us he has that manhood which is inferior to the Father; while from the Father he has equal Godhead with the Father. Accordingly, on account of this unity of Person which is to be understood as existing in both the natures, we read, on the one hand, that "the Son of Man came down from heaven," inasmuch as the Son of God took flesh from that Virgin of whom he was born; and on the other hand, the Son of God is said to have been crucified and buried, inasmuch as he underwent this, not in his actual Godhead; wherein the Only-begotten is coeternal and consubstantial with the Father, but in the weakness of human nature.[190]

What is clear in this text is the equation of "the Lord Jesus Christ," "the Son of Man," "the Son of God," "the Only-begotten," and the fact that all of these terms refer to a divine subject. For Leo, just as for Cyril, the only person in Christ is the person of God the Word.[191]

It should be concluded that Chalcedonian Christology is a Christology in which the divine person God the Word, possessing eternally the divine nature, adds to himself complete human nature, and thus becomes man. The only person present in Christ according to Chalcedon is the person of God the Word. Any doctrine of God's unity that would prevent such an understanding of the incarnation must be judged christologically inadequate. Either that, or Chalcedon must be abandoned.

A BRIEF PREVIEW

This chapter has sought to introduce the subject of the unity of the triune God and to provide sufficient historical, theological, and Chris-tological background to adequately critique contemporary understandings of God's unity. The next four chapters will examine and critique the positions of four twentieth century theologians. Chapter 2 will look at the position of Karl Rahner, perhaps the leading Roman Catholic theologian of that century, whose position combines a classic thomistic emphasis on the unity of God with more modern movements in philosophy. Chapter 3 will examine the position of Millard Erickson, a prominent evangelical author. His position is at the farthest extreme from Rahner's, for he teaches that there are three

---

190. Leo, *Tome of Leo* (*NPNF2* 14:256–57).
191. Grillmeier, *Christ in Christian Tradition*, 532.

distinct subjects and substances in the Godhead. Chapter 4 will consider the work of John Zizioulas, a Greek Orthodox whose work emphasizes the communal nature of the Godhead as grounded in the person of God the Father. Chapter 5 will deal with the work of Wolfhart Pannenberg, who draws upon a unique philosophical perspective and a broad grasp of Christian tradition to develop his doctrine of divine unity. Chapter 6 will serve as a constructive conclusion. It will summarize the results of the critical chapters and attempt to draw from them elements for a successful evangelical doctrine of divine unity. It will then launch from those elements and present a complete understanding of trinitarian unity that is adequate according to the criteria which have been presented here.

2

Karl Rahner and Trinitarian Unity

KARL RAHNER IS WIDELY recognized as one of the most influen-tial theologians and one of the most important contributors to trinitar-ian theology of the twentieth century. Veli-Matti Kärkkäinen writes, "The late Karl Rahner is the main figure in contemporary Roman Catholic theology."[1] He is often associated with Karl Barth, for the two share both an importance to the revival of trinitarian studies and concern over the understanding of the term "person" as it is applied in trinitarian discus-sion.[2] Reflecting on the impact his work has had, Catherine LaCugna writes, "Rahner's book launched one of the most significant theological developments of the last few decades: the restoration of the doctrine of the Trinity to its rightful place at the center of Christian faith."[3] Rahner served as editor of Denzinger's *Enchiridion Symbolorum*, co-editor of *Lexicon für Theologie und Kirche* and *Sacramentum Mundi: An Encyclopedia of Theology*, and according to Cornelius Ernst was "perhaps the most influ-ential theologian in German-speaking Catholicism" in 1961.[4]

Rahner's work on the doctrine of the Trinity has garnered similar acclaim. Gregory Havrilak writes, "Following Barth, Rahner's classic work *The Trinity* appeared as the most innovative contribution to trini-tarian theology until the advent of Moltmann."[5] Rahner's musings on the Trinity are not confined to this seminal work, but appear through-

1. Kärkkäinen, *Doctrine of God*, 142; cf. Havrilak, "Karl Rahner and the Greek Trinity," 61.

2. Bartel, "Plight of the Relative Trinitarian," 153; Moltmann, "Unity of the Triune God," 160; Moltmann, *Trinity and the Kingdom of God*, 144; Hill, *Three-Personed God*, 146; Fox, *God as Communion*, 25–26.

3. LaCugna, introduction to *The Trinity*, xxi.

4. Ernst, introduction to *Theological Investigations*, 1:5.

5. Havrilak, "Karl Rahner and the Greek Trinity," 61.

out his *Theological Investigations* and other writings. Rahner has made several significant contributions to the doctrine of the Trinity. Rahner's Rule, which states, *"The 'economic' Trinity is the 'immanent' Trinity and the 'immanent' Trinity is the 'economic' Trinity,"*[6] has guided many in a new generation of trinitarian scholarship, and even those who have not followed it have found it hard to ignore.[7] Rahner is not afraid to offer constructive criticism of the traditional Catholic doctrine of the Trinity; according to Phillip Cary, he "is probably the most influential of the Western theologians who profess to find the Greek doctrine of the Trinity superior to the Latin."[8]

However, while the high points of Rahner's doctrine of the Trinity are well known, the specifics of his doctrine are less so.[9] This chapter will examine how Rahner understands the unity of the Trinity. It will begin by examining the methodology of his trinitarian thought. It will then show how Rahner understands the divine Trinity to be united, to be one, after which it will present the concerns against which Rahner explicates his doctrine of the Trinity. After highlighting the contributions Rahner has made to the doctrine of the unity of God, a thorough critique of Rahner's doctrine of the unity of the Trinity will be offered.

KARL RAHNER'S UNDERSTANDING OF DIVINE UNITY

LaCugna notes that Rahner deviates from Latin tradition by not beginning his doctrine of the Trinity with contemplation of the single divine essence. For Rahner, she writes, "The unity of the divine persons is found not in a common essence (as with Augustine or Thomas) but in the person of the Father and in the perichoretic interrelatedness of the divine persons."[10] This is something of an overstatement, as Rahner does discuss the importance of the single divine essence for the oneness of God.[11] However, it is true that he begins with the person of the Father, and sees

---

6. Rahner, *Trinity*, 22.

7. Badcock, "Karl Rahner, the Trinity," 143; LaCugna, introduction to *The Trinity*, xiv.

8. Cary, "Classical Trinitarianism," 365.

9. Badcock, "Karl Rahner, the Trinity," 143.

10. LaCugna, introduction to *The Trinity*, xx. Havrilak, however, disagrees with this conclusion. Havrilak, "Karl Rahner and the Greek Trinity," 63. See Augustine, *De Trinitate* 1.2.4 (*NPNF1* 3:19); Aquinas, *Summa Theologiae* 1a.3.3, 1a.11 (BF 2:29–31, 157–69). Olson and Hall take a similar view of Aquinas in Olson and Hall, *The Trinity*, 64.

11. For example, Rahner, *Trinity*, 61, 66, 69.

the unity of God as a unity of a plurality of Father, Son, and Holy Spirit.[12] The reason why he shifts the starting point, if not emphasis, in locating the unity of God is found in his methodology.

Rahner's Methodology

Rahner's theological methodology is an interesting topic in itself. He approaches theological questions with a transcendental methodology. This is perhaps best seen in his *Foundations of Christian Faith: An Introduction to the Idea of Christianity*, in which he seeks to root the basics of the Christian message in a transcendental philosophy.

As has already been noted, Rahner's Rule, which identifies the economic and immanent Trinity, has garnered widespread attention. This is, however, only one aspect of Rahner's methodology as he approaches the doctrine of the Trinity. This section will examine not only Rahner's Rule, but also Rahner's understanding of symbol and of divine self-communication, both of which are foundational to his understanding of the Trinity and its unity.

Theology of Symbol

Rahner describes his theology, or perhaps more accurately, ontology, of symbol in an essay in the fourth volume of his *Theological Investigations*.[13] Rahner's basic thesis is that "all beings are by their nature symbolic, because they necessarily 'express' themselves in order to attain their own nature."[14] There is a necessary plurality in being, but a plurality which each being overcomes in unity.[15] This plurality comes when a being creates a symbol of itself and in so doing constitutes itself, makes itself fully real.

Why is a symbol needed? It is needed because "the being of that which is, is *knowability*."[16] A being only exists to the extent that it is knowable, particularly to itself. Rahner states, "The essence of being is knowing and being known in an original unity, which we call the (conscious)

---

12. Ibid., 45–46.

13. Rahner, "Theology of Symbol."

14. Ibid., 224.

15. Ibid., 229.

16. Rahner, *Hearers of the Word*, 39.

being-present-to-itself of being."[17] For a being to know itself, it must be present-to-itself as an other. As Rahner puts it, "The symbol strictly speaking (symbolic reality) is the self-realization of a being in the other, which is constitutive of its essence."[18] Thus the symbol is not primarily the means by which others know a being; the symbol is first and foremost the means by which a being knows itself.[19] By knowing and possessing their symbols, beings come to know themselves and possess themselves.[20]

This theory has a clear application in trinitarian theology. The Son can be understood as the Father's self-expression, or in Rahner's terms, his symbol.[21] In a manner reminiscent of Clement, Origen, and the later Alexandrian Athanasius, Rahner argues that the divine Logos is necessary because "the Father is himself by the very fact that he opposes to himself the image which is of the same essence as himself, as the person who is other than himself; and so he possesses himself. But this means the Logos is the 'symbol' of the Father, in the very sense which we have given the word."[22] The Father could not know himself, and therefore could not be himself, if he did not express himself in an other, his Word, his Son.[23]

Theology of Self-Communication

The theology of symbol raises a question. How can a being possess itself in its symbol if its symbol is other than itself? For the theology of symbol to work, there must be an inherent unity of a being and its symbol. Rahner attributes to Aquinas the insight that there can be no unity of things which are inherently multiple.[24] Thus, there must be an essential connection between the Father and his symbol, the Son.

---

17. Ibid., 39–40.

18. Rahner, "Theology of Symbol," 234.

19. Leithart, "Sacramental Theology," 6.

20. Rahner, "Theology of Symbol," 230.

21. Leithart, "Sacramental Theology," 7–8.

22. Ibid., 236; Cf. Clement of Alexandria, *Stromata* 5.1 (*ANF* 2:444); Origen, *De principiis* 1.1.9 (*ANF* 4:245); Athanasius, *Orationes contra Arianos* 1.6.21–22 (*NPNF2* 4:318–19).

23. Leithart, "Sacramental Theology," 6.

24. Ibid., 227. Here, as elsewhere, Rahner is notably lacking in citations. Where possible, references to Aquinas's works have been provided by the author. Rahner may have in mind Aquinas, *Summa Theologiae* 1a.44.1 (BF 8:5–9).

Rahner finds such a connection in the ancient category of formal causality.[25] Because the Father is the formal cause of the Son, what is effected is not different than the cause itself, but is the reality of the cause. He notes Aquinas's reference to "resultance," an outflowing of a being's faculties as the being projects "from itself the 'otherness' of its faculties, which according to St Thomas is really distinct from the substance."[26] The Son shares the being of the Father, though he remains other than the Father.

As a symbol, the Son is not only the basis of the Father's self-knowledge, but also of human knowledge of God. Remember that being and knowability are inextricably linked for Rahner. This leads to Rahner's understanding of revelation as God's self-communication. What is communicated in revelation is not knowledge about God, but God himself. The Father "communicates the Son as his own, personal self-manifestation."[27]

In developing his understanding of revelation as self-communication, there are two points about revelation on which Rahner is perfectly clear. First, the revelation of God is the self-communication of God the Father. Second, what the Father communicates to man in revelation is nothing other than God himself. These two assertions are, of course, tied together. It is "*Jesus'* Father, who sends the Son and who gives himself to us in the Spirit, in his Spirit."[28] In the Son, man contacts the revelation of the Father, and therefore the Father himself. As Rahner writes, "The Son is first . . . the self-communication of the Father to the world in such a way that in this Son he is radically *there* and that his self-communication entails, as an effect produced by itself, its radical acceptance."[29] Rahner makes clear that it is not the Godhead as a whole but the Father who is

25. Formal causality was one of the four types of causes presented by Aristotle. See *Physics* 2.3 (332–34); *Metaphysics* 5.2 (1600–1). Aquinas uses and elaborates on Aristotle's system. For examples, see *Commentary on Metaphysics* 5.2 (43–46); *Summa Contra Gentiles* 1.26 (81). These citations are from Thomas Aquinas, *St. Thomas Aquinas: Philosophical Texts*. In the latter, Aquinas states that if God were the formal cause of all things, all things would be one. Presumably, he means God.

26. Ibid., 232–33. Cf. Aquinas, *Summ. Theol.* 1a.77.6 (BF 11:111). That the application of resultance, which Aquinas associates with the soul, to God cannot result in division is clear from 1a.77.3 (BF 11:97), where Aquinas notes that the soul differs from God in that "in God there is neither power nor activity that is not his essence."

27. Rahner, *Trinity*, 35.

28. Ibid., 18.

29. Ibid., 63.

communicating himself to man, for "the Son is the self-expression of the Father, the word of the Father (not of the Godhead)."[30] This is also true of the revelation provided in the Holy Spirit. God's revelation of himself has a "double mediation," in which the work of the Son and the Spirit are distinct yet interrelated.[31] However, for it to truly be God who is communicated, these mediators cannot be created, else "God would not really be communicated as he is in himself."[32]

Rahner's Rule

This understanding of revelation, in which God communicates himself, and not something else, is the basis for Rahner's Rule, the axiom, "*The 'economic' Trinity is the 'immanent' Trinity and the 'immanent' Trinity is the 'economic' Trinity.*"[33] Some have suggested that this is best understood as simply a methodological device.[34] However, this seems to set at naught Rahner's own intentions. He writes, "The goal of our efforts is rather to bring out a prior and original identity and unity of the two realities, in relation to which the immanent and economic Trinity offer developments, clarifications and aspects of this underlying unity."[35] The Trinity that appears to man in revelation must be the Trinity that is God, else revelation would not in fact be self-communication. However, man encounters God as "the Trinity, in which the Father is the incomprehensible origin and the original unity, the 'Word' his utterance into history, and the 'Spirit' the opening up of history into the immediacy of its fatherly origin and end. And precisely this Trinity of salvation history, as it reveals itself to us by deeds, is the 'immanent' Trinity."[36]

Rahner's doctrine of the Trinity, then, purports to be built upon historical events. The coming of Christ and the Spirit are the data from which Rahner attempts to construct his doctrine of the Trinity, and his understanding of the unity of the Trinity. In part because of this

---

30. Ibid., n. 17.

31. Ibid., 37, 84; Rahner also speaks of a "threefold aspect" to revelation but that calculation seems to come from adding the ground of revelation to the two mediations.

32. Ibid., 37.

33. Ibid., 22.

34. LaCugna, introduction to *The Trinity*, 15.

35. Karl Rahner, *Theological Investigations*, 16:259.

36. Rahner, *Trinity*, 47.

historical starting point, Rahner's understanding of the divine unity begins with the person of the Father.

The Father as the One God

According to Rahner, both Scripture and the Greek fathers used the word "God" primarily for the Father.[37] In fact, it is Rahner's assertion that whenever *ho theos* is found in the New Testament, it refers to the Father.[38] Using Scholastic terminology, Rahner argues that *theos* means (*significatio*) the Father, and that it is only because the Son and Spirit share his essence that *theos* can be used to refer (*suppositio*) to them.[39] Therefore, when one speaks of the unity of God, one is discussing a unity centered in the Father. Biblical monotheism means that "the *Father* of our Lord *Jesus* Christ is the unique God."[40]

This fits nicely into Rahner's theology of symbol and of self-communication. Because it is the Father who expresses the Son and receives him back again in the Spirit, he is their source and the basis for their unity. The Son and Spirit are "manners of givenness of the Father."[41] Because in them the one Father is communicating himself, they must be one. However, that oneness does not destroy their distinction. As Rahner writes, "Both basic modalities condition one another. They derive from the nature of the self-communication of the unoriginate God who remains incomprehensible, whose self-communication remains a mystery both as possible and as actual. But the two modalities are not simply the same thing."[42] Because the Father is revealing himself in the Son and the Spirit, their unity is not merely the unity of a numerically singular essence, though it is grounded in that unity. Rahner notes:

37. Ibid., 16. While Rahner does not cite any particular work, there are numerous instances where the church Fathers identified the one God specifically with God the Father. For example Justin, *Apologia i* 6 (*ANF* 1:164); *2 Clement* 20 (*ANF* 7:523); Irenaeus, *Adversus haereses* 1.10.1, 5.17 (*ANF* 1:330, 544–46); Tatian, *Oratio ad Graecos*, 4 (*ANF* 2:66).

38. Rahner, *Theological Investigations*, 1:136. Rahner does grant that John 20:28 appears to be an exception, but discounts it because *ho theos* is being predicated.

39. Ibid., 126–27. For a discussion of Scholastic semiotics, see Bocheński, *History of Formal Logic*, 153–88, especially 162–73. See also Kretzmann, "Semiotics, History of," in *Encyclopedia of Philosophy*, especially 365–75.

40. Rahner, *Theological Investigations*, 1:102.

41. Rahner, *Trinity*, 74.

42. Ibid., 99.

For when we mean the expression "on the *one* God" literally, this treatise does not speak only of God's essence and its unicity, but of the unity of the three divine persons, of the unity of the Father, the Son, and the Spirit, and not merely of the unicity of the divinity. We speak of the mediated unity, of which the Trinity is the proper consummation, and not of the unmediated unicity of the divine nature. For when we think of this nature as numerically one, we are not yet thinking *ipso facto* of the ground of God's tri-unity.[43]

Because the Father is one, and because his revelation in the Son and Spirit cannot be other than God and still be self-communication, the Trinity is united in the person of the Father. The Father, as the font of divinity, is the basis for Trinitarian personal unity.[44]

The Single Divine Essence

While Rahner emphasizes the Father as the source of divine unity, he nevertheless retains the traditional Catholic understanding of the singular divine essence.[45] Both the Son and the Spirit are united to the Father in the one divine essence. The one God has a "numerical unity of his nature."[46] The Son is "of the Father's own divine and total essence, of his 'substance,' of his 'nature.'"[47] Likewise Rahner writes of the Holy Spirit, "As self-communication of God he is God as given in love and powerful in us in love. Hence he possesses the one and same essence as the Father, he is God, yet distinct from Father and Son. He proceeds from the Father and the Son through an eternal communication of the divine essence as the act of the Father and the Son."[48] Thus the three are one because each is "really identical with the one, simple essence of God."[49] Rahner writes of the Father, Son, and Holy Spirit, that "they are one and the same God in

---

43. Ibid., 45–46, emphasis original.

44. LaCugna, introduction to *The Trinity*, xx.

45. As Bracken notes, Rahner here adheres to the relative trinitarian scheme of Aquinas, who in part follows Augustine. See Bracken, *What are They Saying?* 5. Cf. Aquinas, *Summ. Theol.* 1a.28 (BF 6:23–40); Augustine, *Trin.* 5.8–16 (*NPNF*1 3:91–96).

46. Rahner, *Theological Investigations*, 1:132.

47. Rahner, *Trinity*, 61.

48. Ibid., 66.

49. Ibid., 69.

the unlimited fullness of the one Godhead and in possession of one and the same divine essence."[50]

Of course, for this unity to be trinitarian unity, it cannot be such that it eliminates the possibility of distinction within the Godhead. Rahner again follows tradition by asserting that the three within the Godhead are relations of opposition. Each person of the Trinity is a subsistent relation of opposition. In God, fatherhood and sonship, opposed relations, subsist as Father and Son. And, as Rahner says, since "every relation is really identical with God's absolute essence, the persons are distinct only through their *esse ad* (their being relative to) and the three opposed relative *esse ad* are of the same perfection."[51] The unity of the divine essence is the absolute reality of the Trinity; the distinctions among the persons are relative realities.[52]

It is this unity of essence which provides a basis for the perichoresis of the persons. Rahner writes, "On account of the unity of the essence, of the processions and of the relative oppositions, which constitute the persons, we speak of the mutual inexistence [existence in one another] of the three persons (circumincession, circuminsession, περιχώρησις)."[53] This is important, because sometimes the concept of interpenetration is used to unite the members of the Godhead who would otherwise be essentially three.[54] For Rahner, the three share one life because they share one essence, and not vice versa.

What is this one divine essence? It is not only the location of the traditional divine attributes, but is the single divine subject. Commenting on the relation of person and substance, Rahner writes:

> there exists in God only *one* power, *one* will, only one self-presence, a unique activity, a unique beatitude, and so forth. Hence self-awareness is not a moment which distinguishes the divine "persons" one from the other, even though each divine "person," as concrete, possesses a self-consciousness. Whatever would mean three "subjectivities" must be carefully kept away from the concept of person in the present context.[55]

50. Rahner, *Foundations*, 136.

51. Rahner, *Trinity*, 70–71.

52. Ibid., 70.

53. Rahner, *Trinity*, 79.

54. This is true of the position of Millard Erickson, for example. See pp. 75–80.

55. Rahner, *Trinity*, 75.

This is also the analysis of Robert Doud, who writes, "Rahner describes God as a single subject."[56] That this subject is included in the concept of essence is clear when Rahner writes, "This unicity of essence implies and includes the unicity of one single consciousness and one single freedom, although of course the unicity of one self-presence in consciousness and freedom in the divine Trinity remains determined by that mysterious threeness which we profess about God when we speak haltingly of the Trinity of persons in God."[57] God is only one person, in the modern sense of the term.[58]

However, the consciousness, the personality, of this one divine subject is not something other than one of the divine persons. The one divine essence, the Godhead, is the Father.[59] Rahner writes, "We are told that we are dealing with God in his radical incomprehensible Godhead (Father), that this Godhead is really given to us in the Son and in the Holy Spirit."[60]

Thus, Rahner's understanding of the divine unity comes full circle. The Father, as both the source of the Son and Spirit, and as the reality of the divine essence, the true divine substance, unifies the Godhead. Because the Son and the Spirit are the Father's self-communication, they share his essence, and are one with him in it. Because each is self-identical with the one Godhead, they are simply one. Further exposition of Rahner's understanding of divine unity will come in response to Rahner's trinitarian concerns.

Rahner's Concerns

It is common knowledge that theology does not take place in a vacuum. Rahner mentions four dangers to a proper trinitarian theology against which he sets his own doctrine of the Trinity. Rahner's responses to these four dangers, "mere" monotheism, tritheism, Sabellianism, and a belief in a quaternity, help clarify Rahner's understanding of the Trinitarian unity.

56. Doud, "Rahner's Christology," 146.

57. Rahner, *Foundations*, 135.

58. Rahner, *Trinity*, 89.

59. This is also the conclusion of Moltmann: "For Rahner the one, single God-subject is the Father." Moltmann, *Trinity and the Kingdom*, 147.

60. Rahner, *Trinity*, 52.

"Mere" Monotheism

Rahner begins his work, *The Trinity*, with a lament. He points out that neither the life of the average Christian nor the typical theology textbook would change if the concept of "Trinity" ceased to exist. Rahner writes that "despite their orthodox confession of the Trinity, Christians are, in their practical life, almost mere 'monotheists.'"[61] Textbook theology is in a similar state. Rahner continues, "We must be willing to admit that, should the doctrine of the Trinity have to be dropped as false, the major part of religious literature could well remain virtually unchanged."[62] Thus, Rahner's efforts are intended to make the Trinity relevant again, both to the individual believer and theology as a whole.[63] Cary sees this as part of Rahner's motive for identifying the economic and immanent trinities.[64]

Rahner argues that the simple fact of the Incarnation is not enough to make the Trinity relevant, because, since Augustine, the traditional doctrine has been that any one of the three persons of the Trinity could have become incarnate.[65] For Rahner, this is an unacceptable view of divine unity. In it, the incarnation is not necessarily the incarnation of the Logos, but is understood by many to be the incarnation of God.[66] This amounts to a practical denial of the Trinity, at least according to Rahner's Rule, because the economy, in which only the Logos becomes incarnate, would then tell men nothing about the reality of God.[67]

Rahner therefore appears to question several elements of Catholic tradition. Cary draws attention to three: Augustine's Rule, Anselm's Rule, and appropriations.[68] The first is what Cary calls "Augustine's Rule," "*omnia opera trinitatis ad extra indivisa sunt*" (all external actions of the Trinity

---

61. Ibid., 10.

62. Ibid., 10–11.

63. Bracken, "Holy Trinity, II," 260.

64. Cary, "Classical Trinitarianism," 366.

65. Rahner, *Theological Investigations*, 4:106. Rahner does not cite where Augustine stated this, and Cary denies that this is a fair reading of him, or any other traditional author. Cary, "Classical Trinitarianism," 370–71. Bartel sees the uniqueness of the Son's incarnation as a traditional element of trinitarian theology, though he denies that these theologies could coherently account for it. Bartel, "Relative Trinitarian," 133.

66. Rahner, *Trinity*, 11.

67. Rahner, *Theological Investigations*, 4:90.

68. Cary, "Classical Trinitarianism," 372.

are undivided).[69] Anselm's Rule is that in the Godhead everything is one except where relations of opposition preclude.[70] Since the Bible seems to indicate that certain acts of God are performed by certain persons of the Trinity, Anselm's Rule, which Cary sees as equivalent to the Cappadocian belief in the unity of the divine operation, requires the doctrine of appropriations, which states that activities in the world predicated of a single divine person are only "appropriated" to that person and are not properly his alone.[71]

Rahner, however, does not directly reject any of these claims, a fact which Cary acknowledges.[72] Rahner affirms the unity of external operations and, at least implicitly, Anselm's Rule as affirmed by the Council of Florence.[73] What Rahner does believe, as Robert Jenson notes, is that the way the West has understood the "*omnia opera trinitatis ad extra indivisa sunt*" formula has disconnected each divine person from his saving work by grouping them indiscriminately and attributing them to a single operation.[74] So, Rahner seeks to narrow the proper field of external operations, or, to put it more clearly, to broaden the field of what hypostatic relations are possible between the members of the Trinity and humans. The unity of the Trinity cannot be such that it precludes men from relating to each of the divine persons in a peculiar way. Rahner notes that in the incarnation, a clear exception to the doctrine of appropriations occurs. While others have suggested that this is the only possible exception, that the only hypostatic relation would be a hypostatic union,[75] Rahner argues that this

69. Ibid., 368. Cary notes that Augustine's Rule is a guiding principle throughout the work *De Trinitate*, manifest particularly in 1.4.7, 2.10.18–19 (*NPNF1* 3:20, 46). Of course, Augustine did not deny that each member of the Trinity might have a distinct role in their undivided activity. See Augustine, *Trin.* 1.4.7 (*NPNF1* 3:20). Maurice Wiles states that this clause is "a summary of orthodox conviction on the matter." Wiles, *Making of Christian Doctrine*, 128.

70. "The unity should never lose its consequences except when a relational opposition stands in the way, nor should the relations lose what belongs to them except when the indivisible unity stands in the way." *On the Procession of the Holy Spirit*, 1. In Anselm, *Anselm of Canterbury*.

71. Cary, "Classical Trinitarianism," 388. Augustine states that the Son sends himself, though that action is appropriated to the Father. Augustine, *Trin.* 2.5.9 (*NPNF1* 3:41).

72. Ibid., 372.

73. Rahner, *Trinity*, 76, 73. See p. 32, n. 135 above.

74. Jenson, *Triune Identity*, 157.

75. For example, Hill, "Uncreated Grace," 351–53.

is an unfounded presupposition. It is possible that creation relates to the one God in a threefold way.[76] It is only in this way that the Trinity becomes relevant, and believers escape "mere" monotheism.

Tritheism

Rahner is careful that the escape from "mere" monotheism does not drive believers into tritheism. He points out that believers are always in danger "of believing that there exist in God three distinct consciousnesses, spiritual vitalities, centers of activity, and so on."[77] As noted earlier, a key element of God's unity is his unity of essence, which includes consciousness. Rahner dislikes the trinitarian use of the word "person," which today implies "the idea of three centers of consciousness and activity, which leads to a heretical misunderstanding of the dogma."[78] He therefore consistently emphasizes that there is only one subject in God, one personality:

> [W]hen *today we* speak of person in the plural, we think almost necessarily, because of the modern meaning of the word, of several spiritual centers of activity, of several subjectivities and liberties. But there are not three of these in God—not only because in God there is only *one* essence, hence *one* absolute self-presence, but also because there is only *one* self-utterance of the Father, the Logos. The Logos is not the one who utters, but the one who is uttered. And there is properly no *mutual* love between Father and Son, for this would presuppose two acts. ... There is in God a knowledge of these three persons (hence in each person about himself and about the two other persons), a knowledge about the Trinity both as *consciousness* and as *"object"* of knowledge (as known). But there are not three consciousnesses; rather, the one consciousness subsists in a threefold way. There is only one real consciousness of God, which is shared by Father, Son, and Spirit, by each in his own proper way. ... However, it is not conscious for three subjectivities, but it is the awareness of distinctness in one only real consciousness.[79]

To quell this notion of three personalities, which he considers tritheism, Rahner suggests that the term "person" be replaced with "distinct manner of subsisting." Such a phrase avoids the misunderstandings "per-

76. Rahner, *Trinity*, 24–30.
77. Ibid., 43.
78. Ibid., 57.
79. Ibid., 106–7.

son" provokes, is suggestive of relation as the basis of the divine persons, and "underlines God's unity and unicity."[80]

Sabellianism

Rahner seems to realize that his theology opens him to the charge of modalism, or Sabellianism.[81] Two elements of his system seem to attract this charge. The first is the one just mentioned, that he minimizes the concept of person as applied to the three. He describes person as a virtual reality.[82] He denies that the term can be used univocally of the three, because "the ways in which each person is a person are so different that they allow for only a *very loosely* analogical concept of person, as *equally* applicable to the three persons."[83] In such a system, the reality referred to by "person" or "distinct manner of subsisting" seems rather tenuous.

Rahner's second problem is that he often presents the Son and Spirit as no more than the ability of God to communicate, to reveal himself. Rahner writes:

> The "Spirit" would then signify the divine possibility of direct self-communication to man as mystery. The "Son" means that God can give historical shape to this ultimate truth, which is himself, and bestow it upon humanity in a man who freely accepts his salvation in death and thus makes the divine self-gift of the mystery a definitive and credible reality.[84]

For Rahner, the second person of the Trinity "is exactly identical with God's *ability* to express himself in history."[85] The Spirit and Son are "manners of givenness," and the Spirit himself is "God as given in love."[86] In denying the Son and Spirit distinct personalities and then presenting them as faculties of God, Rahner does seem open to the charge of modalism.

---

80. Ibid., 109–13. Bracken suggests that this language emphasizes unity to the point of moving Rahner back towards "mere" monotheism. Bracken, *What are They Saying?* 14–15.

81. Moltmann sees him in danger of lapsing into "Idealistic modalism," and Hill classifies him as a "Modal Trinitarian." Moltmann, *Trinity and the Kingdom*, 144; Hill, *Three-Personed God*, 146. Cf. Thompson, *Modern Trinitarian Perspectives*, 132.

82. Rahner, *Trinity*, 70.

83. Ibid., 29.

84. Rahner, *Theological Investigations*, 16:240.

85. Rahner, *Foundations*, 304.

86. Rahner, *Trinity*, 74, 66.

Rahner's defense is fairly simple. He claims, "*Economic* Sabellianism is false."[87] It is modalism that believes a solely singular God has arbitrarily manifested himself in three modes which is heresy. Rahner believes he escapes this charge, because the distinctions between the persons, though virtual, are truly and fully attributed to God as he is. And this is the defense to which he repeatedly returns. His doctrine is proper because it recognizes that revelation in the Spirit and Christ "is one of radical *self-manifestation* in uncreated grace and in the hypostatic union."[88] It recognizes that the persons are not "merely the result of a mental distinction deriving from our intelligence," but instead are really the entry of God into human situations in the Son and the Spirit.[89] Rahner's defense amounts to the claim that the manners of divine subsistence are more than modes because they are real to God, and not just to mankind.[90] If the Son were merely the way God appeared in Christ, the way God expressed himself, rather than his very ability to do so, that would be modalism. How successful this defense is will be seen later in this chapter.

Quaternity

It has already been noted that Rahner emphasizes the importance of identifying the Father with the Godhead. It is true that Rahner follows tradition in asserting that each divine person, as only relatively distinct, is identical with the Godhead, but it is also true that the Father enjoys a clear priority in Rahner's thought.[91] One must agree with Hill, who asserts that Rahner "represents the First Person as conceptually identical with the Godhead in a way that Son and Spirit are not."[92] Rahner appears to make this assertion in part to forestall any implication of a quaternity in God.

Rahner notes that the Council of Florence rejected the possibility of a quaternity, and that therefore a proper understanding of divine unity

---

87. Ibid., 38. It is difficult to refute Rahner about what qualifies as "Sabellian." Ancient descriptions of Sabellianism proper are rarely extensive, as shown by Athanasius, *Expositio fidei* 2 (*NPNF2* 4:84), *C. Ar.*, 23.4 (*NPNF2* 4:395), and Basil, *Epistulae* 214.3 (*NPNF2* 8:254). The term is often used to impugn other heresies by association, as in Dionysius of Rome's *Adv. Sab.* (*ANF* 7:365–66). Unfortunately, there has been no recent work attempting to reconstruct the teaching.

88. Ibid.

89. Ibid., 55, 88–89.

90. Ibid., 112; Rahner, *Theological Investigations*, 4:69–70.

91. Cf. Aquinas, *Summ. Theol.* 1a.39–40 (BF 7:99–158).

92. Hill, *Three-Personed God*, 73.

could not posit a divine essence distinct from the divine persons which serves as their foundation.[93] Cary points out that "the unity of what is divine cannot flow from a higher principle of unity, for then that higher principle would itself be God. This implies for the doctrine of the Trinity that the *ousia* of God cannot be made into a higher principle uniting the Three."[94] Therefore, according to Rahner, person and essence cannot each be absolute realities.[95] However, Rahner also takes seriously that there is only one consciousness in God, one center of activity. This cannot be found in the essence as essence, else it would be something "behind" the Father, Son, and Spirit, thus making a quaternity. This seems to be part of why Rahner locates the divine personality in the Father, seeing him as "the original source of both the processes within the godhead and of the creation of the world."[96]

Rahner develops a view of divine unity centered upon the Father. The Father, as the one who speaks the Son as his symbol, and receives him again in the Spirit, ties the three together personally. The Father, as the original bearer of the divine essence, unites the Son and the Spirit, who are identical with that same essence. The divine Trinity are undivided in their external work in the world, which is the execution of the will of the Father, who sends the Son and the Spirit to communicate himself to man. The next section will test this understanding of divine unity.

A CRITIQUE OF RAHNER'S UNDERSTANDING OF UNITY

It should be clear that Rahner has made a significant contribution, both in methodology and in content, to the contemporary discussion of the doctrine of the Trinity. He has developed a view of the Trinity, and particularly the unity of the Trinity, which draws upon Roman Catholic tradition without lapsing into a simple aping of received tradition. Several positive elements in this understanding of the trinitarian unity will here be highlighted.

Rahner deserves credit for reminding the trinitarian theologian that any proper understanding of the unity of God is bounded about by heresy. The unity of the divine three cannot collapse them into one ("mere"

93. Rahner, *Trinity*, 70; Denzinger, *Enchiridion Symbolorum*, 337.
94. Cary, "Classical Trinitarianism," 382.
95. Rahner, *Trinity*, 68–70, 58.
96. Rahner, *Theological Investigations*, 16:240.

monotheism), nor can it posit the three as pertaining only to the human reception of the revelation of the one God (economic Sabellianism). However, the divine unity must be strong enough to avoid the charge of tritheism. This study of Rahner's theology has shown that, for him, the triune God is thoroughly one; of the theologies to be examined here, Rahner's has the most extensive grounding for the divine unity. He is one because of the causal priority of the Father. This causality is formal, meaning that the Son and Spirit are also one with the Father in the one divine essence, with which each is identical. God is one in that he has one will, one purpose, one consciousness, one center of activity; he is one person in the modern sense. Yet this one person is not one who lurks behind the Trinity, for there are not four in God. He is instead the person of the Father, who truly gives himself to men in the Son and Holy Spirit.

Seen this way, it is difficult to conceive of a system which has a stronger view of God's unity and is also adequately trinitarian. If for no other reason, Rahner is valuable because he provides a benchmark for the maximal understanding of the trinitarian unity. This text will now address the question of the adequacy of Rahner's system. It will present critiques of Rahner which others have offered, and find that several do not detract from the strengths of Rahner's position. However, it will conclude that Rahner's thought presents a false generalization of the Greek tradition, has problems with internal consistency, threatens God's aseity, flirts with modalism, and requires a non-Chalcedonian Christology. Gary Badcock writes that it is in Rahner's doctrine of the Trinity that "his most glaring theological inadequacies can be seen."[97] This section will support that assertion.

Historical Difficulty

Readers conversant with the Catholic trinitarian tradition will recognize much of Rahner's doctrine of the Trinity. A large portion of *The Trinity* is devoted to an exposition of "The Main Lines of Official Trinitarian Doctrine."[98] Despite his attempts to integrate what he sees to be the Greek tradition into the doctrine of the Trinity, he nevertheless retains the core of the trinitarian doctrine expounded by Augustine and Aquinas, relative

97. Badcock, "Karl Rahner, the Trinity," 154.
98. Rahner, *Trinity*, 49–79.

trinitarianism.[99] Rahner can be seen to uphold, in his own way, the trinitarian maxims of Augustine, Anselm, and Aquinas, as discussed above.[100]

However, it is true that Rahner deviates from the work of Aquinas, and possibly Augustine, by giving priority to the Father as the font of divinity.[101] Rahner looks to the earliest Christian thinkers for support. He writes, "If, with Scripture and the Greeks, we mean by ὁ Θεός in the first place the Father (not letting the word simply "suppose" for the Father), then the trinitarian structure of the Apostle's Creed, in line with Greek theology of the Trinity, would lead us to treat first of the Father and to consider also, in this first chapter of the doctrine of God, the 'essence' of God, the Father's godhead."[102] He writes that "when the New Testament thinks of God, it is the concrete, individual, uninterchangeable Person who comes to mind, who is in fact the Father."[103] Because both the Scriptures and the church Fathers meant "the Father" when they wrote "God," it is best to think in a similar manner, and recognize that the recitation of the Lord's Prayer is offered to the Father, and that saints are adopted by the Father. These activities do not relate to "God" as the undifferentiated unity.[104]

Rahner seems to believe that it is obvious that "God" signifies only the Father in both Scripture and the Greek Fathers; uses to identify the Son and Holy Spirit are *suppositio*, not *significatio*. Rahner acknowledges that there are several instances where the Bible speaks of the Son as *theos*: Rom 9:5, John 1:1, 1:18, 20:28; 1 John 5:20, Titus 2:13. However, he denies that these passages allow for "God" to signify the Son for two reasons. First, with the exception of John 20:28, none of these passages refer to the Son as "*ho theos*." Second, in John 20:28, "*theos*" is predicated of the Son; it is not used to refer to him as the subject. Rahner notes that there are many instances where the Son is not referred to as "God," and states that the Holy Spirit is never called "God" in Scripture. He contrasts this with the

---

99. Bartel, "Relative Trinitarian," 153; Augustine, *Trin.* 5.8–16 (*NPNF1* 3:91–96); Aquinas, *Summ. Theol.* 1a.39–40 (BF 7:99–158).

100. See pp. 20–23 above.

101. Hill, *Three-Personed God*, 73, 77; Rahner, *Trinity*, 16. There is disagreement as to whether Augustine thought of the Father as the font of divinity. See Olson and Hall, *Trinity*, 44–45.

102. Rahner, *Trinity*, 16.

103. Ibid., 17.

104. Rahner, *Theological Investigations*, 1:147. That this is not the unanimous position of Catholic scholars can be seen by the response of Hill. Hill, "Uncreated Grace," 352.

Father, who is consistently and clearly presented as "God," especially in benedictions.[105] He also argues that the Old Testament references to God should be understood not as references to the undifferentiated Godhead, but the Father.[106] Rahner does little to demonstrate that the Greeks used the term *ho theos* to signify only the Father, though the example of Origen, who denied the Son the article, does come to mind.[107]

However, it is not at all obvious that "God," or even "the God," only signifies the Father in Scripture. First, it should be noted that Rahner gives no explicit criteria for determining when a word functions as *significatio* or *suppositio*, and therefore can give no defense for these criteria. It certainly seems arbitrary to discount John 20:28 on the assertion that the exclamation is predicating "God" of Jesus, not naming him.[108] Second, there appear to be examples that meet the implicit criteria that for "God" to signify the Son it must be subjective and articular. John Behr believes that the article is grammatically present in two of the instances Rahner mentions, Rom 9:5 and John 1:1.[109] If this is the case, Rom 9:5, in which *ho theos* is nominative, satisfies Rahner's implied standards for *significatio*. Third, regarding the Old Testament usage of "God," Behr notes that, for Paul, the numerous references to Jesus as Lord carry "the full significance of the Divine Name, *YHWH*."[110] If this is the case, Paul understood the Old Testament to refer not just to the Father, but also to the Son. Fourth, it is hard to understand Acts 5:3–4 as anything other than an identification of the Holy Spirit as "God," as the latter term is clearly substituted for the former.

Finally, the suggestion that "God" applies to the Father by *significatio* and the other persons, or the Godhead, by *suppositio* makes little sense within Rahner's system. The Father, Son, and Spirit are the self-same identical Godhead. Therefore, if "God" refers by *significatio* to the Father's nature, it refers in the exact same way to the Son and Spirit, because there is only one nature. On the other hand, if it refers to the person of the Father, it is singularly unapt to refer by *suppositio* to the Son or Spirit, for,

105. Rahner, *Theological Investigations*, 1:134–41.

106. Rahner, *Trinity*, 59–60; Karl Rahner, "Trinity, Divine," 295.

107. Origen, *Fragmenta in evangelium Joannis* 2.2, (*ANF* 9:323). Rowan Williams notes Origen's general reluctance to call the Son *ho theos*. Williams, *Arius*, 136.

108. Rahner, *Theological Investigations*, 1:137.

109. Behr, *Way to Nicaea*, 59, 61.

110. Ibid., 64.

if person is to be understood as relation of opposition, their persons are precisely that in which they are not like the Father. It seems that Rahner's assertion that the Bible thinks of the Father as "God" in a way prior to that of the Son or Spirit is an unproven simplification.

The same can be said about the language of the Greek Fathers. While some of them may have seen "God" as referring properly only to the Father, that does not appear to be the consensus. Archibald Robertson writes of Athanasius, "To Athanasius, the Godhead is complete not in the Father alone, still less in the Three Persons *as parts* of the one οὐσία, but in *each* Person as much as in *all*."[111] It is true that Athanasius gives the Father a generative priority within the Godhead,[112] and generally he uses "God" as a substitute name for "Father." However, he does not appear to view this usage as an absolute rule. Athanasius uses "God" to refer to both the Father and the Triad.[113] He also writes of the Son, "He too is the First, as the Fulness of the Godhead of the First and Only, being whole and full God."[114]

The Cappadocians show a similar willingness to use "God" to refer properly to the Father, the Godhead, the Son, or the Spirit. In fact, Gregory Nazianzen seems to see "God" as referring most properly to the divine nature, not the individual divine persons. He writes that "there is One Essence of God, and One Nature, and One Name . . . and that whatever is properly called by this Name really is God; and what He is in Nature, That He is truly called."[115] Perhaps even more clear is his assertion, "As far then as we can reach, He Who Is, and God, are the special names of His Essence."[116]

Gregory of Nyssa denies that the special name of the divine essence is "God," instead arguing that the greatest name is unuttered, because

---

111. Archibald Robertson, introduction to *NPNF2* 4:xxxi. Williams recognizes the continued influence of Origen's emphasis on the Father in Alexandria, but also notes that Athanasius believed the Son was essential to the Father. See Williams, *Arius*, 155, 228–89. Weinandy believes Athanasius saw God not so much as Father or Son, but the Father begetting the Son. Weinandy, *Father's Spirit of Sonship*, 11–12.

112. Athanasius, *C. Ar.* 1.5.14 (*NPNF2* 4:314).

113. Ibid., 1.6.17 (*NPNF2* 4:316); 3.25.15 (*NPNF2* 4:402).

114. Ibid., 3.23.6 (*NPNF2* 4:397).

115. Gregory Nazianzen, *Orationes* 3.13 (*NPNF2* 7:305).

116. Ibid., 4.18 (*NPNF2* 7:316); cf. Gregory Nazianzen, *Or.* 34.8 (*NPNF2* 7:336).

it belongs to the ineffable divine essence.[117] However, he does believe that a reference to the one God "does not indicate the Father alone, but comprehends in its significance the Son with the Father."[118] In fact, aside from "Father" all the Father's titles refer properly to the Son.[119] Gregory responds to the charge of tritheism by identifying the one God with the Triad, writing "what room is there for the charge of tritheism against those by whom one God is worshipped, the God expressed by the Name of the Father and the Son and the Holy Ghost?"[120] Thus, "God" signifies any of the divine three, for "if you speak of God, you signify the same Whom you understood by the other attributes."[121]

Basil shows a similar understanding of how God should be used, and what the "one God" is. His exposition of 1 Cor 8:5–6 does not read "the Father" in sole apposition to "one God." Instead, Basil asserts that Paul uses "one God" to refer to the divine nature before discussing the persons of the Father, Son, and Holy Spirit.[122]

John of Damascus, who seeks primarily to preserve the teaching of his Greek predecessors, clearly understands "God" to refer primarily to the Godhead. He writes, "We, therefore, both know and confess that God is without beginning, without end, eternal and everlasting, uncreate, unchangeable, invariable . . . that God is One, that is to say, one essence, and that He is known, and has His being in three subsistences, in Father, I say, and Son and Holy Spirit."[123] While many ancient creeds begin with, "We believe in God the Father," John begins one paragraph with, "We believe, then, in one God," and includes in the next the two phrases, "(We believe) in one Father," and "in one Son."[124] The practice of discussing the nature of the one God prior to dealing with the persons of the Trinity, which Rahner traces to the replacement of Lombard by Aquinas,[125] actually begins much earlier, and in the Greek tradition.

---

117. Gregory of Nyssa, *Contra Eunomius*. 2.3 (*NPNF2* 5:103).

118. Ibid., 2.4 (*NPNF2* 5:104).

119. Ibid., 2.6 (*NPNF2* 5:108).

120. Ibid., 2.14 (*NPNF2* 5:130).

121. Gregory of Nyssa, *Trin.* (*NPNF2* 5:327).

122. Basil, *Ep.* 8.3 (*NPNF2* 8:117).

123. John of Damascus, *Expositio fidei orthodoxa* 1.2 (*NPNF2* 9:1–2).

124. Ibid., 1.8 (*NPNF2* 9:6).

125. Karl Rahner, *Karl Rahner*, 159; Rahner, *Trinity*, 16.

It appears that Rahner, despite his best efforts, cannot claim the usage
of the Greek Fathers to support his contention that "God" properly signifies only the Father. How important is this criticism? Taken by itself, not
very. However, it suggests that the emphasis Rahner places on the Father's
priority within the Godhead is similarly an exaggeration, or even distor-
tion, of the position of the Greek Fathers. It also suggests that, if this is the
case, Rahner is unaware of it. While much of Rahner's trinitarianism has
significant historical support, his extreme identification of the Father with
the Godhead goes well beyond the positions of those to whom Rahner
claims to look for support. In this area, at least, Rahner's understanding of
the unity of the Trinity departs from the historical tradition.[126]

Logical Difficulties

It has already been stated that theology must operate within the dictates
of logic, and that the doctrine of the Trinity is no exception. At this point,
two logical objections will be raised to Rahner's understanding of trinitarian unity. The first is a broad critique of relative trinitarianism, of which
Rahner's system is only one example.[127] The second concerns Rahner's
system only, and is a suggestion that Rahner's trinitarian system is illogi-
cal because it contains elements which lead to contradictory conclusions.
While the first critique will be shown to be flawed, the second will reveal
serious difficulties in the logic of Rahner's position.

The Coherence of Relative Identity

As has already been noted, Rahner's understanding of trinitarian unity
depends on the concept of relations of opposition. It requires that the
Father, Son, and Spirit can be identical in an absolute sense, and still be
distinct in a relative sense, be distinguished in opposition to one another.
This is the concept of relative identity. According to relative identity, it is
coherent to say that two x's are identical, but in some sense not the same.

There is something inherently counterintuitive about relative identity, and one philosopher who has recently attempted to show the incoherence of relative identity is Timothy Bartel.[128] Bartel believes his argument

126. While Cary sees more extensive problems with Rahner's use of the Greeks, this
is likewise his conclusion. Cary, "Classical Trinitarianism," 392.

127. As noted above, Aquinas presents the classic relative scheme. See Aquinas, *Summ.
Theol.* 1a.39–40 (7:99–158).

128. Bartel, "Relative Trinitarian," 129–55.

"fatally damages many of the historic interpretations of Trinitarian doctrine. For example, we must dismiss the Trinitarian theories of Augustine, Aquinas, Boethius, and any other theologian who maintains that each person of the Godhead is somehow numerically identical with the divine essence."[129] Rahner holds such a position, and Bartel notes that his argument effectively disproves the position of Rahner which he sees as a form of "the One Person Theory."[130]

Bartel begins his argument by pointing out that many see a logical contradiction in the following four trinitarian statements:

1. There is exactly one divine being
2. The Father is divine
3. The Son is divine
4. The Father is not identical with the Son[131]

Taken together, the first three statements entail the identity of the Father and the Son, which the fourth denies. The traditional response, Bartel notes, has been to state that identity is polygamous, or sortal-relative. That is, the statement "*x* is the same as *y*" is incomplete; only a statement like "*x* is the same *S* as *y*," which specifies a sortal, or, as Peter Geach calls it, a criterion of identity, is able to be evaluated.[132] Thus, the statement, "The Father is the same essence as the Son," is not the same statement as, "The Father is the same person as the Son." This is the theory of relative identity.

However, Bartel believes that the relative trinitarian faces insuperable difficulties. He must reject Leibniz's Law, the Indiscernibility of Identicals.[133] He must deny the eternal begetting and procession of the Son and the Spirit. He must deny that only the Son could become incarnate. The position which remains, Bartel suggests, is no better than Sabellianism.[134] Rahner would likely agree with the assessment of such a position; clearly he felt the need to assert that only the Son could become

129. Ibid., 153. Bartel believes his critique leaves only social models of the Trinity as viable options.
130. Ibid.
131. Ibid., 129.
132. Geach, *Reference and Generality*, 39.
133. Leibniz, *Discourse on Metaphysics*, 14; Leibniz, *Monadology*, 222, 377.
134. Bartel, "Relative Trinitarian," 133.

incarnate. The question is, however, if Bartel is correct as to what a relative trinitarian must deny.

Bartel's first point is that the relative trinitarian faces trouble with Leibnitz's Law. Put briefly, it states that x is identical to y if and only if x and y share all properties. Bartel argues that the intuitive clarity and value of this Law require its acceptance.[135] Gordon H. Clark argues that this theory of individuation is the only one tenable.[136] Thus, a doctrine of the Trinity which requires a rejection of Leibnitz's Law must itself be rejected.

Having said that, Bartel does allow that some revision of Leibnitz's Law may be permissible, especially in light of the Incarnation. After testing several forms, Bartel concludes with a relative version of Leibnitz's Law which he finds permissible:

(RLL) For any x and any y and any sortal f and any property P: if x is the same f as y, then x has P $qua\, f$ if and only if y has P $qua\, f$.[137]

This allows the Incarnate Christ to have some properties as God, and others as man.

However, Bartel denies that this formulation of Leibnitz's Law allows the relative trinitarian to affirm the eternal begetting of the Son or procession of the Spirit. The begetting of the Son, or "begottenness," has traditionally been understood to be a personal property, a *notio*.[138] But this is a property which the Son possesses and which the Father lacks. This Bartel notes, is a problem: "If God the Son has a property *qua* divine that God the Father lacks, then they are simply two different deities."[139] The same holds true for the procession of the Holy Spirit. Bartel points out that the Holy Spirit either depends asymmetrically on the Father for his existence

135. Ibid., 136.

136. Clark, *Trinity*, 104.

137. Bartel, "Relative Trinitarian," 138. Bartel offers another form on 143, but it differs little.

138. Ibid., 143; Rahner, *Trinity*, 78–79. The idea that the persons of the Trinity are distinguished by personal characteristics, sometimes called notions or *notio*, is seen in John of Damascus, who claims to "recognise the difference of the subsistences only in the three properties of independence of cause and Fatherhood, of dependence on cause and Sonship, of dependence on cause and procession." John of Damascus, *Fid. Orth.* 3.5 (*NPNF2* 9:49). See also Aquinas, *Summ. Theol.* 1a.32.2 (BF 6:109–19); Augustine, *Trin.* 5.6–7 (*NPNF1* 3:89–91).

139. Bartel, "Relative Trinitarian," 144.

or he does not. If he does, they are not identical as divine beings, for they have different properties *qua* divine. If he does not, there is no eternal procession. The relative trinitarian seems to be forced to choose between his theory and tradition, but Rahner's position seeks to hold to both.

Bartel concludes with what he believes to be demonstrative proof of the failure of relative trinitarianism. Tradition clearly teaches that only the Son became incarnate. The Incarnation means that the divine mind of the Son was co-personal with Jesus Christ. This is a divine property, but it is a divine property which both the Father and the Spirit are traditionally said to lack. But this would mean they are not the same divine being, for they differ in divine properties. Bartel believes the relative trinitarian must therefore either abandon his trinitarian understanding or assert that the entire Trinity became incarnate.[140] Rahner seems particularly vulnerable to this criticism, since he asserts clearly that the three persons of the Trinity are one consciousness. Yet he is equally adamant that only the Son could, much less did, become man.

Is Rahner caught, along with all other relative trinitarians, in a logical trap? It does not appear so. In fact, several responses have been offered to arguments like Bartel's. Regarding Leibnitz's Law, A. P. Martinich asserts that, "Leibniz, of all people, did not accept, at least during his mature period, the law that bears his name."[141] Martinich points out flaws with any absolute concept of identity, and also notes that many thinkers have rejected absolute substitution of identicals.[142] From the arguments of Peter van Inwagen, one can conclude that a position like Bartel's fails to fully understand the implications of relative identity. First, it fails to recognize that not all relative identity predicates entail identity of properties. Second, it fails to recognize that classical identity is necessary for counting. Where there is only relative identity, the concepts of one and three are no longer univocal. The four statements with which Bartel begins only seem inconsistent because the reader reads the singulars as genuine singulars.[143] Thus, relative trinitarianism is not without its responses to Bartel.

140. Ibid., 150.

141. Martinich, "Identity and Trinity," 180.

142. Ibid. Millard Erickson criticizes Martinich's position for not guarding against tritheism, but here it is serving only as a logical defense of relative identity. See Erickson, *God in Three Persons*, 255–56.

143. van Inwagen, "Not Three Gods," 254, 264.

Since Bartel is writing after Rahner, it is uncertain how Rahner would respond to Bartel's criticism. However, Rahner was aware of the supposed logical difficulties of relative trinitarianism, and his thought contains elements which can serve to disarm Bartel's two other objections. These will be drawn on to show that Bartel does not demonstrate that Rahner's position is inconsistent.

Rahner anticipates the objection to the concept of relative identity. He notes that two absolute realities identical with one another must be identical with a third identical to either. However, he denies that is the case in the Trinity, for the persons are virtual distinctions, relative realities. And because of this, the proper thing to do is to presuppose that two relations of opposition can be distinct despite real identity with the divine nature. Because the nature of identity in the Godhead is a matter of presupposition, rather than proof, one cannot be proven wrong.[144] The positions of Geach, van Inwagen, and Martinich, as well as the fact that Bartel is able to offer several different definitions of identity in his article, all suggest that one's concept of identity is in large part presupposed, and Rahner seems fully within his rights on this point.

But, if relative identity is possible, does it destroy the distinctions between the persons? As has been noted, Bartel allows the coherence of the distinction between Christ as divine and Christ as human. Similarly, Rahner suggests that "we may distinguish between 'essential' and 'notional' realities or statements."[145] Some properties are essential and therefore apply to God and each person singly. However, the notional properties apply to each person as that person; they relate solely to the relation which constitutes the person.[146] Thus, the Son has the personal property of being begotten as person, in distinction from the Father, though he has the property of being omnipotent in identity with the divine essence and therefore the Father. Bartel, however, rejects this possibility because he cannot conceive of hypostasis, or person, as a sortal distinct from deity or *simpliciter*.[147] Clearly, this is the root of Bartel's objection to relative trinitarianism. For God to be one x and three y's only makes sense if x and y are not the same. Bartel rejects relative trinitariansim because he rejects

144. Rahner, *Trinity*, 70–72.

145. Ibid., 77.

146. Ibid., 78.

147. Bartel, "Relative Trinitarian," 146.

the possibility of a genuine distinction between person and essence.[148] Yet this distinction is the keystone of Rahner's doctrine of the Trinity, and it is a distinction which many have found coherent, from the early church until today.

However, distinguishing person from essence as Rahner does still leaves him vulnerable to Bartel's last criticism. Rahner places the divine consciousness in the one divine essence. If, as Bartel states, the Incarnation meant that the consciousness of the Son was the consciousness of Christ, it seems that all the members of the Trinity must have become incarnate.

While a fuller treatment of Rahner's Christology will come later, at this point is suffices to say that Rahner's Christology is not open to such a conclusion. For Rahner, the consciousness, the personality, of Jesus Christ was entirely a human consciousness, a human personality, and not the divine mind.[149]

Thus, it appears that the concept of relative trinitarianism is not incoherent, as long as a credible distinction can be made between person and essence. Rahner is not forced to abandon the personal distinctions between the members of the Godhead. Bartel seems to object to Rahner's doctrine at the deeper level, that of the distinction between person and essence. Yet it seems that the possibility of that distinction, not a perfect explanation thereof, is what is necessary to protect the relative trinitarianism from logical contradiction.[150] As van Inwagen concludes after arguing for relative identity:

> I have left the mystery of the Holy Trinity untouched. It is one thing to suggest that "is the same being as" does not dominate "is the same person as." It is another thing to explain how this could be.[151]

---

148. Bartel's arguments seem more germane to the positions of Anselm and Aquinas, which, as was shown, less credibly distinguish the persons and essence in God. See pp. 21–23 above.

149. Rahner, *Theological Investigations*, 4:112; *Foundations*, 287–92.

150. It might be suggested that the doctrine of property simplicity makes the concept of relative identity incoherent. While that is likely true, property simplicity is an issue in its own right, distinct from the question of trinitarian unity, and as such will not be addressed here.

151. van Inwagen, "One God," 272.

The Conflict between Rahner's Method and his Conclusions

While Rahner is not trapped in a logical contradiction by his relative trinitarian position, a careful examination of his methodology and conclusions will demonstrate that his system fails to meet the test of logical consistency. Rahner attempts to draw from both the Greek and the Latin traditions, and to develop a doctrine of the Trinity with his own transcendental methodology. He mixes the emphasis on God the Father, the definition of person as relation of opposition, and the concept of revelation as self-communication. This section will attempt to show that Rahner's synthesis results in contradictory conclusions.

Moltmann hints at this problem, but fails to properly identify it because he evaluates Rahner's thought from within his own theological system. For example, he suggests that emphasizing the Father's priority results in the disappearance of the Son. He writes, "If salvation history is reduced to the self-communication of the Father, the history of the Son is no longer identifiable at all."[152] But for Rahner, this is not a problem, because the Son is the self-communication of the Father, and the same self. There is no other self in the Son, so he can have no separate history.

However, there is a problem with Rahner's concept of self-communication, the priority of the Father, and a trinitarian understanding of the Son and Spirit. Recall Rahner's defense against Sabellianism. He states that the economic distinctions in God reveal a pre-existent, essential threefoldness within the God who reveals himself:

> The absolute self-communication of God to the world, as the mystery which has drawn nigh, is Father as the absolutely primordial and underivative; it is Son, as the principle which itself acts and necessarily must act in history in view of this free self-communication; it is Holy Spirit, as that which is given, and accepted by us. Since this "as" which is used in relation to us really speaks of the self-communication of God *in himself*, this trinity appertains to God in himself—it signifies a distinction in God himself.[153]

Because God reveals himself to us, and is revealed as three, he, in himself, must somehow be three.

Whether or not this is an adequate defense against Sabellianism, it poses a logical difficulty as soon as one remembers who "God" is for

152. Moltmann, *Trinity and the Kingdom*, 147.
153. Rahner, *Theological Investigations*, 4:70.

Rahner, who is revealing himself. It is always the Father. Rahner clearly asserts that "God" properly signifies the Father.[154] The Son is "the self-communication of the Father to the world," "the self-expression of the Father, the word of the Father (not of the Godhead)."[155] Rahner's theology of symbol identifies the Father as the origin of the Son, his symbol, his self-expression.[156] The God who is revealing himself is the Father; therefore, the distinctions of revelation must be real distinctions within the Father.

That this causes tension can be seen in Rahner's vacillation between references to two-fold and three-fold revelation. Sometimes he indicates that God reveals himself in a double way through the Son and the Holy Spirit. He writes of four pairs that describe God's self-communication: origin and future, history and transcendence, offer and acceptance, knowledge and love.[157] After showing that these pairs can be reduced to one pair, he concludes, "Hence the divine self-communication possesses two basic modalities: self-communication as truth and as love."[158] These two basic modalities are "a double self-communication of the Father, by which the Father communicates *himself*, while, as the one who utters and receives, he posits, precisely through this self-communication, his real distinction from the one who is uttered and from the one who is received."[159] Revelation in the Son and in the Holy Spirit are the two distinct, yet interrelated, moments of God's, meaning the Father's, self-communication.[160] Yet Rahner also speaks of three-fold communication. A single quotation reveals how quickly Rahner switches between the two ideas, "The one God communicates himself in absolute self-utterance and as absolute donation of love. ... Now the testimony of revelation in Scripture tells us that this self-communication of God has a threefold aspect."[161] He writes of three concrete ways in which God is given in revelation, and that these ways, Father, Son,

154. Rahner, *Trinity*, 16–18; Rahner, "*Theos* in the New Testament," in *Theological Investigations*, vol. 1.

155. Rahner, *Trinity*, 63.

156. Rahner, *Theological Investigations*, 4:236.

157. Rahner, *Trinity*, 90–94.

158. Ibid., 97.

159. Ibid., 102.

160. Ibid., 84.

161. Ibid., 36.

and Spirit, are how the hidden God becomes radically present in mystery.[162] At times Rahner speaks of two-fold self-communication, at other times, of three-fold.

This would not be a problem if not for Rahner's defense against Sabellianism, his concept of self-communication, and his equation of the economic and immanent Trinities. But for Rahner, the way God reveals himself must be a revelation of a prior distinction within himself. This leaves Rahner's reader with two possible conclusions. Either the Son and Spirit, the revelation of the Father, are distinctions within the Father, or the Father, Son, and Spirit are distinctions within "GOD," a prior being revealing himself through them.

Both of these potential conclusions are at odds with Rahner's trinitarianism. The latter is a quaternity, a position Rahner's opposition to which has already been discussed, and one he has sought to avoid by thoroughly identifying the Father with God. The first is not trinitarian at all, but a novel binitarianism in which the Son and Spirit are seen as prior internal aspects of the one God, the Father. Rahner states that the divine persons "do not differ from their own way of communicating themselves."[163] Because the Son and Spirit are ways in which the Father communicates himself, they become aspects of the Father, not persons of the Godhead. This goes far beyond the implicit subordinationism of which W. J. Hill accuses Rahner.[164]

One reaches a similar conclusion when one examines the uneasy wedding of relations of opposition and Rahner's concept of self-communication. It has been shown that Rahner consistently suggests that the Father is able to reveal himself, as Father, through the Son and the Holy Spirit. But the doctrine of relations of opposition, which Rahner espouses, indicates that the Son is Son in precisely those aspects in which he is not the Father. Because he shares the Father's essence, he can communicate the essence of the Father. But because he is precisely not the person of the Father, he cannot communicate the Father's person. Hill makes a similar point from within the Catholic tradition, when he writes that "the only communication possible in the case of a divine Person will be that which the Person is in Its distinct hypostatic character. It can only

162. Ibid., 74.

163. Ibid., 36.

164. Hill, *Three-Personed God*, 143.

involve then that whereby a Person stands in relative opposition to the other Two. Should it be something which pertains rather to His identity with the nature, then, by that very fact, it ceases to be proper and becomes common to all three divine Subsistences."[165] Thus, neither the Son nor the Spirit can reveal anything about the Father as Father, as a distinct person, a distinct relation opposed to them; they can only reveal their own persons and the common divine essence.

This may not appear to be a problem, since the Father is the one divine essence. But it reveals again that, for Rahner, the Father cannot be the relation of opposition he is supposed to be. Because he is revealed, as Father, by the Son and Spirit, he ceases to be a relation opposed to them. If, on the other hand, the Son and Spirit reveal the Father in that which they share, the divine essence, then the Father's distinct hypostasis is not revealed and therefore, by Rahner's Rule, has no immanent reality. In either case his person, his virtual distinction from the absolute reality of the Godhead, dissolves, leaving a binity of Son and Spirit within the Father.

This is a severe inadequacy of Rahner's understanding of the unity of the Trinity. It is carefully hidden, for Rahner shifts between "God" and "Father" and between "two-fold" and "three-fold" in his discussions of self-communication. Yet it is now clear that Rahner has combined elements to strengthen his understanding of trinitarian unity which are essentially incompatible with his understanding of self-communication. If the one God, the Father, truly reveals himself, and his essential distinction, through the Son and Spirit, they cannot be relations of opposition against him. If, on the other hand, the revealed Trinitarian distinctions are genuine distinctions defined by relative opposition within the Godhead, then the Father cannot be the source of revelation Rahner presents him as. Rahner's trinitarian system cannot hold together.

Theological Difficulties

Just as any construction of the doctrine of the Trinity stands within a history of dogma, so it also stands within a total theological scheme. The unity of a trinitarian God must fit that God. Two problems have been noted with how Rahner's doctrine of the unity of the Trinity fits the God of the Bible. Some have suggested that, despite his assertions, Rahner's emphasis

165. Hill, "Uncreated Grace," 350–51.

on the triune unity is so great that his system approaches modalism, or Sabellianism.[166] It has also been suggested that Rahner's understanding of the unity of the Trinity, in which God is understood to be a single absolute subject, weakens the aseity of God.[167] These two criticisms will now be examined. The first will be found to be deficient, the second to be apt.

Sabellianism

It has been noted that Rahner attempts to forestall any accusation of Sabellianism against him. For Rahner, "Sabellian" describes a doctrine of God which sees the trinitarian distinctions as entirely human, as "merely the result of a mental distinction deriving from our intelligence."[168] Rahner's defense against this charge is to assert the ontological reality of the distinctions, the relations of opposition, which are the diversity within his trinitarian unity. Rahner therefore escapes from what he defines Sabellianism to be.

It might be argued that this is not the only possible definition of Sabellianism. The Greek Fathers used this term to impugn a variety of positions. Athanasius wrote that Sabellians are those who call the Son "*monoousian* and not *homoousian*," those who allow no distinction between the Father and the Son.[169] Elsewhere, a temporal shift from Father to Son, in which the difference is only nominal, marks the Sabellian position.[170] Gregory Nazianzen notes that many in the East suspected the Latin terms for "person" of Sabellianism, presumably because they believed the terms *persona* and *prosopon* too weak when compared with the more substantial Eastern *hypostasis*.[171] It is thus an open question as to what exactly the term "Sabellian" properly applies.

But it is also a moot question. What is at issue is not whether Rahner is a follower of Sabellius. What is at issue is whether Rahner's emphasis on divine unity has led him to deny the biblical testimony concerning the

---

166. Thompson, for example, cautiously concludes that Rahner, while not a modalist, shows traces of modalism. Thompson, *Modern Trinitarian Perspectives*, 132. Hill classifies him as a "Modal Trinitarian." Hill, *Three-Personed God*, 146, 149.

167. Thompson, *Modern Trinitarian Perspectives*, 27–28.

168. Rahner, *Trinity*, 55. This is also the position of Aquinas. Aquinas, *Summ. Theol.* 1a.28.1.

169. Athanasius, *Exp. Fid.* 2 (*NPNF2* 4:84).

170. Athanasius, *C. Ar.* 3.23.4 (*NPNF2* 4:395).

171. Gregory Nazianzen, *Theol. Or.* 21.35 (*NPNF2* 7:279).

three in God. Any trinitarian system which fails to do justice to the biblical picture of divine persons is inadequate, at least from an evangelical perspective. It is this charge which Moltmann levels clearly at Rahner:

> Neither Barth's formula of the "one personal God in three modes of being" nor Rahner's thesis of the one divine "subject in three distinct modes of subsistence" does justice to the story that is played out between Jesus the Son, Abba his Father, and the Holy Spirit. The personal interrelationship of the Father who loves the Son, the Son who prays to the Father, and the Spirit who confesses and glorifies the Father and the Son—so emphatically underscored in the New Testament—is not grasped by deductively obtained formulas of modern doctrines of the Trinity.[172]

Nor is he alone in making this charge. Michael O'Carroll, who himself would not use "person" univocally in trinitarian discussion, sees Rahner at odds with the biblical witness. He writes, "One obvious difficulty about this phrase [Rahner's "distinct manners or modes of subsisting"], as about the idea suggested by Barth—who did not espouse ancient modalism—is precisely that of the language quoted from the NT. How can a 'distinct mode of subsisting' say 'I', without being taken for the godhead identical with every use of 'I'?"[173] J. Scott Horrell has recently shown that the New Testament supports, if not demands, a doctrine of the Trinity in which the Father and Son possess distinct centers of consciousness, a position directly opposed to Rahner's.[174] Is Rahner's position compatible with the Bible?

Certainly, as noted earlier, Rahner has left the ontological content of "person," or "mode of subsisting," minimal. He has denied that the Son loves the Father with mutual love, and that "person" can be used univocally of the three. In addition, he has denied that "person" carries the same meaning in Christological and trinitarian discourse.[175] Bracken has noted that Rahner appears to be working at cross-purposes at this point. While he warns about "mere monotheism," he denies individual personality to each of the three.[176] The interpersonal categories which Rahner wants to emphasize between God and man, he removes from

172. Moltmann, "Unity of the Triune God," 160. Cf. Boff, *Trinity and Society*, 137.

173. O'Carroll, *Trinitas*, 180.

174. Horrell, "Biblical Model," 405–8.

175. Rahner, *Trinity*, 26–27.

176. Bracken, "Holy Trinity, II," 260.

the immanent trinity.[177] This seems to move away from the picture of the Trinity Rahner, O'Carroll, and Horrell highlight. As Lawrence B. Porter concludes, "Thus Rahner's formula cannot help but render a sterile image of the Trinity as an impersonal system of relations among hypostases in an abstract essence."[178]

Rahner might respond, however, that the biblical picture of the Trinity is seen primarily, if not exclusively, in the incarnate Son. And in the Incarnation, Rahner sees provided another subject who can interact with the Father in the way the Bible indicates. Rahner's Christology focuses on the human subject in Christ, and it is that human subject who loves, obeys, and serves the Father.[179] This allows Rahner to do justice to the obviously personal interaction of the Father and Jesus in the New Testament, though its effects on his Christology will be evaluated later. While the Holy Spirit is clearly distinct from the Father in the New Testament, the nature of that distinction, and its basis in a distinct center of consciousness, is much less clear than in the case of the Son. Thus, Rahner's system is able to be reconciled feasibly with the New Testament record, despite its understanding of a single divine consciousness. The presence of a human consciousness in Christ could conceivably allow the interaction the Bible describes. Despite the biblical reservations one may have about understanding the triune God as a single subject, that position cannot be ruled out immediately; it must be measured against other options.[180]

Aseity

Thomas V. Morris has pointed out two problems with modalism. One, as has just been shown, is the New Testament. The other is the problem of a lonely God.[181] It is this latter problem which Rahner cannot escape.

Morris does not elucidate what he means by the problem of a lonely God, but the nature of the problem can be seen in Richard of St. Victor's

177. Ibid., 258. There is in fact a tension between how the Logos, the Father's self-expression, lacks a personality other than that of the Father, and how humans, a further self-expression of God, have personality. See Rahner, *Trinity*, 32; *Theological Investigations*, 4:239.

178. Porter, "'Persons' in the Trinity," 543.

179. Rahner, *Theological Investigations*, 4:110–12.

180. Hill, *Three-Personed God*, 145.

181. Morris, *Our Idea of God*, 180, 183.

work, which argues for the Trinity by tracing the consequences of the fact that the God of the Bible is a good God. Goodness requires genuine love, genuine love requires another as its object, and perfect love requires a divine object. Therefore God, to be perfectly good, must have perfect love, and thus another divine person of equal worth.[182] No single absolute subject could be the God of love of the Bible, as Richard writes, "Behold how from shared fellowship with a third person in that Trinity it is argued that concordant charity and consocial love are never found anywhere in an isolated individual."[183] Instead, the divine being, to truly love as God ought, must have distinct centers of action, for "in mutual love it is absolutely necessary that there be both one who gives love and one who returns love."[184] Rahner agrees with this, but uses it to ground his denial of mutual love in the Trinity; for Rahner, there cannot be mutual love because there are not two subjects.[185] Richard's discussion of the need for a third in the Trinity implies there is a unanimity within the Godhead, an impossibility for a single subject.[186] Anselm asserts that each member of the Trinity must love the others, and himself, with equal intensity.[187] It is because each member of the Trinity is a loving person that God can be love.[188]

This is clearly not how Rahner understands the divine unity. As Moltmann notes, "Rahner's reinterpretation of the doctrine of the Trinity ends in the mystic solitariness of God."[189] God, in himself, is a single, solitary subject. Certainly, he expresses himself and loves his self-expression, but there is only one "he." God can love himself, but he cannot love selflessly. There is no one else.

This view of God's unity threatens God's aseity, his self-sufficiency. Richard's argument, that true goodness results in genuine love for a genuine other, means that Rahner's God cannot be fully good in and of himself. Creation is necessary for God to achieve the highest level of love, and therefore the highest level of good. For God to experience the kind of love he demands from believers, the sacrificial love that he reveals on the cross,

182. Richard of St. Victor, *De Trinitate* 3.2 (374–75).

183. Ibid., 3.20 (393).

184. Ibid., 3.3 (376).

185. Rahner, *Trinity*, 106–7.

186. Richard, *Trin.* 3.11–12 (385).

187. Anselm, *Monologion* 51 (61).

188. Olson and Hall, *Trinity*, 4.

189. Moltmann, *Trinity and Kingdom*, 148.

he must create other personalities for whom he can give himself. Before creation, he is a lonely God, and therefore, a God who is not fully good. A god who requires creation to be virtuous is not the God of the Bible.

Rahner's understanding of the divine unity falls short theologically. By asserting the unity of the Trinity in a single divine consciousness, he strips the doctrine of its ability to explain how God can be love apart from creation. As such, it critically endangers the doctrine of God's aseity.

Christological Difficulty

It has been shown that Rahner's understanding of the unity of the Trinity is not consonant with the historical tradition it claims, with the doctrine of a self-sufficient God, and even with itself. There is a final problem with Rahner's understanding of Trinitarian unity; it is incompatible with a Chalcedonian Christology, despite the fact that Chalcedon is normative for Catholic Christology.[190]

Rahner's Christology develops naturally from his doctrine of the Trinity. In his doctrine of the Trinity, the Logos, as the Father's self-expression, is not an individual center of consciousness. He is not a subject of action, for he possesses no will. There is only one subject in the Godhead, the Father who is identical with the Godhead. However, Jesus Christ was certainly a subject, a center of consciousness. But the source of this subjectivity cannot be the Logos, for the Logos has no subjectivity of its own. Therefore it is the human element in Christ that supplies the subject for all of Christ's actions.

Rahner wants to avoid any suggestion that the humanity of Christ was a tool of his divinity.[191] Instead, he makes the human reality take precedence. Rahner believes "Jesus had a human self-consciousness which may not be identified in a 'monophysitic' way with the consciousness of the divine Logos."[192] It is the human nature, with its will and personhood, and not the divine nature, which determines the hypostatic union, in human freedom.[193] What role does that leave for the divine Logos in the actions of Jesus? Very little. Rahner writes, "In accordance with the fact that the natures are unmixed, basically the active influence of the Logos

190. Doud, "Rahner's Christology," 144.

191. Ibid., 146.

192. Rahner, *Foundations*, 249.

193. Rahner, *Theological Investigations*, 1:160, 169; *Foundations*, 289.

on the human 'nature' in Jesus in a physical sense may not be understood in any other way except the way the influence is exercised by God on free creatures elsewhere."[194] When the Logos is said to be the person of Christ, that must not be understood as saying that the Logos is the center of Christ's consciousness, or that the Logos is the immediate source of his choices or actions.[195] What the humanity of Christ experienced was "nothing essentially more or less in the line of closeness to and encounter with God, than that which is in fact provided for *each* man in grace: the beatific vision."[196]

Rahner's portrayal of the interaction of the humanity and the divine logos is not entirely unprecedented. As David Coffey writes, many "words of his have a somewhat Nestorian ring about them."[197] They also seem similar to Geoffrey Bromiley's definition of dynamic monarchianism, whose adherents saw "in Jesus a finite man in whom the eternal but impersonal Word found embodiment and who in virtue of this association could be acknowledged as the Son of God."[198]

In Chapter 1, it was shown that Chalcedon affirmed a Christology in which the second person of the Trinity, the Son, added humanity to himself.[199] The person of the Word was the sole person in the man Jesus Christ. Yet Rahner has developed a Christology at odds with Chalcedon. He denies that "person" as used in the doctrine of the Trinity is equivalent to "person" as used in the Christological debate.[200] By doing so, Rahner falsely severs the connection between Trinity and Christology. The Fathers certainly believed that the second "person" of the Trinity was the "person" born of Mary in the Incarnation.[201] Rahner denies that "person" in the Christological formula carries the modern sense of a conscious subject.[202] However, for Chalcedon, because the conscious subject of Christ is the second person of the Trinity, "person" must carry the meaning which Rahner denies it,

194. Rahner, *Foundations*, 289.

195. Ibid., 292.

196. Rahner, *Theological Investigations*, 4:112.

197. Coffey, "The 'Incarnation' of the Holy Spirit," 473. For a discussion of Nestorius, see Grillmeier, *Christ in Christian Tradition*, 1:447–72.

198. Bromiley, *Historical Theology*, 68.

199. See pp. 30–33 above.

200. Rahner, *Trinity*, 26–27.

201. Porter, "'Persons' in the Trinity," 532.

202. Rahner, *Foundations*, 292; Hill, *Three-Personed God*, 222.

and must do so in both cases. For that to work that person must be the divine person of the Logos, the single subject of the life, death, and resurrection of Christ. As Clark notes, according to the orthodox doctrine since Chalcedon, Christ has two natures, and therefore two wills, but does not have a human person.[203] Bromiley makes a similar point when he writes that, in orthodox Christology "the Word constitutes the unity of the being of Jesus."[204] Rahner's Christological position, grounded in his doctrine of the Trinity, is clearly opposed to that of Chalcedon, and in fact is reminiscent of Nestorius, whose condemnation was affirmed at that council.

Conclusion

Karl Rahner has done much to restore attention to the doctrine of the Trinity. He has made significant contributions, presenting an understanding of trinitarian unity which is certainly not tritheism. He articulates in a contemporary form the classic doctrine of Aquinas and Augustine, and attempts to relate it to the doctrines of the Greek Fathers and the realities of modern life. He serves as a reminder that relative trinitarianism is not dead, and that a case can still be made for it as long as person and essence are genuinely distinguished.

However, his position must be rejected as unacceptable. A unity of the Trinity which speaks of the Father as God in a way different from the Son or the Spirit is outside the Christian tradition. A Trinitarian unity so strong that it denies that mutual love, and therefore goodness, can occur within God himself destroys the self-sufficiency of God. A doctrine of the Trinity which results in a quaternity or a binity is not a doctrine of the Trinity at all. Finally, any doctrine of the Trinity which leads to a Christology which removes the divine subject in Christ is unacceptable.

203. Clark, *Trinity*, 59.
204. Bromiley, *Historical Theology*, 79.

3

Millard Erickson and Trinitarian Unity

SINCE THE PUBLICATION OF his first book, *The New Evangelical Theology*, in 1968, Millard J. Erickson has been a consistent voice for American evangelicalism. Veli-Matti Kärkkäinen sees him as representing the moderate, and likely the majority, voice in contemporary American evangelicalism.[1] His systematic theology text, *Christian Theology*, has served well and been well received in the evangelical community through several printings and two editions. He has also interacted extensively with postmodernism and postconservatism, seeking to develop an appropriate evangelical response to these two related movements.[2]

His recent work, *God in Three Persons: A Contemporary Inter-pretation of the Trinity*, represents a significant evangelical contribution to the contemporary discussion of the Trinity. James Leo Garrett, Jr., notes that the mere existence of the text makes a contribution. He writes, "No twentieth century author clearly identifiable as an Evangelical Protestant has written a major monograph on the Trinity. No Baptist theologian during the nineteenth and twentieth centuries has written such. . . . Now Millard Erickson, as an Evangelical and a Baptist, has produced such a monograph, and his undertaking is thus inherently noteworthy."[3] In this text, Erickson surveys the history of the doctrine of the Trinity, examines several contemporary responses to the doctrine, presents his own understanding of the doctrine, and finally describes some of the practical implications of his doctrine of the Trinity. Erickson has also supplemented that lengthy

1. Kärkkäinen, *Doctrine of God*, 192.
2. Erickson, *Postmodernizing the Faith*; *Evangelical Left*.
3. Garrett, review of *God in Three Persons*, 78.

work with the simpler text, *Making Sense of the Trinity*. Unfortunately, his work has not garnered significant scholarly interaction.[4]

This chapter will examine Erickson's understanding of divine unity. It will begin by presenting Erickson's social view of the Trinity, noting the stark contrasts it has with the position of Karl Rahner. It will then discuss the two ways in which Erickson sees this social Trinity being united. Finally, it will expose Erickson's position to several critiques.

MILLARD ERICKSON'S UNDERSTANDING OF DIVINE UNITY

In Chapter 2 it was suggested that Rahner's understanding of divine unity provided a maximal picture of that unity. God is one essence, one will, one operation, one consciousness, and one "person" in the modern sense. The Son and Spirit are united to the Father who is their source, and who is the one will at work within them. The word "God" properly refers to the Father alone, who reveals himself to the world through his Son and Holy Spirit. God is one in a very absolute way, but is three only relatively.[5]

Erickson's position falls at the opposite end of the spectrum from that of Rahner. While Rahner makes repeated reference to the singular essence of God, Erickson avoids any reference to a singular essence when presenting his understanding of the trinitarian unity. Erickson replaces Rahner's singular personality and consciousness with an understanding of "three persons, three centers of consciousness."[6] Erickson rejects all talk of the Father as source within the immanent Trinity, instead writing, "Rather than one member of the Trinity being the source of the others' being, and thus superior to them, we would contend that each of the three is eternally derived from each of the others, and all three are eternally equal."[7] Against Rahner's assertion that "God" refers properly only to the Father, Erickson states that it is the Trinity as such which is properly identified as "God." Other uses of "God," as in "the Father is God," are predicables. This means "the Father is God" is equivalent to "the Father

---

4. For example, Letham, *Holy Trinity* refers repeatedly to Rahner and Pannenberg, and mentions Zizioulas several times. Erickson, however, does not appear in the index. One notable exception is Kärkkäinen, *Trinity*, 214–34.

5. For these elements in Rahner, see pp. 41–44 above.

6. Erickson, *God in Three Persons*, 331.

7. Erickson, *Making Sense of the Trinity*, 90.

possesses deity."[8] For Erickson, God is not a singularity with virtual distinctions, but a "true unity, [a] union of those that are more than one."[9] Erickson's understanding of divine unity is radically different from the relative trinitarian position of Rahner.

Erickson puts forth the first of the three understandings of trinitarian unity based upon a social model of the Trinity which this paper will examine. This is a model of the Trinity which has gained considerable popularity in recent years.[10] Jürgen Moltmann, Richard Swinburne, and many others work with a social model, developing it along both biblical and philosophical lines.[11] J. Scott Horrell gives a useful definition of a social model of the Trinity: "In summary, as rooted in the NT, a *social model of the Trinity is that in which the one divine Being eternally exists as three distinct centers of consciousness, wholly equal in nature, genuinely personal in relationships, and each mutually indwelling the other.*"[12] Obviously, a wide variety of models could fit this definition, as the next three chapters will show. For, while the manner in which God is three is spelled out rather clearly, little is said about how God is one.

The contemporary use of the social model is often traced back to Leonard Hodgson, who suggested that the unity of the Triune God could not be understood as mathematical simplicity.[13] Instead, the proper way to understand God's unity is as an "organic unity," or an "internally constitutive unity."[14] Hodgson attempts to explain this unity as "the unity of a being whose unity consists in nothing else than the unifying activity which unifies the component elements."[15]

---

8. Erickson, *God in Three Persons*, 265–66.

9. Ibid., 231.

10. Schwöbel, "Introduction," in *Persons, Divine and Human*, 12; Horrell, "Biblical Model," 404.

11. Moltmann, *Trinity and the Kingdom*, 149–77; Swinburne, *Christian God*, 180–89; Gresham, "Social Model," 326–27.

12. Horrell, "Biblical Model," 408, emphasis original.

13. Gresham, "Social Model," 326; Bracken, "Holy Trinity, I," 166. Of course, Hodgson had sources. He mentions Webb, *God and Personality* in Hodgson, *Towards a Christian Philosophy*, 150. See also Welch, *In This Name*, 133–38; Hodgson, *Doctrine of the Trinity*, 90–96.

14. Hodgson, *Doctrine of the Trinity*, 90, 108.

15. Ibid., 94.

To exemplify this type of unity, he points to the psychological theories of John Laird.[16] Human selves are known in the three interrelated activities of thinking, feeling, and willing. These activities are distinct from each other, yet they are inseparably alloyed together, for they are "elements in a more or less unified whole, and in spite of the fact that they are only observably existent when active, there is a continuity as well as a unity in each interpermeating group, that unity and continuity which is to be found in the individual life of each human being."[17] He points out that there is no fourth unifying principle or reality, but that the three are, rather mysteriously, the self. Hodgson uses this as a model of divine unity, a unity based on interpenetration and mysterious self-constitution.[18]

This unity of the Trinity cannot be reduced to a unity of an individual, however. It is instead a social unity. Time and again, Hodgson refers to "the social life of the Blessed Trinity" and "the social life of the divine Trinity."[19] It is a life in which both unity and diversity are real, and which forms a model for human society. Love serves to unite the "social whole" together into one life without effacing variety.[20] Hodgson is clear that the diversity in God cannot be understood as inequality, even in terms of cause or source. He writes, "I now wish to add that in this unity there is no room for any trace of subordinationism, and that the thought of the Father as the Source or Fount of Godhead is a relic of pre-Christian theology which has not fully assimilated the Christian revelation."[21]

As will become evident, Erickson's understanding of the Trinity parallels Hodgson's at several points. This summary statement is exemplary:

> The Trinity is a communion of three persons, three centers of consciousness, who exist and always have existed in union with one another and in dependence on one another. . . . They share their lives, having such a close relationship that each is conscious of what the other is conscious of. . . . There is therefore a mutual submission of each to each of the others and a mutual glorifying of one another. There is complete equality of the three. . . . At the same

16. Laird, *Problems of the Self.*
17. Ibid., 86.
18. Ibid., 87–90.
19. For example, Hodgson, *Essays in Christian Philosophy*, 43, 103, 108, 109, 156.
20. Ibid., 133.
21. Hodgson, *Doctrine of the Trinity*, 102.

time, this unity and equality do not require identity of function. There are certain roles that distinctively belong primarily to one, although all participate in the function of each.[22]

Erickson believes "the Trinity must be understood as fundamentally a society. The Godhead is a complex of persons."[23]

Erickson begins his own construction of a doctrine of the Trinity with a lengthy survey of the Scriptures.[24] While he deals with both the Old and New Testaments, he is particularly attentive to the depiction of the Trinity in the Gospel and Epistles of John. He reaches several conclusions from this part of his study. John clearly views the Son as deity (John 20:28). This is done without equating him with God. Instead, both Jesus and the Holy Spirit are represented as distinct from the Father. Erickson writes, "There are indications in the Gospel of interaction among the members of the Trinity. This is especially the case of the relationship between the Father and the Son. A definite distinction is present between the two, indicated both by the narratives involving dialogue between Father and Son and the discussions of the nature of that relationship."[25] Despite this diversity, there is a closeness seen in the loving interaction of the three (John 14:9–21), in addition to outright statements of unity (John 10:30). This unity is further reflected in the coordinated work of the three (John 7:16, 18; 16:13–15) and in the fact that one's relationship to the Father is determined by his relationship to the Son (John 5:17–21, 8:19, 14:23).[26]

In addition to the biblical evidence for a social Trinity, Erickson roots his position in the fact that God is the metaphysical ultimate, writing, "There is one eternal, uncreated reality: God. . . . God is spirit, not matter."[27] Citing Carl F. H. Henry, he associates spirit with mind, drawing the conclusion that "the fundamental characteristic of this universe is personal."[28] Persons are what matter in reality. He concludes, "If, then, the most significant members of the creation are persons in relationship, then

22. Erickson, *God in Three Persons*, 331.

23. Ibid., 221.

24. Ibid., 157–210; cf. Erickson, *Making Sense of the Trinity*, 17–42.

25. Erickson, *God in Three Persons*, 210.

26. Ibid.

27. Ibid., 219.

28. Erickson, *God in Three Persons*, 219–20; Henry, *God, Revelation and Authority*, 5:105.

reality is primarily social."[29] It is therefore best to understand the creator of reality, God, as a social being.

Erickson believes that the "Trinity is three persons so closely bound together that they are actually one."[30] By person, Erickson does not mean a Rahnerian relation of opposition, but a self-aware subject, a center of consciousness, and more.[31] As suggested above, person functions in Erickson's metaphysic as the primary ontological reality, in many ways replacing the traditional concept of substance as the seat of a being's attributes.[32] After writing that the unique role of persons is the key to his metaphysic, he considers human persons:

> This means that we should think of ourselves not so much as substances with attributes, but as subjects who display certain characteristics. . . . In a sense, we are not even subjects with attributes attached, but the whole set of qualities which go to make up what we are, including both past and future qualities and all of our thoughts, actions, experiences, and relationships. . . . What must be stressed is that each of us is a person, a subject; and everything we are, have been, and will be, is part of that person.[33]

As he has based this metaphysic on the role of divine persons in creation, it would be a mistake to isolate this understanding of "person" to the human context.

Erickson boldly emphasizes the threeness of God. He writes, "The conception we have been employing in this construction tends to emphasize the uniqueness and distinctness of the three persons more than do some theologies."[34] He approvingly cites Pannenberg, who speaks of the self-distinction amongst the members of the Trinity, and refers to each as a center of action.[35] Like Pannenberg, Erickson believes that in the Trinity "there is a distinctness of consciousness capable of originating thoughts and relationships among the members of the Trinity. The way in which

29. Erickson, *God in Three Persons*, 221; Erickson, *Making Sense of the Trinity*, 57.

30. Erickson, *God in Three Persons*, 221.

31. Cf. pp. 43–44, 47–48 above with Erickson, *Making Sense of the Trinity*, 61.

32. Irenaeus, *Adversus haereses* 2.13.3 (*ANF* 1:374); Athanasius, *De decretis* 22 (*NPNF2* 4:164–65); and Augustine, *De Trinitate* 2.2.4 (*NPNF1* 3:39) all espouse this traditional position.

33. Erickson, *Word Became Flesh*, 525–26, 529.

34. Erickson, *God in Three Persons*, 226.

35. Pannenberg, *Systematic Theology*, 1:319; Erickson, *God in Three Persons*, 227, 232.

each refers to the other, and interacts with the other, suggests a greater multiplicity of identity than has sometimes been thought of in trinitarian theology."[36]

Despite his emphasis on the three in God, Erickson works to avoid tritheism. He writes, "We therefore propose thinking of the Trinity as a society, a complex of persons, who, however, are one being."[37] One being here does not mean the singular metaphysical substance it means in Tertullian, Anselm, or Rahner.[38] Erickson is clear that the divine nature the three in God share is a generic nature "of which they are the only instances."[39] In fact, Erickson seems to abandon a substance/attribute model for God altogether, instead placing the attributes "in" the persons.[40]

Erickson does not refer to the Trinity as "one being" because of a singular divine substance. Instead, Erickson sees two primary means by which the members of the Trinity are "one being": love and interdependence. Because the cause of the universe is ultimately personal, Erickson says "the most powerful binding force in the universe is love."[41] The God of the Bible is described as love, and while this does not exhaustively identify his being, it is a "very basic characterization of God."[42] The love of the Father, Son, and Holy Spirit for one another is both a basic attribute of each and a mutual exchange which unites them as Trinity. Erickson writes, "Love is such a powerful dimension of God's nature that it binds three persons so closely that they are actually one."[43]

Erickson anticipates the objection that love is an inadequate means of uniting the Triune God. He notes that this objection is based on human experience, in which love is necessarily limited by the physical separation of bodies, the existential separation of diverse experiences, and the spiri-

---

36. Erickson, *God in Three Persons*, 227.

37. Erickson, *Making Sense of the Trinity*, 58.

38. Tertullian, *Adversus Praxean* 2, 7, 22 (*ANF* 3:598, 602, 618); Anselm, *Monologion* prologue, 16, 17, 25 (5, 28–30, 41–42); Rahner, *Trinity*, 75.

39. Erickson, *God in Three Persons*, 225, 266.

40. Erickson, *God the Father Almighty*, 231; Erickson, *Word Became Flesh*, 528–30. Like many who attempt to move away from that metaphysic, however, Erickson occasionally assumes it, as when he denies that God changes in "essence, status, or quality." See Erickson, *The Word Became Flesh*, 542.

41. Erickson, *God in Three Persons*, 221.

42. Ibid.

43. Erickson, *Making Sense of the Trinity*, 58.

tual separation of selfishness.[44] God, however, does not suffer from these problems, but instead experiences a perfectly shared life. Because they lack corporeality, diverse experiences, and selfishness, the Father, Son, and Spirit eternally experience perfect communion and the perfect identity of experiences.[45] Erickson believes that in the Trinity, "Each of these three persons then has close access, direct access, to the consciousness of the others. As one thinks or experiences, the others are also directly aware of this. They think the other's thoughts, feel the other's feelings."[46] The perfectly shared divine life occurs amongst three who have the same "goals, intentions, values, and objectives," and who are secure in their communion because they know it is eternal and unbreakable.[47]

It is this concept of shared life which Erickson identifies with the ancient terms *perichoresis* and *circumincessio*. John of Damascus used *perichoresis* to describe the mutual interpenetration of the members of the Trinity, and the term has been appropriated by recent theologians such as Moltmann and Leonardo Boff.[48] Erickson takes the term to mean "that each of the three persons shares the lives of the others, that each lives in the others."[49] This sharing of life includes cooperation in every action, whether or not one member seems to be particularly active in that action. Creation, for example, while attributed primarily to the Father, is also the work of the Son and Spirit.[50] Through love based on a total sharing of life, the three persons in God are bound together in a unity like, but infinitely stronger than, the unity of a husband and wife, or the unity amongst believers.[51]

44. Ibid., 59–60; Erickson, *God in Three Persons*, 222.

45. Erickson, *God in Three Persons*, 223–24. During the Incarnation, the second person of the Trinity did possess a limited body, but Erickson sees this as a temporary and minor obstacle to the point at hand.

46. Ibid., 225.

47. Ibid., 226.

48. John of Damascus, *Fidei Orthodoxa* 1.8, 1.14 (*NPNF2* 9:11, 17; *PG* 94:829, 860); Erickson, *Making Sense of the Trinity*, 57; Moltmann, *Trinity and the Kingdom*, 150; Jürgen Moltmann, *History and the Triune God: Contributions to Trinitarian Theology*, trans. John Bowden (New York: Crossroad, 1992), 86; Leonardo Boff, *Trinity and Society*, trans. Paul Burns (Maryknoll: Orbis, 1988), 137.

49. Erickson, *God in Three Persons*, 229.

50. Ibid., 235; Erickson, *Making Sense of the Trinity*, 64.

51. Erickson, *God in Three Persons*, 227. Erickson states that there is "some univocal element" among these examples of unity.

The other element of Erickson's understanding of divine unity is the interdependence of the three in God. He repeatedly asserts that the three in God cannot exist, let alone be God, without one another, and writes about their "mutual production."[52] He writes of the three, "None has the power of life within himself alone. Each can only exist as part of the Triune God."[53] The life of God is a life in which "the life of each flows through the others, and in which each is dependent on the others for life, and for what he is."[54] The Father, Son, and Spirit are one because their existence is tied to their closeness.

Erickson presents several analogies to demonstrate this interdependence. One is that of Siamese twins, in which the organs of one member sustain the life of both.[55] Another is that of a married couple with such a strong relationship that they, as a couple, have an identity which is more important to them than their identity as individuals, and in fact influences their individual behavior.[56] Erickson's most well developed analogy is that of the heart, lungs, and brain of the last man alive. These organs are interdependent; without any of them, the other two die. They are human organs as long as they are alive, for they make up the only human alive, and therefore the totality of human nature, rather than simply one "human" among many. But only together, assuming the rest of a human body needed for life, do they compose that human. Erickson concludes the illustration, writing, "Each is human, so long as in union with the other two, but together the three, the organism, is a human, a human being. Note that I said the three is, rather than the three are, for together they constitute a new entity, a single being, which is more than the sum of the parts."[57] Like these three organs, the three persons in the Godhead depend upon one another for their existence.

Erickson is aware that claims of dependence within the Godhead have traditionally taken the form of an asymmetrical dependence of the Son and the Spirit on the Father as their source or cause. He describes this as the "Greek" position, and examines its formulation by Rahner and

52. Ibid., 233, 235, 264; Erickson, *Making Sense of the Trinity*, 62.
53. Erickson, *God in Three Persons*, 264.
54. Erickson, *Making Sense of the Trinity*, 61.
55. Ibid., 63; Erickson, *God in Three Persons*, 233–34.
56. Erickson, *God in Three Persons*, 269–70.
57. Ibid., 269; also Erickson, *Making Sense of the Trinity*, 62–63.

LaCugna.[58] While Erickson acknowledges that such positions claim biblical support, he believes that they are "based on identifying too closely the economic Trinity (the Trinity as manifested to us in history) with the immanent Trinity (God as he really is in himself). Rather than one member of the Trinity being the source of the others' being, and thus superior to them, we would contend that each of the three is eternally derived from each of the others, and all three are eternally equal."[59] Erickson believes it is an exegetical leap, and therefore a mistake, to read a few statements about the economic work of the Trinity back into eternity.[60]

In addition, Erickson presents the work of B. B. Warfield to show that the New Testament does not clearly subordinate the Son to the Father. Warfield notes that Paul prefers to refer to the first and second members of the Trinity as God and Lord rather than Father and Son, and that the triadic formulae of the New Testament show no particular pattern of authority. Nor is Father/Son language indicative of subordination or derivation; according to Warfield, in the Semitic context, the emphasis was on equality.[61] Concerning the question of why the person of the Trinity became incarnate who did, Erickson looks to Warfield's assertion of a covenant arrangement in God concerning the responsibilities of each divine person in the economy.[62] The New Testament does not definitively assert any sort of eternal subordination within the Godhead, nor can such a subordination be read from the functional subordination seen in the economy.[63]

There is therefore some epistemic distance between the immanent Trinity and the economic Trinity. The relations within the Trinity which

58. Erickson, God in Three Persons, 291–99. That Erickson chooses these as his representatives of the "Greek" view is odd, though they do see the Father as source of divinity. Case, review of God in Three Persons, 236. John Zizioulas, an Orthodox metropolitan, might be a more logical representative of the Greek view.

59. Erickson, Making Sense of the Trinity, 90. See also Erickson, God in Three Persons, 309.

60. Erickson, Making Sense of the Trinity, 86. While Erickson cites only John 14:28 here specifically, he mentions begetting and proceeding as concepts that should not be read back into eternity. It is ironic that Welch believes that reading economic statements into eternity is the mistake all social trinitarians make. See Welch, In This Name, 262.

61. Erickson, God in Three Persons, 301–302; Warfield, "Biblical Trinity," 50–52.

62. Erickson, God in Three Persons, 303; Warfield, "Biblical Trinity," 53–54.

63. For a similar argument, see Bilezikian, "Hermeneutical Bungee-Jumping," 57–68. For an opposing view, see Kovach and Schemm, "Eternal Subordination," 461–76.

make its persons interdependent should be conceived of as symmetrical, and no immanent distinctions should be presumed to exist within the Godhead.[64] Erickson writes, "I would propose that there are no references to the Father begetting the Son or the Father (and the Son) sending the Spirit that cannot be understood in terms of the temporal role assumed by the second and third persons of the Trinity, respectively. They do not indicate any intrinsic relationship among the three."[65]

This means that the titles "Father," "Son," and "Holy Spirit" are purely economic; the roles played by the three persons in redemption could have been exchanged. While Erickson does freely use the terms to identify the three, especially in his systematic theology, he does not indicate that these titles are in themselves eternal.[66] Instead, when one reads Erickson's constructive Christology, one reads about the incarnation of "the Second Person of the Trinity," the incarnation of "God."[67] There are few, if any, references to the incarnation of "God the Son" or "the eternal Word." There is nothing about the "Second Person of the Trinity" which suits him to the incarnation, and it appears Erickson identifies him by that title because it is the option which serves to pick out the divine person incarnate as Jesus which makes the least distinction amongst the members of the Trinity. As Erickson's summary statement indicates, "There is complete equality of the three."[68]

Erickson sees the Trinity as a society of three eternally divine, perfectly equal, fully personal centers of consciousness. As a divine society, the Trinity is united by a love of infinite power, which binds the three into one. This perfect love is based on the perfect sharing of lives amongst the three persons. This sharing of life includes an intrinsic symmetrical interdependence of the members. They depend upon one another for their life and deity. As such, they are one. The next section will critique this understanding of unity.

64. Erickson, *God in Three Persons*, 309–10; Erickson, *Making Sense of the Trinity*, 86.

65. Erickson, *God in Three Persons*, 309.

66. For example, Erickson, *Christian Theology*, 362–63.

67. For example, Erickson, *Word Became Flesh*, 544, 549, 552, 553, 625, 546.

68. Erickson, *God in Three Persons*, 331.

A CRITIQUE OF ERICKSON'S UNDERSTANDING OF UNITY

What is one to make of Erickson's contemporary interpretation of the Trinity? At the very least, it can be appreciated that an American evangelical has offered one.[69] Erickson attempts to develop a metaphysic and a view of the Trinity which does justice to the modern, and he would say biblical, emphasis on the role of persons in reality. His understanding of unity is one which allows a robust understanding of the divine persons. His description of the love and shared life within God resonates with human ideals of intimate fellowship and worship.

Yet this very resonance is the problem. There is nothing in Erickson's description of the divine unity which is not an amplified part of human existence. Christians share lives and love sacrificially. Organs depend upon one another, as do equal co-owners of a business. These examples, taken to whatever degree, seem too mundane to adequately characterize the unity of God.

Erickson's understanding of trinitarian unity will now be exposed to critiques in three broad areas. First, a pair of historical critiques will compare Erickson's understanding of God's unity with the decision of Nicaea and Erickson's understanding of *perichoresis* with that of John of Damascus. In both cases, his position will be found to be at odds with the tradition. Then three critiques will show that his egalitarian understanding of the persons in God fails to account for divine decision-making, is incompatible with a scheme of interdependence, and compromises God's aseity. Several of these criticisms will be drawn from the works of other social trinitarians. Finally, a multi-faceted theological critique will show his position compromises God's unity.[70] These critiques will not so much conclude that Erickson's position is entirely untenable, but that it currently lacks the explanatory power desired in a doctrine of trinitarian unity.

---

69. Case, review of *God in Three Persons*, 64.

70. The Christological objection Colin Brown levels against all social trinitarian positions, that they require a kenotic Christology, will not be considered. See Brown, "Trinity and Incarnation," 90. While Erickson does support a kenotic-by-addition Christology in *Word Became Flesh*, there is nothing in Erickson's social position which would prevent an adherent from utilizing the *extra Calvinisticum* concept which Brown endorses on 90–91. See Calvin, *Institutes of the Christian Religion*, 2.13.4 (20:481).

Historical Difficulties

Erickson is aware of the long history of Christian thought within which he stands. His explicitly doctrinal works consistently devote significant portions to the historical development of the doctrine in question.[71] This does not mean that Erickson binds himself to all the history he surveys; he generally attempts to draw key principles from historical theology and incorporate them into his contemporary restatements of doctrine. For example, he attempts to preserve the values behind the doctrine of divine simplicity without being encumbered by the scholastic version thereof, which he believes is problematic.

This section will propose two historical critiques of Erickson's understanding of trinitarian unity. First, it will examine how well he captures the key elements of the Nicene Creed in his own position. Then, it will examine whether his appropriation of John of Damascus's term, *perichoresis*, does justice to John's understanding of the divine unity.

The Nicene Creed

The exposition of the Nicene Creed in Chapter 1 concluded that the Council of Nicaea intended to endorse two elements by which the Son is eternally united with the Father.[72] The Son is derived from the Father and therefore naturally related to him. The Son also shares the Father's numerically singular essence.

Erickson's position does not retain either of these insights. He denies an asymmetrical relationship of any sort between the Father and Son in eternity, preferring to think of them as mutually produced.[73] He also rejects the concept of a numerically singular essence shared between Father and Son, preferring to consider their shared essence to be generic deity, that is, a description of "God" which they all meet.[74] It seems neither of

71. Roughly one-eighth of *Word Became Flesh* and one-sixth of *God in Three Persons* are dedicated to historical survey. Important figures are sometimes missed. Garrett notes the absence of Augustine from the patristic survey in *God in Three Persons*, and suspects it is because of Erickson's own social position. See Garrett, review of *God in Three Persons*, 79. Distortions also occur, as when Erickson seems to set the Cappadocians against positions endorsing the monarchy of the Father and the identity of the divine substance. As shown on pp. 17–19 above, the Cappadocians held to both. See Erickson, *God in Three Persons*, 230.

72. See pp. 11–17 above.

73. Erickson, *Making Sense of the Trinity*, 62.

74. Erickson, *God in Three Persons*, 225, 266.

the elements which the Fathers at Nicaea used to secure the divine unity make it into Erickson's position.

It should be noted, in fairness, that Erickson aligns himself with J. N. D. Kelly, who denies that Nicaea meant to affirm a numerically singular metaphysical essence in God.[75] However, Erickson also fails to carry on the Nicene teaching of the Son's derivation. As noted in Chapter 1, a position on God's unity which does not comply with a particular historical position, even one as accepted and important as Nicaea, is not rejected *a priori*. However, such a position does bear a strong burden of proof. As the next two sections will show, Erickson's trinitarian position is unacceptable on logical and theological grounds. What is interesting is that his deviations from the two elements of unity endorsed at Nicaea contribute to the logical and theological difficulties which his position faces.

John of Damascus

As noted above, Erickson appropriates John of Damascus's term *perichoresis* to describe the shared life of the Trinity.[76] He takes the term to mean that the three in God share one divine life, they live in one another. He believes John uses the term to elucidate the Cappadocian assertions that the three in God share one life, and that this position is preferable to one which locates the divine unity in the Father's monarchy or the single divine essence.[77] He therefore appears to claim the Damascene as historical support for his own position, which locates the divine unity in the one shared life of God.

This seems to concur with John's usage of the term. According to him, the three do not commingle, but cleave together, and "they have their being [have *perichoresis*] in each other without any coalescence or commingling."[78] He goes on to compare them to three suns "cleaving to each other without separation and giving out light mingled and conjoined into one."[79] A longer quotation clarifies the point:

---

75. Kelly, *Early Christian Doctrines*, 234.

76. Erickson, *Making Sense of the Trinity*, 57.

77. Erickson, *God in Three Persons*, 229–30; for example, Gregory of Nyssa, *Contra Eunomius*, 1.36 (*NPNF2* 5:84–85).

78. John of Damascus, *Fid. Orth.*, 1.8 (*NPNF2* 9:11), author's translation in brackets (*PG* 94:829).

79. Ibid.

The subsistences dwell and are established firmly in one another. For they are inseparable and cannot part from one another, but keep to their separate courses [having *perichoresis*] within one another, without coalescing or mingling, but cleaving to each other. For the Son is in the Father and the Spirit: and the Spirit in the Father and the Son: and the Father in the Son and the Spirit, but there is no coalescence or commingling or confusion. And there is one and the same motion: for there is one impulse and one motion of the three subsistences, which is not to be observed in any created nature.[80]

Thus *perichoresis* indicates the interpenetrating life of the Father, Son, and Spirit. They cleave tightly together without losing their distinction, operate with one another without ceasing to be three.

There is a difference, however, in the way John uses *perichoresis* and the way Erickson uses it. For John, *perichoresis* appears as a consequence of the divine unity already established by the derivation of the Son and Spirit from the Father in the singular divine essence. John begins his exposition of the Trinity by discussing the One God, who is "one essence, one divinity, one power, one will, one energy, one beginning, one authority, one dominion, one sovereignty, made known in three perfect subsistences and adored with one adoration."[81] The one essence of God precedes discussion of the persons.

The next paragraph discusses the persons. The Father is the sole beginning and cause of all. The Son is consubstantial with the Father, and is in and with him because he is "everlastingly and without beginning begotten of Him."[82] John continues to elucidate the meaning and nature of the Son's generation from the Father for several paragraphs before addressing the fact that "the Holy Spirit proceedeth from the Father's essence."[83] It is only after this that his use of *perichoresis* and the analogy of the suns appears. The same pattern recurs in book 14, where he again uses *perichoresis*. There is one divine nature of the Father which the Son and Spirit derive from and share with him. Because of this, they share one interpenetrating life.[84]

---

80. Ibid., 1.14 (*NPNF2* 9:17), author's translation in brackets (*PG* 94:860).

81. Ibid., 1.8 (*NPNF2* 9:6).

82. Ibid.

83. Ibid., (*NPNF2* 9:8).

84. Pannenberg also notes that *perichoresis* presupposes, rather than determines, the unity of God. See Pannenberg, *Systematic Theology*, 1:334.

Erickson's use of *perichoresis* is not in line with John of Damascus's. While John sees it as a consequence of a divine unity established by other means, Erickson attempts to use it to bind together divine persons not already one. John would reject any such attempt, because he believes "it is a natural necessity that duality should originate in unity."[85] Thus, while Erickson is free to use the concept of *perichoresis*, it must be recognized that his use of the concept does not imply the same metaphysical underpinning it has in John of Damascus.

Egalitarian Difficulties

The social model of the Trinity lends itself to an egalitarian interpretation, because the three in God seem to confront one another fully formed.[86] As was noted, Hodgson rejected any sort of derivation or subordination amongst the three, and Erickson does the same. Horrell states that social trinitarians generally deny an "*essentialist* monarchy" in God.[87] Despite his assertion, Horrell argues for an eternal functional relationship within the Godhead, and he is not alone among social trinitarians.[88] Cornelius Plantinga, Jr. and Richard Swinburne both argue for relations of origin within the Godhead, and Swinburne is particularly clear that those relations imply an eternal structure of authority within the Godhead.[89]

This section will indicate that an egalitarian position causes a problem for any egalitarian social model of the Trinity, for it cannot account for the unity of action generally proposed by such models. It will also demonstrate that Erickson's attempts to secure the divine unity in terms of interdependence are thwarted by his egalitarian position. Finally, it will show that Erickson's egalitarian position contradicts his doctrine of God's aseity, for it makes the creation of the universe necessary for God to be three.[90]

85. Ibid., 1.5 (*NPNF2* 9:4).

86. Throughout this section, "egalitarian" means the lack of any immanent distinction amongst the members of the Trinity. They have the same experiences, attributes, history, etc., and are not distinguished by relations of origin.

87. Horrell, "Biblical Model," 408, emphasis original.

88. Ibid., 411–16.

89. Plantinga, "Social Trinity and Tritheism," in *Library of Religious Philosophy*, 1:29–31; Swinburne, "More Than One God?" 232–36; Swinburne, *Christian God*, 174–76. The alteration in Swinburne's position between these two works is not relevant here.

90. Kärkkäinen has noted that the first of these is abstract speculation in *Trinity*, 232.

How are Divine Decisions Made?

The God of the Bible makes decisions and acts. One of the marks of his uniqueness and glory is that he does so without any advisors, but only "after the counsel of his own will."[91] A social model of the Trinity recognizes that there is not one active agent involved in these decisions, but three. How do the three divine persons make joint decisions?

A traditional, hierarchal view of the Trinity can account for divine decision making in at least two ways. It can suggest that the Father, as head, makes all decisions in consultation with the Son and Spirit. Swinburne believes that this is too authoritarian an understanding of the Trinity, and instead suggests that the Father eternally assigns the Son and Spirit functional spheres which they, recognizing his headship, accept. Within each person's sphere, he makes decisions with the full backing of the other two persons, who in turn expect backing within their own spheres.[92] In both cases, the economic roles of the Trinity are reflections of their eternal roles.[93] Can Erickson's position similarly account for divine decision making?

Swinburne has noted that an omnipotent divine being has infinite choices of action amongst morally neutral options, some of which, however, are mutually exclusive. Members of the Trinity, thinking about the same things at the same time, could simultaneously propose mutually exclusive options. God could have called Abraham elsewhere, or made the earth spin in a different direction.[94] While one may contest particular examples, if God is free at all, there are certainly areas in which God could

---

All three of these critiques are somewhat speculative, and may seem to impose questions upon God that actually require no answer. Against this impression, two things should be noted. First, most readers approach the discussion of the Trinity with some firm convictions based upon the traditional model of derivation and unity of essence. However, because Erickson's position disavows these elements of Nicene trinitarianism, questions which make no sense in light of Nicaea may pose genuine problems to Erickson's position. Second, even if an inability to answer speculative questions does not count against Erickson in an absolute sense, when compared with the traditional position which can answer such questions, Erickson's position can be shown to be relatively inferior. The first criticism is explicitly presented as a question of explanatory power.

91. Eph 1:11. Cf. Isa 40:13–14, Rom 11:34, 1 Cor 2:6, Eph 1:5, 9.

92. Swinburne, *Christian God*, 173–75, 177; Swinburne, "More Than One God?" 231–32.

93. For other variations on this theme, see Pannenberg, *Systematic Theology*, 1:320–26, 2:363–67, 2:390; Zizioulas, "Communion and Otherness," 353.

94. Swinburne, *Christian God*, 171–72.

have done otherwise than they in fact have done. How can Erickson's three perfectly equal persons make such a decision between mutually exclusive options? Voting cannot work, because God has more options than persons.[95]

This issue also arises, perhaps with greater strength, concerning the morally significant events of salvation history. For example, the Trinity decides that one of its members will become incarnate to save man. Erickson states that the person of the Trinity who became incarnate did so by the mutual decision of the three persons.[96] But how would such a decision take place? The concept of thoroughly egalitarian divine persons suggests not only that they will agree about what must be done in moral situations, but that each will desire to play the same role. If it is a shameful thing for God to die, would not each member simultaneously volunteer to save his loved ones from facing death? Certainly, a perfect person would not foist death on another if he himself were an equal candidate. Or, if it is a glorious thing for God to die, how could a perfect divine person claim such an honor for himself? Would not each member recuse himself, that one of his loved ones might receive this honor? Whatever the proper response of a divine person would be to the possibility of living the life of Jesus of Nazareth, the three persons in Erickson's model should share it. Apart from immanent distinctions within the Godhead, how could such a mutual decision be made?[97]

Erickson follows Warfield in connecting the economic roles to a prior covenant, which seems to grant that an explanation is needed. But this only pushes the problem back a step.[98] How were the covenant roles decided? Consider the "moment" when God thinks a covenant is needed, and each loving person simultaneously proposes a covenant in which he plays the most humble role. If no single role is most appropriate for a perfect divine person, but the roles of Father, Son, and Spirit are necessary, there are still six possible covenant arrangements. Given no immanent reason for any divine person to fill any specific role, there is

95. Swinburne, "Could There be More Than One God?" 232.

96. Erickson, *Making Sense of the Trinity*, 74–75.

97. One might respond that Erickson forbids only hierarchal immanent distinctions, but it is hard to see how hierarchal economic distinctions can be based on non-hierarchal immanent distinctions.

98. Erickson, *God in Three Persons*, 303; Warfield, "Biblical Trinity," 53–54; Richard Swinburne, "More Than One God?" 231–32.

a 55.5% chance each member would propose a different arrangement.[99] Since there are no intrinsic differences amongst the three, there are no reasons why any particular covenant should be adopted.

It is reasonable to ask how a society makes decisions, even a divine society. An egalitarian social model of the Trinity does not offer an answer to that question, while a hierarchal model does. The latter is shown to have an advantage in explanatory power, and therefore a greater chance of being the correct trinitarian model.

How Are the Divine Persons Interdependent?

Perhaps the strongest element of Erickson's understanding of the unity of the persons in God is their interdependence. Time and again he makes assertions that "each is dependent on the others for life, and for what he is," that "each is dependent on the others for his own life and his being deity," that "[e]ach is essential to the life of the whole."[100] Yet he never directly addresses why it is that they are interdependent. He seems to suggest that they are interdependent because they share experiences,[101] but it is hard to see how each of three divine persons must share the experiences of the other two in order to exist. Several types of interdependence, each of them suggested by one of Erickson's analogies, will now be examined.

The most obvious form of interdependence is that suggested by Erickson's analogy of a heart, brain, and lung.[102] It is the interdependence of things each of which is unable to sustain its own life independently, but whose diverse competencies complement one another. Thus the heart moves blood, the lung places oxygen within it, the brain controls both heart and lung, and blood nourishes all of them. Welch, a critic of the social theory, believes that this type of unity, organic unity, is the best that a social trinitarian can offer. He points out that it is deficient because it makes the members of the Trinity parts of God, incomplete and therefore

99. Three persons can fill three roles in six ways, giving six possible covenant arrangements. If each proposes one arrangement, there are 216 (6³) possible composite propositions. Of those, only 6 are unanimous, 90 have two persons in agreement, and 120 have no members agreeing.

100. Erickson, *Making Sense of the Trinity*, 61, 62; Erickson, *God in Three Persons*, 233; see also 235, 264.

101. Erickson, *Making Sense of the Trinity*, 62.

102. Ibid., 62–63; Erickson, *God in Three Persons*, 269.

finite, and clearly not God.[103] Kärkkäinen similarly notes that, at best, this analogy makes the three parts of a fourth reality, which is a conclusion at odds with Erickson's total position.[104] Erickson, however, could not be presenting the divine unity in these terms at all, because for him the persons of the Trinity are perfectly equal. Each has all the perfections of either of the others.[105] The Trinity therefore cannot be interdependent in such a complementary way.

A second form of interdependence is suggested by Erickson's analogy of Siamese twins.[106] It is the interdependence of multiple things which share a dependence met by a single source. In the case of the twins one heart gave life to both of them. A more complete example might be three pools fed from a single spring. If one of the pools is opened to the sea, the spring would be unable to keep any of them full. However, while the three persons clearly correspond to the three pools, or the two twins, Erickson's understanding of the divine unity has no answer for what corresponds to the one spring, or the one heart. It has been noted that Erickson studiously avoids any suggestion that there is one metaphysical substance underlying the three persons in the Godhead.[107] While they do share a life, Erickson clearly means by this a series of experiences, not a life-giving source other than themselves.[108] Thus, the interdependence of the three cannot be a shared dependence upon another reality.

The final form of interdependence possible is that suggested by Erickson's perfectly married couple, the *Zweieinigers*.[109] It is the interdependence of multiple things which together possess something impossible for them to have separately. Now, in Erickson's model, the three in God possess a sharing of life which they could not possess separately. Yet how can that sharing of life be necessary? On what basis can the First Person of the Trinity be required to share his life with two other divine

103. Welch, *In This Name*, 254, 256, cf. Thompson, *Modern Trinitarian Perspectives*, 142.

104. Kärkkäinen, *Trinity*, 231.

105. Erickson, *God the Father Almighty*, 230.

106. Erickson, *God in Three Persons*, 233–34; Erickson, *Making Sense of the Trinity*, 63.

107. Erickson, *God in Three Persons*, 225, 266.

108. Ibid., 331.

109. Ibid., 269–70.

persons, or not exist? The Father, as a person, is deity.[110] So are the Son and the Holy Spirit. Who or what can impose the requirement of sharing life upon them? If it is a lack in the persons, how can they be considered perfect? If the necessity comes from an outside source, it would be her, and not the Father, Son, or Spirit, who is in fact God.[111]

Nor does the divine love emphasized by Erickson require unity to exist. The ancients used the social model to depict God's diversity, not his unity.[112] Richard believed in the single perfect divine essence, argued that perfection required love, and concluded that love required there to be three in God. Love necessitated distinction within God, not unity. If, as in the traditional view, love is what God self-sacrificially does for another, it certainly does not require unity with the object loved. Aquinas writes, "And then again the divine love is a binding force, inasmuch as God wills good to others; yet it implies no composition in God."[113] The loving nature of the Father does not require him to be one with the Son, and vice versa.

Erickson might respond that the three together, as God, "constitute a new entity, a single being, which is more than the sum of the parts."[114] The problem is that this idea is taken from the heart, lung, brain analogy, in which the parts are radically diverse. Erickson, however, has argued for the total equality of the divine persons, and the result of combining identical objects is simply the sum of the parts. If one gold coin is added to two identical gold coins, the result is exactly three gold coins. In the case of persons it may be the case that adding equal persons results in less than the sum of the parts. Consider two philosophers with identical education, background, and training. If the two collaborate, will the result be twice as good as what one could have done alone? It seems highly unlikely.

Erickson's assertions of a unifying interdependence among the equal members of the Godhead amount to little more than that. He provides no suitable illustration or explanation for what such an interdependence might mean. At best, he seems to argue in a circle, first asserting that God

110. Ibid., 266; Erickson, *God the Father Almighty*, 230; Erickson, *The Word Became Flesh*, 529.

111. Cf. Cary, "On Behalf of Classical Trinitarianism," 382.

112. Gresham, "Social Model," 331–32. For example, Richard of St. Victor, *De Trinitate* 3.2 (374–75).

113. Aquinas, *Summ. Theol.* 1a.20.1 (BF 5:55–59); also 1a.20.2 (BF 5:59–63).

114. Erickson, *God in Three Persons*, 269.

is one in part because he is interdependent and then arguing that he is interdependent because he must be interdependent to be one.

The regrettable fact is that it is Erickson's egalitarian position which prevents him from developing a coherent understanding of interdependence. Traditional, hierarchal models of the Trinity can easily account for the divine unity. But the argument seen in Origen and Athanasius, that God as eternal Father eternally requires a Son, cannot be made by Erickson.[115] While Father implies Son, or at least child, three undifferentiated persons do not imply one another. There is no *res* that is the single divine essence which can be necessarily triune. There are just the three persons. A God conceived of as eternally Father, Son, and Spirit shows concrete relations which bind him together that simply do not appear amongst persons one, two, and three. The analogy of heart, lung, and brain has potential which Erickson cannot tap. Father implies Son without taking anything away from the perfection of the Father.

Wolfhart Pannenberg, whose position will be examined in detail in Chapter 5, is a staunch opponent of ontological subordinationism.[116] Nevertheless, he builds his understanding of the mutual interdependence of the members of the Godhead on their eternally distinct relations. The Father is always the Father, who eternally generates the Son. The Son is always the Son, who subordinates himself to the Father in eternity and in creation and thereby establishes the Father's monarchy.[117] John Zizioulas makes a similar argument.[118] Neither Father, Son, nor Spirit can be who he is alone because they are different, not because they are the same.

How Are the Divine Persons Three Apart from Creation?

The orthodox doctrine of the Trinity is not that God appears to be three to us, but that he is three in himself, that he is eternally three. As Erickson writes, "The Trinity is a communion of three persons, three centers of consciousness, who exist and always have existed in union with one an-

---

115. Origen, *De principiis* 1.1.9 (*ANF* 4:245); Athanasius, *Orationes contra Arianos* 1.6.21–22 (*NPNF2* 4:318–19).

116. Pannenberg, "Christian Vision of God," 57; Blocher, "Immanence and Transcendence," in *Trinity in a Pluralistic Age*, 106; Schwöbel, "Rational Theology in Trinitarian Perspective," 504.

117. Wolfhart Pannenberg, *Systematic Theology*, 1:320–26, 2:363–67, 2:390.

118. Zizioulas, "Communion and Otherness," 353.

other and in dependence on one another."[119] Early Christians resisted efforts to reduce the Son and Spirit to temporal prolations or expansions of the Father.[120] However, Erickson's denial of eternal asymmetrical relations amongst the divine persons raises the question, "How are there actually three divine persons apart from creation?"

To answer that question, one needs a theory of individuation, a theory to indicate what makes two things two, and not one. Gordon H. Clark points out that, historically, there have been three basic theories of individuation.[121] One is individuation by space and time; two objects in the same place at the same time are not in fact two, but one. The application of this theory to God is clearly limited, as Erickson believes him to be not limited in spatial or temporal terms.[122] The second theory is individuation by difference of substance or matter. Clark believes this theory is in fact unintelligible, but even if it were not, it does not seem to be applicable here. Taken in terms of matter, this theory is not applicable to the persons in God, and Erickson prefers a personal ontology to one based on substance. Swinburne notes, and rejects, another possible option for individuation of divine persons, that of "thisness," in which a divine individual somehow "underlies" his properties.[123] Erickson appears to reject such a position as well, writing that "God is his essence, he is his attributes, the predicates that attach to him" and that God's "attributes, then, are not qualities added to this nature. They are facets of his complex and rich nature."[124]

This leaves one option for individuating the persons in God, that of property individuation.[125] Leibniz believes that "it is not true that two substances may be exactly alike and differ only numerically."[126] Two different things have different properties. These properties can be either monadic properties, properties inherent in the thing itself, like color, or

119. Ibid., 331.

120. Origen, *Princ.* 4.1.28 (*ANF* 4:376–77); Athanasius, *Contra Arianos* 4.13–14 (*NPNF2* 4:437–38).

121. Clark, *Trinity*, 103–4; Locke, *An Essay Concerning Human Understanding*, 27 (pp. 328-348); Kant, *Critique of Pure Reason*, 368–69, 422–25; Leibniz, *Discourse on Metaphysics*, 14; Leibniz, *Monadology*, 222, 377.

122. Ibid., 107; Erickson, *Christian Theology*, 298–304.

123. Swinburne, *Christian God*, 166, 33–50, 163–69.

124. Erickson, *God the Father Almighty*, 229, 231.

125. Clark, *Trinity*, 107; Swinburne, *Christian God*, 163.

126. Leibniz, *Discourse on Metaphysics*, 14.

knowledge, or they can be relational properties.[127] It appears this is the theory of individuation that Erickson accepts. He writes of persons, "In a sense, we are not even subjects with attributes attached, but the whole set of qualities which go to make up what we are, including both past and future qualities and all of our thoughts, actions, experiences, and relationships. . . . What must be stressed is that each of us is a person, a subject; and everything we are, have been, and will be, is part of that person."[128] In short, a person is the sum of his properties. Erickson then points out that it is appropriate to think of persons as the individuating factor for both animate and inanimate objects. Erickson even speaks of himself as the sole instantiation of the essence, or set of properties, Millard J. Erickson.[129]

A property understanding of individuation leads naturally to a principle called "The Identity of Indiscernibles."[130] Two things which lack thisness but that have all the same properties are, in fact, one thing, and not two. Traditional models of the Trinity have distinguished the members of the Trinity by noting their distinct relational properties. The fact that the Father is eternally Father, that the Son is eternally begotten, and that the Spirit is eternally proceeding distinguishes the three persons. John of Damascus indicates that the One God is Three in the properties of unbegotten, begotten, and proceeding.[131] Gregory Nazianzen writes about the distinguishing properties and asserts that "Father" refers to a personal relation.[132] Zizioulas writes that not only divine persons, but that all persons are distinguished and constituted by their unique relationships.[133]

Erickson, however, rejects any eternal relational distinctions amongst the divine persons. They are fully divine and therefore share the same monadic properties. Because of their shared life they think all the same thoughts. There is no difference in experiences to hinder the perfect divine love. Because of their egalitarian communion, they

127. Swinburne, *Christian God*, 163–65.

128. Erickson, *Word Became Flesh*, 529.

129. Ibid., 529–30.

130. Leibniz, *Monadology*, 222. Swinburne discusses six possible forms of this in *Christian God*, 34–38. This is another form of the law discussed in Chapter 2, pp. 57–60 above.

131. John of Damascus, *Fid. Orth.* 1.8 (*NPNF2* 9:184).

132. Gregory Nazianzen, *Or.* 5.9, 29, 21.35, 3.16 (*NPNF2* 7:320, 327, 279, 307). Cf. Tertullian, *Adv. Prax.* 10 (*ANF* 3:604–605).

133. Zizioulas, "On Being a Person," 41–43.

share the same relational attribute, that of being equally related to two other identical divine persons.[134] Because they share all the same properties, the three in God logically and existentially collapse into one self-related subject. Logically, if one accepts this application of the Identity of Indiscernibles. Existentially, because Erickson has left the three in God with no Other against which to differentiate themselves.[135]

Clark believes the only way three co-equal members of the Trinity can manifest distinct properties, and thereby distinguish themselves, and not be one, is by thinking each is himself. The Son never thinks, "I am the Father," nor does the Father think, "I have become Incarnate."[136] But for Erickson, everything distinct in these thoughts is economic; Father, Son, and incarnation are not intrinsic to God.[137] Even Erickson's more guarded language of first, second, and third persons is meaningless apart from the economy. It is appears that only in relation to the creation can the three in God distinguish themselves and not be simply one.[138]

This means that for God to actually be three persons, or, to put it more judiciously, to realize his intrinsic threeness, the economic relations of the three within creation become necessary, thus making creation necessary, and each of the three in God dependent upon creation. Yet Erickson specifically rejects that notion, writing that "God did not *have* to create."[139] For Erickson, the fact that God is life frees him from any dependence upon any created thing.[140] He believes that the Triune nature of God is essential to his very being, yet his egalitarian position

---

134. The fact that each is related to two other divine persons does not mitigate this conclusion, because the three are, in eternity, mirror images of one another. Consider an iron sphere in a circular universe with a circumference of one mile. To its right and left are precisely identical iron spheres at a distance of one mile, even though each iron sphere is itself.

135. Zizioulas, "Communion and Otherness," 358.

136. Clark, *Trinity*, 106.

137. Erickson, *God in Three Persons*, 309; Erickson, *Making Sense of the Trinity*, 90. This is not a problem for Clark, who affirms that the Father is source of the Son and Holy Spirit and who denies God is free not to create. See Clark, *Trinity*, 113, 135, 111.

138. Swinburne argues that only relations to other divine beings could individuate divine beings, but it seems possible that a distinct relation to creation could "retroactively" differentiate a divine being. Of course, Swinburne also affirms God's freedom, which this destroys. See Swinburne, *Christian God*, 164–65.

139. Erickson, *Christian Theology*, 399, emphasis original.

140. Ibid., 297–98.

makes creation necessary as a means of individuating the three in God. Thus, Erickson's egalitarian understanding of divine unity has not been reconciled with the doctrine of God's aseity. Erickson has rejected the connection of the economic distinctions in the Trinity with immanent distinctions, and proposed no other distinctions to replace them. This leaves no means for the three in God to be distinguishable, and therefore not identical, apart from creation.

Erickson's egalitarian understanding of the three persons in God comes into conflict with his understanding of the divine unity at three points. First, it endangers the unity of operation in the Godhead by removing any means for the divine society to resolve conflict or to make decisions among equally righteous divine choices. Second, it prevents any clear account of interdependence, a central element in Erickson's doctrine of divine unity, from being developed. While it may not be absolutely necessary for a doctrine of triune unity to provide a means for decision making or specify the manner of interdependence, these problems at least show a relative weakness in Erickson's position. Finally, Erickson's failure to provide any immanent distinctions within the Trinity contradicts his belief in God's independence from creation by making God depend upon creation to actually be three. The next section will demonstrate that Erickson's understanding of divine unity also falls short theologically.

Theological Difficulty

Erickson notes that there are three responses theologians have offered to the criticism that the doctrine of the Trinity, which states that God is three and one, is logically incoherent. The first is to minimize the threeness in God and thus move towards modalism. The second is to stress the threeness in God and thus move towards tritheism. The third is to redefine person and nature in a way which makes three persons and one nature more compatible.

The choice which Erickson makes seems obvious from his description of the second set of options: "These emphasize the three persons, especially noting the passages of Scripture in which the three interact or refer to one another, and see the three interrelated in a closeness of communion and harmony that binds them to one another."[141] This is, of course, a concise summary of Erickson's own method and conclusions.

---

141. Erickson, *God in Three Persons*, 132. Interestingly, Erickson warns that these can become virtual tritheism.

Thus the primary theological objection to Erickson's understanding of divine unity is that it is too weak, that it risks tritheism. Many would raise such an objection against any theology which posits three centers of consciousness in God.[142] Karl Barth states that to propose three personalities in God "would be the worst and most extreme expression of tritheism."[143] This seems to be based on the assumption that Welch expresses when he writes that the best the social analogy can do is provide "three ultimate personalities, agents, perceivers, centers of consciousness—hence three beings."[144] Because a social model of the Trinity proposes three conscious persons, and a person is a distinct being, a social model proposes three beings and therefore three gods. It is tritheism.

This assertion, however, simply begs the question of what constitutes an adequate understanding of divine unity. Plantinga connects it with the extreme, aggressive form of the doctrine of simplicity prominent during the Middle Ages.[145] Thus, the simple presence of three robust persons in the Godhead will not be considered tritheism here, as long as some other adequate ground of trinitarian unity is present.

Erickson describes his defense against the accusation of tritheism after discussing the interdependence and lovingly shared life of the three persons in God. He writes, "The guarantee against that [tritheism], which would be three separate, distinct, and independent individuals, is in the closeness and interaction among them that we have described above."[146] He is not a tritheist because his three divine persons love one another, share one another's life, and depend upon one another.

Is such an understanding of divine unity sufficient? Two other social trinitarians deny that it is. Plantinga believes that a model of the Trinity in which each member possesses the generic divine nature is insufficient. He writes, "We ought to resist every Congregational theory of trinity membership."[147] A social model of the Trinity must include a "quasi-genetic" kinship to ground the divine unity. The Son, for example, must be recognized as derived from the Father and "permanently related to the

---

142. For example, Gresham, "Social Model," 330, 342; Rahner, *Trinity*, 43; Hill, *Three-Personed God*, 254.

143. Barth, *Church Dogmatics*, 1/1:351.

144. Welch, *In This Name*, 259.

145. Plantinga, "Social Trinity and Tritheism," 38–39.

146. Erickson, *God in Three Persons*, 228.

147. Plantinga, "Social Trinity and Tritheism," 28.

Father in an ineffable closeness akin to a child-parent relation."[148] In *The Christian God*, Swinburne argues that two members of the Trinity must be necessarily and eternally created by the first member as distinct substances.[149] More recently, he has amended his position and strengthened the divine unity. He writes, "The Son and the Spirit are eternally 'from the substance' of the Father in that they derive their being from him; the Son and Spirit arise by a division of the Father which does not diminish him."[150] Robert Letham, though cautious about the weakness of Pannenberg's understanding of God's unity, commends him for asserting the eternal monarchy of the Father, stating, "This saves him from tritheism."[151]

The thinking of these authors seems to be in line with that of Thomas V. Morris, who proposes three necessary elements for an adequate social trinitarianism. He writes, "To avoid polytheism of the sort rejected by the early church fathers, social trinitarians must insist on the unity of the divine essence (the persons all share the attributes of deity), the unity of the divine substance (they all share in the being of the Father), and the unity that exists on the level of divine activity."[152] Michael O'Carroll emphasizes Morris's second criteria, defining tritheism as, "A fundamental error which does not take the crude form of affirming three gods, but which undermines the unity of substance, identifying it exclusively and separately with each person, denying therefore the consubstantiality, the unicity of the nature with the three separate persons."[153] By rejecting both the derivation of Son and Spirit from the Father, and the reality of a singular divine substance, Erickson fails to measure up to Morris's second criteria, and falls squarely into O'Carroll's definition of tritheism.

Why do Erickson's aspects of divine unity, perfect love, interdependence, and shared life fail to adequately unify the One God? It may be that Erickson's understanding of unity is too mundane. Erickson states that the unity of God is like the unity of believers, or a married couple, differing only in its infinite intensity.[154] All the aspects of unity exist uni-

148. Ibid., 29.
149. Swinburne, *Christian God*, 173–80.
150. Swinburne, "More Than One God?" 236.
151. Letham, *Holy Trinity*, 318.
152. Morris, *Our Idea of God*, 180.
153. O'Carroll, *Trinitas*, 212.
154. Erickson, *God in Three Persons*, 227.

laterally between God and the world, or God and the individual human, implying that God is in some sense one with every human person. The Bible speaks of God's amazing love for the world of humanity (John 3:16). Erickson recognizes the utter dependence of all creation on God, who is "immanently at work in his creation, constantly willing it to remain."[155] Erickson speaks of the members of the Trinity thinking one another's thoughts.[156] Yet it seems difficult to distinguish this from the fact that God knows the thoughts of all men (Gen 6:5; 1 Chr 28:9). Erickson may mean that each thinks the other's thoughts as if he himself had thought them, but that would prevent, not allow, interpersonal relations. Interpersonal relations are impersonal if one cannot distinguish one's self from another. All mankind is loved infinitely by God, depends upon God, and in some sense shares life with God. Indeed, those who hold to a particularly strong view of providence see God at work in every specific action of men.[157]

Believers manifest even more elements of the divine unity. God loves them, and they are able to love God (1 John 4:15–18). God dwells in them, and they dwell in God. Their lives are connected with the life of Christ, because Christ lives in them (Gal 2:20). The righteous believer's life is to some extent shared by God. For example, it is the Holy Spirit who produces love, joy, peace, patience, kindness, goodness, faithfulness, gentleness, and self-control in the Christian life (Gal 5:22–23). Erickson writes, "These qualities cannot in their entirety be produced in human lives by unaided self-effort. They are a supernatural work."[158] The individual Christian shares love and life with God, to a certain extent.

It appears that resurrected believers share love and life with God to a greater extent. According to Erickson, Christ's resurrected body no longer hindered his perfect connection with the Father and Son as his physical body had.[159] Erickson describes the final state of believers as a state of "closeness and communion with God" in which the redeemed "continue to exercise the perfect character which we will have received from God."[160] Presumably this perfect character will include a maximal

---

155. Erickson, *Christian Theology*, 418.

156. Erickson, *God in Three Persons*, 225.

157. For example, John Calvin, *Institutes of the Christian Religion*, 1.26, 2.4 (20:197–210, 20:309–316).

158. Erickson, *Christian Theology*, 891.

159. Erickson, *God in Three Persons*, 223.

160. Erickson, *Christian Theology*, 1240.

love for God and maximal indwelling by him. Thus, the resurrected believer will possess, in a finite degree, the love and shared life, understood as shared experiences, of the Trinity, and at least a unilateral dependence upon God. Presumably, then, God will be one with him, in the trinitarian sense of one, to a certain degree.

Erickson certainly affirms the absolute qualitative distinction between creator and creature. Erickson demands that the three divine persons share a single generic nature, so no creature can actually become one with the Trinity in exactly the same way they are one. But Erickson's three are not so much unified by that nature as they are made acceptable candidates for unity thereby.[161] The strength of the unity still depends on love, dependence, and shared experiences, and a trinitarian unity which consists entirely of elements seen, in one way or another, between God and created reality seems inadequate. Perhaps this is why the authors noted above demand a unity based on uncreated derivation or shared metaphysical substance; these clearly distinguish creator from creature.

Erickson's understanding of divine unity also seems too weak to satisfy the demand for a single creator proposed in Chapter 1.[162] Erickson has three persons, three centers of action, each of which is his own omnipotence. If all three create, there would seem to be three creators. If two of them do not create, they are not God. Only the creator is.

Erickson recognizes this problem, noting that creation is generally attributed to the Father. The Old Testament usually simply ascribes creation to God. In the New Testament, all three work in creation.[163] 1 Cor 8:6 indicates all of creation depends upon both the Father and the Son. Erickson concludes, "The logical problem is how the Son or the Holy Spirit can be the one who creates, if that is done by the Father."

Erickson proposes to look at creation like the building of a house.[164] Such a construction has several causes: a mortgage company, owners, an architect, a contractor, material suppliers, and individual laborers. He concludes, "Actually, of course, all of these build or cause the house, but each in a different way. So, it is possible to think of the Father as the originator or source of the creation, the Son as the designer or organizer of the

---

161. Erickson, *God in Three Persons*, 225.

162. See pp. 25–29 above.

163. Erickson, *Making Sense of the Trinity*, 65.

164. Ibid., 66–67; Erickson, *Christian Theology*, 398.

creation, and the Spirit as the executor of the act of creation, the one who actually carries it out."[165]

The problem is that there are still three creators. The Father by his omnipotence and wisdom originates. The Son by his omnipotence and wisdom designs. The Spirit by his omnipotence and wisdom executes. Three distinct persons, each a metaphysical reality of its own, bring about creation. None of the three is the unique creator of the universe, and therefore none of them can be the God who speaks to Israel.

To approach the problem another way, consider how Erickson's workers would speak of their activity. Certainly the contractor of a house would not say, "I alone created this house, I, and no other." Yet that is what the Lord says in Isaiah 45: "I am the Lord, and there is none else. I form the light, and create darkness: I make peace, and create evil: I the Lord do all these things. . . . I have made the earth, and created man upon it: I, even my hands, have stretched out the heavens, and all their host have I commanded" (Isa 45:6–7, 12). The speaker here clearly is accepting responsibility for all elements of the creative act. Yet who is the speaker? It cannot be the Trinity. For Erickson, the persons in the Trinity are the acting agents. Presumably, it is the Father speaking for the Trinity in his economic role. But how is it appropriate for him to claim full responsibility for a creative act jointly decided upon by the Trinity, designed by the Son, and carried out by the Spirit?

The Bible does not allow for multiple creators. Yet this is what Erickson proposes in his analogy. While he certainly explains how each member of the Trinity can be said to have a role in creation, he does not explain how they can be considered a single creator. Swinburne notes that this also poses a philosophical problem, writing, "To suppose that there were two or more ultimate sources of being, neither of which was dependent on the other, would be to make a suggestion contrary to what is indicated by arguments for the existence of God."[166]

It must be concluded that Erickson's understanding of the divine unity is theologically inadequate. While the label of tritheism cannot be foisted upon every social position, one which denies both that the Son and Spirit are derived from the Father and that the three in God share a metaphysical substance seems to at least invite the term. The first of these

---

165. Erickson, *Making Sense of the Trinity*, 67.

166. Swinburne, *Christian God*, 173. Erickson's idea of mutual interdependence does not apply here, as Swinburne has in mind an asymmetrical dependence.

denials prevents Erickson from reconciling his position with the biblical belief in a sole personal creator. Because each of the members of the Trinity is a person who is his own attributes, creation cannot be ascribed to a single source, but must be divided amongst the persons. Finally, the elements with which Erickson seeks to establish the divine unity are too much a part of God's relationship with creation to seem adequate to make the triune God genuinely one.

CONCLUSION

Erickson presents a social model of the Trinity which views the three persons in God as three centers of consciousness united by love, a shared life, and egalitarian interdependence. His position does justice to the New Testament interrelations of the divine persons and the reality of love within the Godhead. His metaphysic notes the importance of persons within creation. In addition, Erickson serves in this paper as a "purely" social view of the Trinity; no unity is suggested other than that of a perfect society.

Unfortunately, Erickson's position must be in large part rejected as inadequate. He eschews the historical position, exemplified by both Nicaea and John of Damascus, which bases divine unity on a unity of substance caused by derivation. His alternate egalitarian position provides no reasonable account for united action among three equal, omnipotent persons. It makes the three in God so identical that they become indiscernible and dependent upon creation for self-distinction. It also undermines his strongest element of unity, that of interdependence, because it provides no account of how interdependence could occur between equal divine beings. His position also appears to verge on tritheism. It seems impossible to reconcile with the Bible's demand for a single creator. It bases the divine unity on elements which, perhaps unilaterally, reach across the divide between creator and creation. That it lacks the assurances of unity seen in Nicaea, and in the work of other contemporary social trinitarians, only serves to confirm the tritheistic impression.

A final word should be said about the tentative nature of some of these conclusions. Several of them are reached because this author cannot derive from Erickson's thought an adequate explanation, model, or example. Some of these issues are ones Erickson has not addressed, and may be ones which he could easily settle.[167] But until he does, his trinitarian doctrine should be considered unacceptable.

.

---

167. Case also notes the gaps in Erickson's work, writing "serious questions and arguments tend to receive superficial treatment and Erickson's own proposals often seem unoriginal or simply off the mark." Case, review of *God in Three Persons*, 234.

4

John Zizioulas and Trinitarian Unity

THE RECENT INTEREST IN the doctrine of the Trinity has not only sought to properly understand the Trinity in itself, but also to utilize a proper understanding of the Trinity to better approach worldly issues. While the development of the doctrine of the Trinity was initially guided in part by soteriology,[1] several contemporary authors believe the doctrine should directly shape how believers address social, ecological, ecclesial, and political issues.[2]

John Zizioulas is one of the founding fathers of this "trinitarian methodology." Wolfhart Pannenberg, Leonardo Boff, Jürgen Moltmann, and Catherine Mowry LaCugna have all drawn from his work.[3] John Polkinghorne sees a potential correlation between Zizioulas's concept of being-as-communion and the "togetherness-in-separation" concept of quantum physics.[4] Zizioulas's work on the Trinity has been widely influential.

Zizioulas is an Orthodox Metropolitan, and as such writes with an eye on the Orthodox tradition.[5] While his works are primarily dedicated to eucharistic, ecclesial, and ecumenical interests, he believes that these cannot be detached from a proper understanding of the Trinity.[6] As

---

1. Badcock, *Light of Truth*, 171; Erickson, *God in Three Persons*, 15–18.

2. Gunton, *Promise of Trinitarian Theology*; Zizioulas, *Being As Communion*; Boff, *Trinity and Society*.

3. Boff, *Trinity and Society*; Moltmann, "Unity of the Triune God," 157–171; LaCugna, *God for Us*. Kärkkäinen, *Doctrine of God*, 137.

4. Polkinghorne, *Faith of a Physicist*, 155.

5. Zizioulas, "Apostolic Continuity and Orthodox Theology," 75.

6. Fox, *God as Communion*, 189. See, for example, Zizioulas, "Development of Conciliar Structures"; Zizioulas, "Mystery of the Church," 294–303; Zizioulas, "Orthodox-Protestant Bilateral Conversations."

Zizioulas writes, "Orthodoxy concerning the being of God is not a luxury for the Church and for man: it is an existential necessity."[7] For a man to live properly, both as a human and a member of the church, he must properly understand what God is like.

This chapter will examine the sense in which Zizioulas believes God to be one. It will begin by presenting his understanding of the patristic ontological revolution which makes a successful doctrine of the Trinity possible. It will then discuss the elements he believes unify God. After noting the contributions his position makes to a proper understanding of divine unity, it will critique Zizioulas's position historically, logically, and theologically.

JOHN ZIZIOULAS'S UNDERSTANDING OF DIVINE UNITY

Like Millard Erickson, Zizioulas believes the proper model for the being of God is a social model, based on an ontology of personhood.[8] Also like Erickson, he attempts to draw on the insights of the Cappadocian fathers to develop his doctrine of the Trinity.[9] Unlike Erickson, however, Zizioulas maintains and develops the Cappadocian understanding of the Father as the cause of the Trinity, and does so within a metaphysic which he attributes to the Cappadocian fathers.

The Cappadocian Revolution

Zizioulas believes that one of the fundamental difficulties the early church faced in understanding the biblical depiction of God was a monistic ontology.[10] The problem was that "the being of the world and the being of God formed, for the ancient Greeks, an unbreakable unity ... while biblical faith proclaimed God to be absolutely free with regard to the world."[11] Like all philosophical theologies, Greek thought could only

---

7. Zizioulas, *Being as Communion*, 15.

8. Ibid., 17–18; Erickson, *God in Three Persons*, 219–220; Zizioulas, "On Being a Person" in *Persons, Divine and Human*, 33–35.

9. Erickson, *God in Three Persons*, 230.

10. Zizioulas, "Human Capacity," 403; Collins, *Trinitarian Theology*, 178; Leithart, "'Framing' Sacramental Theology," 13. John Wilks points out that one of the difficulties in evaluating Zizioulas's work is his paucity of citations to the Greek Fathers, but that lack is not limited to his use of the patristics. See Wilks, "Trinitarian Ontology," 74.

11. Zizioulas, *Being as Communion*, 16.

reason back to God from the world,[12] and inevitably connected God with the world.

According to Zizioulas, this monism presented two interrelated obstacles to a proper understanding of personhood. First, the Greek philosophical systems emphasize the universal over the particular. Plato subordinates individuals to abstract ideas.[13] Aristotle, though he seems to reject the total preeminence of the abstract, makes no provision for the persistence of the particular except in terms of species.[14] In the case of humans, for example, Aristotle totally unites the human soul with the body.[15] When the human body dies, the particular human person ceases to be, and only the species of humanity remains.[16] For both authors, the true existence of the particular, and therefore the personal, was contingent upon participation in a universal. This helps explain the philosophical use of the word *ousia*, a word "which accounts at the same time for the being of the particular and of what transcends it, hence Aristotle's oscillating between first and second substance."[17] This leaves personhood as a mere adjunct to the prior, more important category of being.[18] Yet Zizioulas believes this is intuitively wrong, for "there is something about the human phenomenon that seems to resist strongly any definition of man from the point of view of his 'substance' or qualities."[19]

The second obstacle to a personal ontology is related to this exaltation of the universal. According to Zizioulas, in this Greek system, persons were never free, but were always dependent upon the impersonal. God, to the extent he was believed to exist, was dependent upon pre-existent matter for the creation of the world.[20] Even after the act of creation, God continues to be bound by the order of the world and the world's relation to him.[21] God was also limited by his own being. As Paul Collins notes, "In classical metaphysics the category of being was primary, and freedom

12. Pannenberg, *Basic Questions in Theology*, 2:125.

13. Zizioulas, *Being as Communion*, 27–29. Plato *Phaedo* 100–105 (86–91).

14. Zizioulas, "On Being a Person," 36.

15. Aristotle *On the Soul* 2.1 (1:656–57).

16. Zizioulas, *Being as Communion*, 28; Aristotle *On the Soul* 2.4 (1:661).

17. Zizioulas, "On Being a Person," 37.

18. Zizioulas, *Being as Communion*, 33, 35.

19. Zizioulas, "Human Capacity," 406.

20. Ibid., 16.

21. Ibid., 29–30.

was to be understood in relation to that category, as indeed the highest expression of being."[22]

Human persons likewise lack freedom. Zizioulas points to the use of the word *prosopon* for a character in Greek tragedy. He writes of such a *prosopon*, "His freedom is circumscribed, or rather there is no freedom for him—since a 'circumscribed freedom' would be a contradiction in terms—and consequently his 'person' is nothing but a 'mask,' something which has no bearing on his true 'hypostasis,' something without onto-logical content."[23] The ontological vacuity of *prosopon* prompted Greek Christians, beginning with Origen, to use *hypostasis* for the three in God.[24] The Latin *persona*, like *prosopon*, is a limiting, rather than freeing, term. It describes a person's place or role in the Roman social or legal system rather than affirming his ontological priority to and freedom from any system. This thought, expressed in Greek or Latin, resulted in the same conclusion. Zizioulas writes, "Other powers, not the quality of person-hood, laid claim to the ontological content of human existence."[25] God was viewed in a similar manner.

Thus Zizioulas sees Greek monism, with its corollary of person-destroying limitation by impersonal absolutes, as irreconcilable with the biblical picture of a free, personal creator. This difficulty was one which the early apologists were unable to escape. Justin, Clement, and Origen could not avoid monism because they were themselves philosophers, rather than pastoral theologians.[26] However, the later Greek fathers, like the Cappadocians, were pastors, were interested in a new ontology, had a Christian creation cosmology, and were therefore able to develop a new ontology in line with the Bible.[27] It was this accomplishment which "was perhaps the greatest philosophical achievement of patristic thought."[28]

This ontological revolution centered around two philosophical moves. First, the Fathers denied the ontological necessity of the created world, making it the product of creative freedom. Second, and more dra-

22. Collins, *Trinitarian Theology*, 169.

23. Zizioulas, *Being as Communion*, 32; cf. Zizioulas, "On Being a Person," 37.

24. Zizioulas, *Being as Communion*, 37.

25. Ibid., 35.

26. For works on the life and thought of these authors, see Chadwick, *Early Christian Thought*; Barnard, *Justin Martyr*; Crouzel, *Origen*.

27. Zizioulas, *Being as Communion*, 16–17, 35.

28. Ibid., 16.

matically, "Not only was the being of the world traced back to personal freedom, but *the being of God Himself* was identified with the person."[29] Zizioulas attributes this second movement primarily to the Cappadocians, and particularly Basil, but believes both moves are in fact biblical, because in "the Bible being is caused in a radical way by *someone*—a particular being. There is no attempt in the Bible to describe this 'someone' in terms of being, for this would lead to associating Him with the world and thus depriving Him of the capacity of cause in the absolute sense."[30] Contrary to Greek monism, but in accord with the Bible, the Cappadocians make a single person the cause of all that is.

And this single person, to be a person, must be truly free.[31] It is not a natural freedom, which is the freedom to act fully in accord with a given nature. It is instead absolute freedom, freedom from any form of givenness, a freedom which can only be possessed by one who is "uncreated."[32] Such a freedom is possible only for one who constitutes his own being.[33]

Zizioulas believes that the Cappadocians developed an ontology of personhood, with three major implications. The first is that "person is no longer an adjunct to a being, a category which we *add* to a concrete entity once we have first verified its ontological hypostasis. *It is itself the hypostasis of the being*."[34] Person now becomes the primary ontological category, because "it is not a quality added, as it were, to beings, something that beings 'have' or 'have not' but it is *constitutive* of what can ultimately called a 'being.'"[35] The second is that persons become the cause of existence, which is no longer explained in terms of substance. According to Zizioulas, an individual person is "precisely that which *constitutes* being, that is, enables entities to be entities."[36] The final implication derives from

29. Ibid., 39, emphasis original.

30. Ibid, 40, emphasis original. Zizioulas cites later pages for Basil's thought, and there refers only to Basil, *Epistulae* 38.2 (*NPNF2* 8:137). He seems to have in mind Basil's denial that the divine nature exists without being in one of the persons. Cf. Zizioulas, "On Being a Person," 38.

31. Wilks, "Trinitarian Ontology," 64.

32. Zizioulas, *Being as Communion*, 42–44.

33. Ibid.; Zizioulas, "On Being a Person," 42; Nonna Verna Harrison, "Zizioulas on Communion and Otherness," 273.

34. Zizioulas, *Being as Communion*, 39, emphasis original.

35. Zizioulas, "Human Capacity," 409, emphasis original.

36. Zizioulas, *Being as Communion*, 39, emphasis original.

the social nature of personhood. Because a "person cannot exist without communion," there can be "no true being without communion. Nothing exists as an 'individual,' conceivable in itself."[37] Zizioulas writes, "One person is no person."[38]

Zizioulas builds his understanding of reality, and therefore the Trinity, from this metaphysic. It is a far cry from the monistic, impersonal, freedom-destroying substance metaphysic of Greek philosophy. By recognizing that creation is unnecessary, it places the causal agent, the person, in the primary ontological spot. Because persons exist only in communion, this ontology also carries the category of communion to the highest level, the inner life of God.

The Divine Communion

Zizioulas's personal ontology, applied to the personal creator of all reality, demands that for God to exist, he must be a communion. He writes, "The substance of God, 'God,' has no ontological content, no true being, apart from communion."[39] The idea of God existing in isolation is self-contradictory. To exist he must be a person, and to be a person he must exist in relation.[40] In such a system, "*To be* and *to be in relation* becomes identical."[41] Richard Fermer summarizes this point in Zizioulas well, writing, "The three persons are one God, in that none of them can be conceived outside their relationship to one another: their personhood is constituted through their relational communion and their unity through the personal relations in which they have their being."[42]

The fact that God must be inherently relational is the first element in Zizioulas's understanding of the divine unity. It is similar to Erickson's understanding of the three in God as inherently interdependent.[43] However, Zizioulas clearly expresses the basis for that interdependence: persons

37. Ibid., 18, cf., Zizioulas, "Human Capacity," 409–10.
38. Zizioulas, "Mystery of the Church," 299.
39. Zizioulas, *Being as Communion*, 17.
40. Zizioulas, "Communion and Otherness," 358.
41. Zizioulas, *Being as Communion*, 88, emphasis original. Colin Gunton also takes this position in Gunton, "Augustine," 42.
42. Fermer, "Limits of Trinitarian Theology," 162.
43. Erickson, *God in Three Persons*, 233, 235, 264. For a full discussion, see pp. 91–94 above. Of course, chronologically it is Erickson who resembles Zizioulas, and not vice versa.

require relation. Zizioulas also differs from Erickson in that he recognizes the need for real difference, absolute otherness, among the members of the Trinity for their unity to be a communion.[44]

Zizioulas equates this communion with the perfect love and knowledge that exist within the Trinity.[45] Zizioulas writes, "The expression 'God is love' (I John 4:16) signifies that God 'subsists' as Trinity, that is, as person and not as substance. Love is not an emanation or 'property' of the substance of God . . . but is *constitutive* of His substance, i.e. it is that which makes God what He is, the one God."[46] Because it is love, communion, which is "creating absolute and unique identities," it is appropriate to speak of "an ontology of love as replacing the ontology of οὐσία."[47] He similarly equates knowledge with communion, writing simply, "Knowledge and communion are identical."[48]

It is important to note that this position minimizes the content and importance of *ousia*, substance. It is love, communion, which constitutes God, and not *ousia*. *Ousia*, substance, is replaced with love as establishing the reality of all extant beings, especially God. Nonna Harrison writes, "Zizioulas strongly affirms the ontological primacy of the person such that the place of nature and energy is minimized as much as possible."[49] This is seen, for example, when he denies that God has authority based upon anything objective, but solely on the fact that he has entered into communion with men.[50] This does not mean that Zizioulas denies the reality of the divine *ousia*. He in fact affirms it, apparently in the generic sense, for he believes it functions to appropriately distinguish God from the world.[51] But he does remove from it any application to the unity of God. In its place, along with the divine communion, he places the person of the Father.

---

44. Zizioulas, "Communion and Otherness," 353; Fox, *God as Communion*, 48–49.

45. Collins, *Trinitarian Theology*, 109.

46. Zizioulas, *Being as Communion*, 46. Zizioulas does not specifically define love, but seems to use it in the sense of personal relations of closeness and intimacy that affirm.

47. Zizioulas, "On Being a Person," 41; see also Zizioulas, "Human Capacity," 410.

48. Zizioulas, *Being as Communion*, 81.

49. Harrison, "Zizioulas on Communion and Otherness," 278. Cf. Letham, *Holy Trinity*, 463.

50. Zizioulas, "Appendix D.," 165–66.

51. Zizioulas, *Being as Communion*, 89.

The Free Father

Zizioulas realizes that, in moving away from a divine unity secured by *ousia*, he is moving away from the usual understanding of the "one nature and three persons" formula, an understanding which locates the unity of God in the one divine substance. Yet he believes this is a justified move:

> [T]his interpretation [that *ousia* means substance] represents a misinterpretation of the Patristic theology of the Trinity. Among the Greek Fathers the unity of God, the one God, and the ontological "principle" or "cause" of the being and life of God does not consist in the one substance of God but in the *hypostasis*, that is, *the person of the Father.* The one God is not the one substance but the Father, who is the "cause" of both the generation of the Son and of the procession of the Spirit.[52]

The one God of all the universe is the Father. Like Rahner, Zizioulas looks to the Father as the source of unity within the Godhead.[53] However, while Rahner looked at the Father as identical with the divine essence and the source of the Son and Spirit, Zizioulas conceives of the relationship between the Father and the divine nature quite differently; the Father is the cause not only of the other two divine persons, but also of the divine nature itself.[54]

As noted above, one of the requirements for a truly personal ontology is a truly personal creator. One necessary aspect of true personhood is complete freedom, which requires that "the authentic person, as absolute ontological freedom, must be 'uncreated,' that is, unbounded by any 'necessity,' including its own existence."[55] In Zizioulas's system, God the Father cannot be bound by any prior nature.

This does not leave the Father without a nature. Instead, it means he is free, as a person, to bring his own nature into being.[56] The person of the Father is the ultimate primordial reality, because the "ontological 'principle' of God is the Father. The personal existence of God (the Father)

---

52. Ibid., 40–41, emphasis original.

53. Weinandy, *Father's Spirit of Sonship*, 62; Rahner, *Trinity*, 44–45, 74, 99. For a full discussion of Rahner, see pp. 41–44 above.

54. Collins, *Trinitarian Theology*, 195.

55. Zizioulas, *Being as Communion*, 43.

56. Harrison, "Zizioulas on Communion and Otherness," 278.

constitutes His substance, makes it hypostasis. The being of God is identified with the person."[57]

Yet this substance is not something other than the divine communion, the trinitarian reality. Zizioulas writes, "God's being, the Holy Trinity, is not caused by divine substance but by *the Father*, i.e. a particular being."[58] And this trinitarian communion, which is the divine substance, is only possible because the Father as cause brings forth the Son and the Spirit. Zizioulas writes, "If God exists, He exists because the Father exists, that is, He who out of love freely begets the Son and brings forth the Spirit. Thus God as person—as the hypostasis of the Father—makes the one divine substance to be that which it is: the one God. This point is absolutely crucial."[59] The Father does not beget the Son and send forth the Spirit so that they are separate from himself, but so that the three of them, as Trinity, constitute his very being, which is communion. Zizioulas suggests that this is the meaning of Athanasius's doctrine that the Son belongs to the substance of the Father.[60] The one God, the Father, begets the Son and breathes forth the Spirit and thus constitutes himself in relation to them. The unity of God is secured by the person of the Father, who is the cause of the Son and the Spirit, and therefore the Trinity and the communion amongst them.[61]

Thus, like Rahner, Zizioulas traces the two elements of divine unity back to the Father. Aristotle Papanikolaou summarizes this in relation to Zizioulas's ontology:

> The Father as *aitia* supports a relational ontology in two ways: for one, it links the unity of God to the person of the Father rather than to the divine *ousia*. *Monarchia*, the one *arche*, in the Greek fathers was identified with the Father. According to Zizioulas, "the 'one God' is the Father, and not the one substance, as Augustine and medieval Scholasticism would say." This sense of *monarchia* means that God is one because of the Father, which evinces the priority for the Cappadocians of personal categories over substantial categories. Secondly, God's trinitarian existence is the result

57. Zizioulas, *Being as Communion*, 41, Letham, *Holy Trinity*, 372.

58. Zizioulas, "On Being a Person," 40.

59. Zizioulas, *Being as Communion*, 41.

60. Ibid., 84–87. See, for example, Athanasius, *Orationes Contra Arianos* 1.3.9, 1.5.14, 3.23.3 (*NPNF2* 4:311, 314, 395).

61. Zizioulas, *Being as Communion*, 17.

of a person, the freedom and the love of Father, not the necessity of substance. The Cappadocian preference for *aitia* (cause) over *pege* (source) indicates further their affirmation of the priority of a personal over a substantial ontology.[62]

God is one because the one free personal cause of all reality, the Father, brings about the one divine communion of Father, Son, and Holy Spirit, as the constitution of his very existence, and upon which he, as a person, is dependent.

Zizioulas develops an understanding of divine unity based upon an ontology of personhood. He combines the communal interdependence of robust divine persons found in Erickson with Rahner's emphasis on the Father as the one God, the personal unifying cause of the Godhead. The next section will attempt to determine whether this understanding of divine unity is adequate.

A CRITIQUE OF ZIZIOULAS'S UNDERSTANDING OF UNITY

Zizioulas's position bears resemblances to the positions of both Rahner and Erickson. As such, his position shows some of the strengths of both authors'. Like Rahner, Zizioulas focuses on the monarchy of the Father and his role as the cause of the Son and Spirit to present a strong view of divine unity.[63] Like Erickson, Zizioulas develops a robust understanding of personhood to do justice to the biblical description of Father, Son, and Spirit.[64] In addition, he more fully develops a metaphysic which makes that understanding of personhood, and the corollary concept of a personal unity, possible.[65] Zizioulas's understanding of person also allows him to do better justice to the Chalcedonian understanding of the incarnation. He describes the importance of the person of Christ, noting that "it is his *person* that makes divine and human natures to be that particular being called Christ."[66]

However, Zizioulas's position also suffers from several significant weaknesses. His position is weak historically, because he appears to distort

---

62. Papanikolaou, "Divine Energies or Divine Personhood," 368.

63. Rahner, *Trinity*, 44–45, 74, 99.

64. Erickson, *Word Became Flesh*, 525–26, 529.

65. Case laments the brevity of Erickson's metaphysical development in his work on the Trinity. See Case, review of *God in Three Persons*, 235.

66. Zizioulas, "Human Capacity," 436.

the Cappadocian tradition which he claims for support. His position faces logical difficulties as well, because he provides contradictory descriptions of the Father, and seems to leave the divine reality without any grounding. Theologically, his position blurs the distinction between God and the world, leaves the attributes of God ungrounded, flirts with tritheism, and essentially subordinates the Son and Spirit to the Father. These criticisms will now be developed.

Historical Difficulties

John Meyendorff notes that no truly Orthodox theology "either neglects Tradition, uncovered in history, or forgets the truth, which is its *raison d'étre*."[67] Meyendorff claims that Zizioulas's position avoids both errors, transcending the dichotomy to show the integrated nature of doctrine. This, however, may be a bit of an overstatement, especially when it comes to Zizioulas's use of the Cappadocians, and his description of their ontology.

The first cause for concern is the fact that Zizioulas makes several historical errors in his work.[68] For example, he incorrectly attributes a materialistic understanding of the divine nature to Origen, who adamantly rejected such a position, rather than to Tertullian, who espoused it.[69] More concern is caused by the fact that Zizioulas frequently refers broadly to the work of the Cappadocians, but rarely cites the specific work he has in mind.[70] As Wilks notes, "Whilst claiming Patristic support, Zizioulas provides only minimal citations from the Greek Fathers; there are insufficient specific references to them that would enable us to evaluate the evidence for ourselves."[71] When specific texts are used, criteria for their selection are not always offered.[72] One specific corpus Zizioulas cites is

67. John Meyendorff, foreword to Zizioulas, *Being as Communion*, 11.

68. Rowan Williams notes several inaccuracies in Rowan Williams, review of *Being as Communion: Studies in Personhood and the Church*, by John Zizioulas, *Scottish Journal of Theology* 42 (1989) 104.

69. Zizioulas, *Being as Communion*, 75; Origen, *De principiis*, 1.1.4–9 (*ANF* 4:243–45); Tertullian, *Adversus Praxean* 9 (*ANF* 3:603–4); Williams, review of *Being as Communion*, 104.

70. For example, Zizioulas, *Being as Communion*, 17–18; Zizioulas, "Apostolic Continuity," 85; John Zizioulas, "Church as Communion," 7–8.

71. Wilks, "Trinitarian Ontology," 74.

72. Fermer, "Limits of Trinitarian Theology," 164.

the correspondence between Apollinarius and Basil, *Epistles* 361 and 362, which the editors of *Nicene and Post-Nicene Fathers* refer to as "indubitably spurious."[73] While Zizioulas acknowledges the suspect nature of the letters, he claims they represent the thought of Basil seen in other documents.[74] One wonders why suspect documents are used, if other documents with similar content, but more certain authenticity, are available.

As noted above, Zizioulas claims the Cappadocians brought about a revolution in how being is understood and consequently how the unity of the Trinity should be conceived. Wilks asserts that this leaves two issues to sort out. The first is how the Cappadocians understand and use *ousia* and its relation to the trinitarian unity. The second is the Father's place in the Cappadocian understanding of the Trinity.[75]

Zizioulas claims that the Cappadocians understand the being of God to be communion. He states that Basil, in his writings, prefers to write of the unity of God as a communion, rather than a unity of nature.[76] And it is true that Basil writes of a communion or community in God when he discusses what is one in God. But the specific type of communion or community is a "community of essence," and as Fermer points out, such a phrase cannot be understood to equate the two terms community and essence.[77] While Fermer suggests that the phrase could be read as a communion based on essence, even that seems to go beyond Basil's thought. Instead, the better way to understand the phrase, especially in light of Basil's overall thought, is as shared, or common, essence.[78] When Basil specifies what is one in God, he makes clear it is, at least primarily, a singular nature. He writes, "When I say 'alone' I set forth the holy and uncreated essence and substance of God."[79] Wilks renders the proper conclusion, writing, ""The *ousia* is more than the communion together of

73. *NPNF2* 8:326.

74. Zizioulas, "On Being a Person," 38–39. For support of their authenticity, Zizioulas refers to Prestige, *St. Basil the Great*.

75. Wilks, "Trinitarian Ontology," 64–65.

76. Zizioulas, *Being as Communion*, 134; Zizioulas, "Apostolic Continuity," 85, n. 37.

77. Basil, *Ep.* 38.6, 189.7 (*NPNF2* 8:140, 8:231); Fermer, "Limits of Trinitarian Theology," 165. As Zizioulas claims to rely upon all of the Cappadocians, and associates *Ep.* 38 with Basil, whether it was written by Basil or Gregory of Nyssa is not a crucial point here.

78. Basil, *Ep.* 38.2, 214.4 (*NPNF2* 8:137, 254). See also Wilks, "Trinitarian Ontology," 71.

79. Basil, *Ep.* 8.3 (*NPNF2* 8:117); cf. *Ep.* 38.4 (*NPNF2* 8:139).

the *hypostases*. And to claim on the basis of four references (one of which cannot be traced) that Basil prefers communion to *ousia* is to ignore the evidence to the contrary."[80]

This position is also seen in the works of the two Gregorys. Gregory of Nyssa argues that the three in God share a community of nature because they share a community of attributes.[81] This usage indicates both that nature still retains at least some of the Greek philosophical elements Zizioulas criticizes, and that Cappadocian community is not Zizioulan "communion," but a term for what is common in the three.[82] And what is common is a singular, uncreated essence.[83] Gregory Nazianzen also sees "One Godhead" and "One Supreme Substance" as unifying forces in God.[84] He instructs his readers how to properly read biblical assertions of divine unity when he writes, "And when you read, I and the Father are One, keep before your eyes the Unity of Substance."[85] Thus Zizioulas, in arguing that the Cappadocians saw the unity of God in terms of a social communion, rather than an essential unity, conceived in terms of *ousia*, seems to distort the Cappadocian position. This is not to downplay the Cappadocian appreciation for the mutual indwelling of the three in God, only to point out that this communion grew from, rather than replaced, a unity of *ousia*.[86]

---

80. Wilks, "Trinitarian Ontology," 80, 87, n. 118. Zizioulas's citation at this point (*Being as Communion*, 134, n. 23) is quite confusing. He cites primarily Basil, *De Spiritu Sancto*, 18 (*PG* 32:194c). This reference is to the Latin of *Spir.* 68, which does not contain the sentence "The unity (of God) is in the *koinonia tes theotetos*." This sentence actually appears in *Spir.* 45 (*PG* 32:149c; note the inversion), where its meaning is connected to the unity of a king and his image. These share a common form (*morphe*). *Spir.* 68 does state that the Spirit has *koinonia* with God in the context of explaining how glory to the Spirit and in the Spirit mean the same thing. Zizioulas also mentions *Spir.* 68, *Contra Eunomius* 2.12 (*PG* 29:593c), which states that the Son has *koinonia* with the Father, and *Ep.* 52.3, which argues for the son's derivation. Which source Wilks says "cannot be traced," is unclear, but none of them speak of *koinonia* as personal communion forming the essence of the Godhead.

81. Gregory of Nyssa, *On the Holy Trinity* (*NPNF2* 5:327).

82. This is particularly clear in Gregory of Nyssa's arguments in *Contra Eunomius* 4 (*NPNF2* 5:153–71). See also Collins, *Trinitarian Theology*, 187.

83. Gregory of Nyssa, *C. Eun.* 1.35, 5.1 (*NPNF2* 5:81, 173).

84. Gregory Nazianzen, *Orationes* 34.9 (*NPNF2* 7:336).

85. Gregory Nazianzen, *Or.* 34.13 (*NPNF2* 7:337).

86. For example, Gregory of Nyssa, *C. Eun.* 1.21, 2.6 (*NPNF2* 5:61, 106–8).

There are other disagreements between Zizioulas and the Cappadocians on the question of *ousia*. The Cappadocians consistently affirm that the divine *ousia* is incomprehensible.[87] On the other hand, Zizioulas seems confident identifying the divine being as communion.[88] Zizioulas is willing to minimize *ousia* and exalt *hypostasis* as metaphysical categories, but the Cappadocians consistently balanced the two categories.[89]

One final disagreement regards Zizioulas's central thesis, that the Father, as a free person, brings his own *ousia* into being.[90] Gregory of Nyssa, in a debate with Eunomius, refutes that such an occurrence is possible. Eunomius attributes the production of the Son to an energy distinct from the Father. Gregory responds that this energy either is substantial or insubstantial. If it is substantial, then the Father is not truly Father, but this energy is. If the energy is not substantial, however, it cannot produce the Son, because it does not exist. He challenges Eunomius "to explain to us how non-being can 'follow' being, and how what is not a substance can produce a substance."[91] For Gregory, *ousia* retains the meaning of existence, or being. That which has no *ousia* cannot do anything, because it does not exist.[92] Note that the context here is the timeless generation of the Son. Substance must precede substance logically, not just chronologically. To suggest that the Father, as a person without *ousia*, can constitute his own *ousia*, is to defy, not follow, the Cappadocian tradition.

Zizioulas appears to differ significantly with the Cappadocians in his use of *ousia*. He downplays the role of essential unity in Cappadocian thought, and exaggerates the concept of interpersonal communion to replace it. He moves away from the Cappadocian balance of *hypostasis* and *ousia* to a position which exalts the former at the expense of the latter. His attribution of the ontological revolution which his understand-

---

87. For example, Gregory Nazianzen, *Or.* 38.7 (*NPNF2* 7:346); Gregory of Nyssa, *C. Eun.* 1.21 (*NPNF2* 5:61); Basil, *Ep.* 38.3 (*NPNF2* 8:138).

88. Fermer, "Limits of Trinitarian Theology," 174; Zizioulas, *Being as Communion*, 16–18.

89. Zizioulas, "On Being a Person," 41; Zizioulas, "Human Capacity," 410; Gregory Nazianzen, *Or.* 21.13, 21.35 (*NPNF2* 7:273, 279); Gregory of Nyssa, *C. Eun.* 2.2 (*NPNF2* 5:102–103); Basil, *Ep.* 214.4, 236.6 (*NPNF2* 8:254, 278); Wilks, "Trinitarian Ontology," 73.

90. Zizioulas, *Being as Communion*, 41.

91. Gregory of Nyssa, *C. Eun.*, 1.20 (*NPNF2* 5:58).

92. Ibid., 2.5 (*NPNF2* 5:106).

ing of the divine unity presupposes to the Cappadocians therefore is somewhat suspect.

The second issue Wilks notes is the role of the Father in the Godhead. Zizoulas takes a position in many ways similar to that of Rahner, and attributes this position to the Cappadocians. The One God is the Father.[93] The Father is the cause of the Son and Spirit, and brings them into being to constitute his own trinitarian existence.[94]

It was already shown in Chapter 2 that the Cappadocian position is not one which identifies the One God exclusively, or even primarily, with the Father.[95] It also seems that Zizioulas goes beyond the Cappadocian understanding of the causal role of the Father in the Godhead.[96] The Cappadocians speak of the Father as the cause of the Son and Spirit.[97] However, he is not, as Father, the first cause of the universe. It is the One Godhead, in contrast to any one of the three persons, who is the first cause of created reality.[98] The Cappadocians stress that the Father's role as cause cannot be understood as the production of inferiors.[99] To avoid this misunderstanding, the Father's role as cause is balanced with the unity of the divine nature.[100] Gregory of Nyssa writes, "We hear our Lord saying, 'I and My Father are one,' and we are taught in that utterance the dependence of our Lord on a cause, and yet the absolute identity of the Son's and the Father's nature . . . not dividing in the Persons the oneness of their substance."[101] In fact, while Zizioulas sees the causal role of the Father as an element of divine unity, the Cappadocians see it as the means of his distinction. The divine nature is the source of the divine unity.[102]

---

93. Zizioulas, "On Being a Person," 40; Zizioulas, *Being as Communion,* 40.

94. Zizioulas, *Being as Communion,* 40–44; Hopko sees these same two elements in the Cappadocians. See Hopko, "Trinity in the Cappadocians," 265.

95. Gregory Nazianzen, *Or.* 3.13, 4.18 (*NPNF2* 7:305, 316); Gregory of Nyssa, *C. Eun.* 2.3, 2.4, 2.6 (*NPNF2* 5:103, 104, 108); Basil, *Ep.* 8.3 (*NPNF2* 8:117). For a full discussion, see pp. 54–55 above.

96. Wilks, "Trinitarian Ontology," 77.

97. Gregory Nazianzen, *Or.* 3.3, 3.15, 34.10 (*NPNF2* 7:302, 306, 337).

98. Gregory Nazianzen, *Or.* 5.14, 5.33 (*NPNF2* 7:322, 328); Gregory of Nyssa, *C. Eun.* 1.36 (*NPNF2* 5:84).

99. Gregory Nazianzen, *Or.* 40.43 (*NPNF2* 7:375–76).

100. Basil, *Ep.* 38.3 (*NPNF2* 8:138).

101. Gregory of Nyssa, *C. Eun.* 1.35 (*NPNF2* 5:81).

102. Gregory of Nyssa, *On "Not Three Gods"* (*NPNF2* 5:336); Basil, *Ep.* 38.4 (*NPNF2* 8:139); Wilks, "Trinitarian Ontology," 77–79.

It appears that Zizioulas is not as beholden to the Cappadocians as he purports himself to be. He differs significantly from the Cappadocians regarding both the role of the divine *ousia* and of the Father in trinitarian unity. He emphasizes the causal role of the Father as a source for divine unity, while the Cappadocians saw that role as the distinguishing mark of the Father. Of course, the Cappadocians are not necessarily normative. However, Zizioulas claims the Cappadocians for support, even though they significantly disagree with him. Williams concludes that, while Zizioulas insists on "fidelity to a primitive *norm*," his "cavalier treatment of some details of historical evidence will make the whole structure insecure and questionable in the eyes of many."[103] Kärkkäinen, following Miroslav Volf, presents the more judicious conclusion that, even if Zizioulas's position has historical difficulties, his own doctrine should be considered for what it is in itself.[104] This task will now be undertaken.

Logical Difficulties

Zizioulas's position faces two problems of internal consistency. The first relates to his understanding of personhood as freedom, and the possession of personhood by the Father. The second is related to the interplay of relations and persons in Zizioulas's ontology.

The Father and Givenness

Zizioulas believes that a genuine person must be free from givenness.[105] Therefore God the Father, as "the authentic person, as absolute ontological freedom, must be 'uncreated,' that is, unbounded by any 'necessity,' including its own existence."[106] He notes that the human problem is the inability to achieve personhood because of the given human nature.[107] The only way people have of affirming their freedom is by rejecting their nature, which is suicide. God, however, is free, and is so personally, rather than naturally. It is the person of the Father who is free, who "transcends and abolishes the ontological necessity of the substance by being God as *Father*, that is,

---

103. Williams, review of *Being as Communion*, 104, emphasis original.

104. Kärkkäinen, *Trinity*, 97.

105. Zizioulas, *Being as Communion*, 18, 32.

106. Ibid., 43. The suggestion that God does not necessarily exist would trouble many. For a brief discussion, see Nash, *Concept of God*, 107–112.

107. Ibid., 19, 42; Harrison, "Zizioulas on Communion and Otherness," 273.

as He who 'begets' the Son and 'brings forth' the Spirit."[108] In this scheme, the Trinity exists "not because the divine *nature* is ecstatic but because the Father as a *person* freely wills this communion."[109]

To summarize to this point, logically prior to the existence of the Trinity, the Father is a person lacking any substance which limits or determines his behavior. Stipulating for a moment the coherence of this position, it would imply that this person would have limitless options for how it would exist. However, Zizioulas imposes on this person the necessity of communion.

For Zizioulas, there is no being without communion.[110] Individual existence is impossible, for alone a person loses "not only its otherness but also its very being; it simply cannot be without the other."[111] Not only can the Father not be Father without the Son and Spirit, he cannot even be conceived of as existing.[112] The definition of freedom for a person becomes freedom for, or towards, others.

Zizioulas makes a similar move when he redefines freedom as love. Continuing the argument that person is the ultimate ontological principle, and that freedom is necessary for true personhood, Zizioulas limits the type of person who can actually bring about being. He writes, "True being comes only from the free person, from the person who loves freely— that is, who freely affirms his being, his identity, by means of an event of communion with other persons."[113] Freedom, first identified as absolute freedom from givenness, becomes love. Zizioulas writes, "It thus becomes evident that the only exercise of freedom in an ontological manner is *love*. . . . Love is identified with ontological freedom."[114]

This leaves the supposedly free divine person in a quandary. He can cease to exist, or he can "freely" will two other persons into existence to commune with them and therefore exist, but he cannot exist alone. This may sound correct to the traditional trinitarian, who believes God is necessarily, essentially Trinity. But it must be remembered that Zizioulas attempts

108. Zizioulas, *Being as Communion*, 44, emphasis original.
109. Ibid., emphasis original.
110. Ibid., 18.
111. Zizioulas, "Communion and Otherness," 358.
112. Zizioulas, "Mystery of the Church," 299.
113. Zizioulas, *Being as Communion*, 18.
114. Ibid., 46.

to avoid both necessity and essence. The natural freedom of Greek monism is one that he rejects.[115] The divine person has no nature as yet, no essence, no being, until he constitutes it. Why must he become Trinity? There is no metaphysical entity other than this supposedly free person. What is the source of the condition, that this person must experience an event of communion or cease to exist? If such a source can be identified, in what sense is the divine person free, if he must operate under the requirements of the source? After all, Zizioulas has stated that circumscribed freedom is a contradiction in terms.[116]

It appears that Zizioulas's desire to root ontology in a divine person, free from the constraints of nature, cannot coexist with his desire to assert the necessity of communion for existence. Either the divine person is bound by such a necessity, in which case he is not free, or he is free from the necessity of communion, in which case it is not, in fact, necessary.

Person and Communion

Circular causation is impossible. If A causes B, then B cannot cause A. This is because B requires A to exist logically prior to B's occurrence. This is true whether the causation is necessary, so that A must exist for B to exist, or sufficient, so that A suffices to fully account for the existence of B. Events in particular cannot be circularly caused, because events do not just happen. They require a logically prior cause.[117]

Zizioulas's system, however, seems to suggest circular causation within the Godhead. He states that it is communion, relationship, with others which constitutes persons, which causes them to exist. However, he also argues that the persons in God, and particularly the person of God the Father, bring into being the communion which is the being of God.

The first point, that communion causes persons to exist, is a clear element of Zizioulas's thought.[118] He writes, "Personhood is directly related to ontology—it is not a quality added, as it were, to beings, something

115. Ibid., 16; Collins, *Trinitarian Theology*, 169.

116. Zizioulas, *Being as Communion*, 32.

117. This is a common sense position, the defense of which goes well beyond the scope of this paper. For support, see Swinburne, *Christian God*, 82, 89, 147; Moreland, *Scaling the Secular City*, 38–41. Even Hume, who sometimes denied causality, granted the priority of perceived cause to perceived effect in Hume, *Treatise of Human Nature*, 1.3.2 (81).

118. Fermer, "Limits of Trinitarian Theology," 162.

that beings 'have' or 'have not' but it is *constitutive* of what can ultimately called a 'being.'"[119] Personhood causes true being. Personhood, in turn, is caused by communion. It is only "in *communion* that this being is *itself* and thus *is at all*. Thus communion does not threaten personal particularity; it is constitutive of it."[120] That he intends to say communion causes a person to exist is clear when he writes, "That which, therefore, makes a particular personal being be itself—and thus be at all—is in the final analysis *communion, freedom* and *love*."[121] That this reasoning is meant to include God the Father is also clear. Zizioulas writes, "only God can claim to be a personal being in the genuine sense I have just indicated," God here meaning "the *Father*—a term which denotes being in the sense of hypostasis, i.e. of Person."[122] Even in God, "One person is no person."[123] Because communion is what makes the persons of God exist, Zizioulas equates the substance of God with the communion of the three.[124]

Yet Zizioulas also argues for the second point, that communion is constituted by persons. He writes that, in the Trinity, "otherness is *constitutive* of unity."[125] That is, the distinct persons in the Godhead cause their communion.[126] Elsewhere he suggests the logical priority of persons to communion, writing that "personhood implies the 'openness of being', and even more than that, the *ek-stasis* of being, i.e. a movement towards communion which leads to a transcendence of the boundaries of the 'self' and thus to *freedom*."[127] If personhood implies movement towards communion, personhood must be possible away from communion. This same implication, that person is not dependent upon, but instead causes, communion, seems to follow from his assertion that there is nothing logically prior to personhood.[128]

119. Zizioulas, "Human Capacity," 409, emphasis original.
120. Ibid., emphasis original; See also Zizioulas, *Being as Communion*, 88.
121. Zizioulas, "Human Capacity," 410, emphasis original. See also Zizioulas, "Human Capacity," 436.
122. Zizioulas, "Human Capacity," 410, emphasis original.
123. Zizioulas, "Mystery of the Church," 299.
124. Zizioulas, *Being as Communion*, 134.
125. Zizioulas, "Communion and Otherness," 353, emphasis original.
126. Fox, *God as Communion*, 48–49, 205.
127. Zizioulas, "Human Capacity," 408.
128. Zizioulas, "On Being a Person," 33.

It could be suggested that Zizioulas is arguing not for causation in the usual sense, but instead for an inherent simultaneity. The persons simply are in relationship, and the relationships and the persons simultaneously define one another. Zizioulas himself writes, "God is not first one and then three, but simultaneously One and Three."[129] This is Ted Peters's understanding, who writes, "Community and person are correlative. Neither is prior. Each requires the other. Hence, in one and the same moment all of the three divine persons are constituted as individual exist-tents, and God as Trinity is constituted as a divine community."[130] Collins places Zizioulas in the same camp, writing, "Zizioulas understands that the person (*hypostasis*) is both constituted by and constitutes the ontological category of communion."[131] It may be a brute fact that God is persons-in-relation. God is often recognized as being devoid of causal explanation because God has no cause.[132]

Yet this still leaves Zizioulas with two problems. The first is that positions which speak of the persons in God as defined by their relations usually ground those relations in the divine *ousia*, robustly understood.[133] Yet Zizioulas minimizes the concept of the divine *ousia*, relegating it to generic status, and instead conceives of the substance of God as the very communion which is part of the difficulty.[134] As a material example, consider two mountains and the valley between them. They mutually constitute one another. Here on earth, where the surface of the earth is available to ground both mountain and valley, this makes perfect sense. However, speaking of mountains and a valley mutually constituting one another in the void of space is absurd. Similarly, speaking of persons and relations as mutually constitutive when neither is grounded in a clearly self-existent *ousia* is dangerously close to incoherence.

Zizioulas's second difficulty with asserting an inherent simultaneity of person and communion is his own emphasis on the person of the Father as the cause of the divine communion. As long as God's being is neces-

---

129. Zizioulas, "Communion and Otherness," 353.

130. Peters, *GOD as Trinity*, 36–37.

131. Collins, *Trinitarian Ontology*, 59.

132. Moreland notes that God, as a necessary being, does not require a cause. See Moreland, *Scaling the Secular City*, 38.

133. This is true of Rahner, for example. See Rahner, *Trinity*, 69–71.

134. Zizioulas, *Being as Communion*, 134; Fermer, "Limits of Trinitarian Theology," 181–83.

sary, questions of cause are inappropriate.[135] Yet Zizioulas denies that the Trinity is necessary; it is caused.[136] He believes that the Father affirms his own being by an event of communion with the two persons whose cause he himself is.[137] The relational nature of the Trinity is not "a structure of communion existing by itself or imposed by necessity," but instead exists "because the Father as a *person* freely wills this communion."[138] Leonardo Boff asks, "This [constitution by relations], however, raises a problem: how can the Father be a Person if he is so only in begetting the Son? How can he be a begetting subject, if his personality is only formed by the act of begetting?"[139] While he aims this question at Rahner and Barth, it seems equally applicable to Zizioulas. How can the Father, who is not a person outside a communion, be the person who causes the communion?

Zizioulas's position therefore seems to lapse into incoherence. The person of the Father is causally prior to any communion, in part because he is prior to the two with whom he will have communion. However, he cannot be constituted as a specific person, and therefore cannot exist at all, unless he is in communion. Thus communion is causally prior to the Father. Such a position is untenable.

It should be noted that this philosophical looseness appears throughout Zizioulas's work, particularly in connection with the categories of person and communion. At times the Father's being is identified with his person. At other times the Father's being is the communion of the Trinity.[140] Zizioulas also writes that the Bible speaks of God as ὁ ὤν "in order to indicate in an apophatic manner that he is not to be described in any ontological way."[141] This would suggest that no ontology can be developed from or applied to God. At one point, Zizioulas seems to identify the Father with the Trinity, writing, "For this communion is a product of freedom as a result not of the substance of God but of a person, the Father—observe why this doctrinal detail is so important—who is

---

135. Nash, *Concept of God*, 112.

136. Zizioulas, *Being as Communion*, 43.

137. Ibid., 18, 40.

138. Ibid., 17–18, 44.

139. Boff, *Trinity and Society*, 137.

140. Ibid., 17, 39, 41, 134; Zizioulas, "On Being a Person," 42.

141. Zizioulas, "On Being a Person," 38.

Trinity."[142] To summarize, Zizioulas does not consistently maintain the distinction between person and communion, Father and Trinity.

As in the case of the conflict between freedom and communion, Zizioulas again appears to be affirming two conflicting statements. On the one hand, communion makes persons exist. On the other hand, a person, the Father, makes the communion of the Trinity exist. By introducing the category of cause into the uncaused being of God, Zizioulas renders his position logically incoherent.

Theological Difficulties

Zizioulas's position also faces several theological difficulties, four of which will be noted here. They are not all unanswerable. Yet together they raise serious questions as to whether Zizioulas has put forth an adequate understanding of Trinitarian unity.

God and Creation

The first theological difficulty is the place of creation in Zizioulas's ontology. The one God of the Bible is the sole creator of all created reality, and its relationship to him is an important issue. Fermer raises two questions about the role of creation in Zizioulas's system. The first is what existence creation has, if ontology is personal. Zizioulas places person outside of the world and makes person constitute true being, which raises questions about how this impersonal world actually exists.[143]

Zizioulas appears to answer this question by relating the impersonal elements of the world to personal realities. The world was created as the free act of a personal creator. Human persons were intended to serve as priests of creation, thus lifting up the impersonal aspects of creation to the personal. In Christ, the divine and human natures are united, and the priestly role of man fulfilled.[144] Zizioulas writes, "Christ realises the unity of God and the world, through man, in communion."[145] The church, united with Christ, now carries on that mission. The church pursues its purpose, which is to "bring about a communion of the world in the life

---

142. Zizioulas, *Being as Communion*, 44.

143. Fermer, "Limits of Trinitarian Theology," 171; Zizioulas, "Human Capacity," 420; Zizioulas, *Being as Communion*, 39–40.

144. Zizioulas, *Being as Communion*, 39–40; Zizioulas, "Human Capacity," 425.

145. Zizioulas, "Human Capacity," 447.

of God by bringing into the world the love of God the Father, in the form of the grace of our Lord Jesus Christ within the communion of the Holy Spirit."[146] The world is established as real not because it is itself a person, but because of the relationship it has to genuine persons.

Yet this assertion leads to Fermer's second question for Zizioulas, that of how the world is distinguished from God. Zizioulas freely applies his divine ontology to human life, but if God's existence is truly other than that of creation, such a transfer should not be possible.[147] To add to Fermer's point, it is clear that the two elements Zizioulas believes unify the Godhead also relate God to the world. The Father is the causal source of the Son, the Spirit, the divine communion, and the created world.[148] Christ and the church bring the world into the life of God and unite the world to God by communion.[149] If causality and communion make the Son and Spirit one with the Father, do they similarly unite the world to him? At best, this position dangerously blurs the distinction between God and the world.[150]

Zizioulas does believe that God and the world must be distinguished, and he retains the concept of the distinct divine *ousia* for that purpose. He writes, "The identification of God with the Father risks losing its biblical content unless our doctrine of God includes not just the three persons, but also the unique *ousia*."[151] God is distinguished from the world by the *ousia*, which only the Father, Son, and Holy Spirit have. In one respect, this seems like a hollow assertion, since Zizioulas has minimized the reality of the divine *ousia*. However, even if *ousia* is understood generically, in the sense of a unique set of attributes, God and the world can still be distinguished. The world does not have the attributes that God does.

Nature and Attributes

However, this leads to a second area in which Zizioulas's position is questionable. What are the divine attributes, and where are they located? John of Damascus is representative of tradition when he lists divine attributes such as "uncreate [*sic*], unbegotten, imperishable and immortal, everlast-

146. Zizioulas, "Informal Groups," 288.

147. Fermer, "Limits of Trinitarian Theology," 173.

148. Zizioulas, *Being as Communion*, 39–44.

149. Zizioulas, "Human Capacity," 447; Zizioulas, "Informal Groups," 288, 298.

150. This is similar to the critique made of Erickson on pp. 97–98 above.

151. Zizioulas, *Being as Communion*, 89.

ing, infinite, uncircumscribed, boundless, of infinite power" and "creator of all created things," and when he locates those attributes in, or more accurately, identifies them with, the divine *ousia*.[152] But Fermer notes that Zizioulas does not clearly locate the divine attributes in the divine *ousia*.[153] In fact, it is an open question how Zizioulas handles the divine attributes, his assertion regarding "the unique *ousia*" notwithstanding.

The reason is again his description of the Father as a free person. As a truly free person, the Father is not bound by a nature, which seems to mean that the Father does not have any particular attributes. He certainly is not everlasting, immortal, or imperishable, as Zizioulas asserts that "the authentic person, as absolute ontological freedom, must be 'uncreated,' that is, unbounded by any 'necessity,' including its own existence," and presents suicide as one manifestation of personal freedom.[154] Yet an immortal, imperishable being is bound by the necessity of his own existence. He is not free not to exist.

The other attributes listed seem to pose less of a problem for the Father's freedom. It is hard to think of infinity, or omnipotence, as limiting freedom; they almost define it. Where, then, does Zizioulas locate them? The Father, as a free person, has no substance "before" he brings the communion of God into being.[155] Clearly, to bring that communion into being he must possess some capability, and presumably he possesses freedom-defining attributes. But the only metaphysical reality which might serve as the seat of his omnipotence, or his infinity, is his person. Therefore the reader must conclude that it is as a person that the Father is omnipotent, omniscient, infinite, etc. These attributes reside in his person. This seems to fit well into Zizioulas's scheme, as he identifies person as "the ultimate ontological category."[156]

According to Zizioulas, human persons similarly bear human attributes. The Chalcedonian reference to a human nature expresses only that such a nature exists. But the concept "human nature" does not further man's understanding of what it is to be human. The question of whether humans have the ability to please God is not a question about nature,

152. John of Damascus, *Fid. Orth.* 1.8 (*NPNF2* 9:6); Richard Swinburne gives a good brief summary of the divine attributes in Swinburne, "More Than One God?" 225–26.

153. Fermer, "Limits of Trinitarian Theology," 166.

154. Zizioulas, *Being as Communion*, 43, 42, 46; Zizioulas, "Human Capacity," 428.

155. Zizioulas, *Being as Communion*, 17–18.

156. Ibid.

but about person.[157] Memory is not an element of nature, but of person.[158] The body is not part of a human's being, but an aspect of his person.[159] In humans as in God, person is the ontological category.

Is there a problem with placing the divine attributes in the person? This is, after all, how Erickson handles the divine attributes.[160] It is not a perfect solution for Zizioulas, however. It seems to negate the whole thrust of his ontology by effectively merging the person with the substance. Being becomes identified with person.[161] While some attributes are relative attributes, it is usually recognized that at least some of God's attributes are not. God's omnipotence would be an example of a monadic, non-relational property. But this means that even Zizioulas's personal ontology includes within the person something that is not personal, because it is not defined by relation. Rather than a person, established by communion, being based in or derived from an impersonal substance, Zizioulas has a person, established by communion, including within itself a non-relational, and therefore impersonal, reality of attributes.

There is nothing wrong with such a general ontology, but it certainly falls short of an ontological revolution. The impersonal still has an essential place within God, for it is attributes which distinguish him from the world. While Zizioulas wants to emphasize the priority of the personal, it is, as noted above, the Father as non-related freedom, not person-in-relation, who is the cause of the Trinity. It makes one wonder whether this is a conceptual advance over a substantialist metaphysic, or simply a language shift, in which person is assumed to include substance, so that what once was referred to substance is now referred to person.

Freedom and Subordinationism

Many authors note that the "Eastern" view of the Trinity, which emphasizes the role of the Father as the source of deity, tends towards subordinationism.[162] Zizioulas attempts to avoid this conclusion. According to

157. Zizioulas, "Human Capacity," 407.

158. Ibid., 418.

159. Zizioulas, "Human Capacity," 423.

160. Erickson, Word Became Flesh, 525–26, 529; Erickson, God the Father Almighty, 231.

161. Zizioulas, "Human Capacity," 414; 435–36.

162. For example, Boff, Trinity and Society, 234; Hill, Three-Personed God, 73, 78, 143;

Zizioulas, the persons in God share the unique divine *ousia*.[163] They all share the same attributes within their persons, and are not distinguished by their attributes. The distinction, then, among each of Father, Son, and Spirit is not made "by way of difference of qualities but by way of simple affirmation of being who He is."[164] There is therefore no subordination of the Son and Spirit to the Father at the level of *ousia* or attributes.

At first glance, this would seem to rule out the charge that Zizioulas teaches heretical subordinationism, because heretical subordinationism teaches that the Son and Spirit are at a lower level of being, traditionally understood as essence or attributes, than the Father. There is general agreement that the Nicene Creed, for example, meant to prohibit essential subordinationism by its inclusion of *homoousios*.[165] This is distinguished from functional subordination, in which the Son and Spirit obey the Father, either eternally or only within the economy.[166]

However, in evaluating Zizioulas's position, it is important to remember that he believes person to be "the ultimate ontological category."[167] Thus, a distinction between the Father, Son, and Spirit at the level of being would be a distinction in terms of person, rather than *ousia*. Now, obviously Zizioulas believes that the three are different persons. But is one of the three more of a person than the other two? Is he a person to a different degree? Such a distinction would seem to indicate an ontological subordinationism, because ontology is personal for Zizioulas.

Zizioulas posits just such a distinction. It should be recalled how important the concept of freedom is to Zizioulas's understanding of a person, and how the Father possesses such freedom. The Father is a free person, who freely begets the Son and breathes forth the Spirit, willing the

Blocher, "Immanence and Transcendence," 106. Hodgson states that the Eastern position is actual, "pre-Christian" subordinationism in Hodgson, *Doctrine of the Trinity*, 102. Erickson seems to agree in Erickson, *God in Three Persons*, 309.

163. Zizioulas, *Being as Communion*, 89.

164. Zizioulas, "Communion and Otherness," 353.

165. Kelly, *Early Christian Doctrines*, 234–37. Hanson, *Search*, 170; Clark, *Trinity*, 113. It was argued in Chapter 1 that *homoouisios* was meant to state more than that. For a full discussion, see pp. 11–17 above.

166. Pannenberg, "Christian Vision of God," 58; Erickson, *Making Sense of the Trinity*, 90; Kovach and Schemm, "Eternal Subordination," 462–64.

167. Zizioulas, *Being as Communion*, 18; Leithart, "'Framing' Sacramental Theology," 13.

eternal trinitarian communion.[168] It is only because he has no prior limits on his being, but freely constitutes it, that he is an authentic person.[169] But what of the Son and the Spirit? Since the Son and Spirit share the Father's essence, they are not free ontologically in the same sense, but "their freedom consists in absolute love and self-offering to the Father and to each other."[170] The Son and Spirit are not free as the Father is, but are bound by givenness. They are brought forth with their being already constituted by another person. This starkly distinguishes them at the level of person from the Father, who "being uncreated is not faced with a given being: *He, as a particular being* (the Father) brings about His own being (the Trinity). He is thus free in an ontological sense."[171] In terms of freedom, the Son and the Spirit more closely seem to resemble created humans, who have no choice in their being.[172]

The introduction of causation in terms of choice into the Godhead cannot but lead to subordinationism. Traditionally, the generation of the Son and the procession of the Spirit have been understood to be necessary, not freely chosen, acts of the Father. Athanasius, for example, says of the Son that "an offspring is not subject to will, but is proper to the essence."[173] Rowan Williams concludes that Athanasius means that the Father generates the Son "by the necessity of his own being, not by any intrusive compulsion."[174] While Gregory Nazianzen is a bit more obscure, he seems to argue that neither the sonship of the Son nor the fatherhood of the Father can be discussed in terms of will, but that both are essential aspects of their being.[175] Swinburne, a rather more recent author, has likewise argued that there can only be multiple divine beings if the second and third triune persons are necessarily, or essentially, brought forth from the first.[176] In such a situation, the Father does not choose to be Father, and therefore is not distinguished from the Son, who does not choose to be Son. Zizioulas, by emphasizing the choice of the Father, the ontological

168. Zizioulas, *Being as Communion*, 41.

169. Ibid., 42–44.

170. Harrison, "Zizioulas on Communion and Otherness," 279.

171. Zizioulas, "On Being a Person," 42, emphasis original.

172. Zizioulas, *Being as Communion*, 19, 42.

173. Athanasius, *C. Ar.* 1.8.29 (*NPNF2* 4:323).

174. Rowan Williams, *Arius: Heresy and Tradition*, 228–29.

175. Gregory Nazianzen, *Or.* 3.6–7 (*NPNF2* 7:302–303).

176. Swinburne, *Christian God*, 175–180.

primacy of personhood, and the necessity of freedom for full personhood, relegates the Son and Spirit to a subordinate ontological status.

Trinity and Tritheism

These three theological difficulties culminate in a final, decisive problem. Zizioulas's position has a discernible tritheistic slant,[177] and each of the difficulties mentioned above pushes Zizioulas further in that direction. The relationship between God and creation, the location of the attributes of God in the persons, and the ontological subordination of the Son and Spirit to the Father all weaken the understanding of trinitarian unity Zizioulas puts forth.

In Chapter 3, it was suggested that Erickson does not adequately distinguish how God is related to creation and how the Trinity is united as one God.[178] Zizioulas seems even more vulnerable to that charge. To make creation real, he connects it to the Father as its personal cause. He asserts that it is now drawn into the divine communion, and therefore united to God.[179] Yet these two elements are also the two elements of his trinitarian unity. The Father is the personal cause of the Son and Spirit, whom he brings forth to constitute his being as communion. It is this communion which is the being of God.[180] Does God's communion with the world then have a role in determining his being? If not, how can the Son and Spirit truly be considered one with the Father?

While Zizioulas relies upon the one divine *ousia* to distinguish God from the world, it does not appear that his understanding of this one *ousia* can do much to truly unite the three in God. Understood in the generic sense, it does nothing to make the three one God. As Cyril Richardson writes, "If the Father and Son share a common essence, they in no way differ from the gods of polytheism, who all shared a common divinity."[181] And it is difficult to understand Zizioulas's use of *ousia* as anything other than generic; he has stripped it of almost all ontological content.[182] The Cappadocians, who stressed the single divine *ousia* and recognized it as a

---

177. Fermer, "Limits of Trinitarian Theology," 175.

178. See pp. 145–47 above.

179. Zizioulas, *Being as Communion*, 39–40; Zizioulas, "Human Capacity," 425, 447.

180. Zizioulas, *Being as Communion*, 17.

181. Richardson, *Doctrine of the Trinity*, 64.

182. Wilks, "Trinitarian Ontology," 80.

metaphysical reality were themselves accused of tritheism.[183] How much more vulnerable to that charge is Zizioulas, who has a more truncated understanding of that *ousia*?[184]

The difficulty becomes obvious when one asks Zizioulas what is one in God. There are three persons, and person is the "ultimate ontological category." These three persons have, as aspects of their persons, all of the divine attributes. What is one is communion. Yet it is a communion in which the created order is included.[185] What makes the Trinity one God is something which does so without distinguishing him from creation.

The third theological difficulty, that of ontological subordination-ism, also pushes Zizioulas's position towards tritheism. Time and again, Zizioulas reminds the reader that it is the Father who is the one God.[186] Yet Thomas Weinandy notes that, by making the one God the Father, Zizioulas prevents the Son and the Spirit from being the one God.[187] At the level of ultimate ontology, that of person, they are distinguished from him by not being free from givenness. Instead, like the created order, they are brought forth according to an extant being. To unite them to the one God, the Father, with a communion that likewise includes creation does not appear to justify considering them one God with the Father.

CONCLUSION

John Zizioulas is an ecclesial theologian seeking to draw insights for life in this world from true knowledge about the being of God. He combines the Cappadocian assertion that the Father is the cause of the Son and Spirit within the Godhead with a personal ontology. He desires to avoid the impersonalism which he believes afflicts the classical Greek substantialist metaphysic and Christian theology which relies upon this metaphysic. He therefore rejects the *mia ousia* as the unifying element in God, replacing it with the person who is the one God, the person of the Father. The Father, as cause of the Son and Spirit, brings them forth in communion with himself, thereby constituting his own being within that communion.

183. Gregory Nazianzen, *Or.* 40.43 (*NPNF2* 7:376).

184. Wilks, "Trinitarian Ontology," 80–81.

185. Zizioulas, "Human Capacity," 447.

186. For example, Zizioulas, *Being as Communion*, 40, 41; Zizioulas, "On Being a Person," 40; Zizioulas, "Mystery of the Church," 299.

187. Weinandy, *Father's Spirit of Sonship*, 63.

Yet it appears that, rather than starting with the Cappadocian view of the Trinity and applying it to other issues, Zizioulas reads other interests back into the doctrine of the Trinity. The Cappadocians did not consider the Father the free cause of his own existence, nor did they believe him to be free to not exist. For them, the perfect, concrete, divine *ousia* was not a burden to be avoided, but a reality which served to unify the Father, Son, and Spirit they worshiped. Zizioulas so thoroughly deviates from the tradition he claims to embrace that it is difficult to overlook this fault, and difficult to grant Zizoiulas's position historical credence.

It also does not appear that Zizoiulas has thought through how his ontology fits together. How the Father can be personal logically prior to the communion that constitutes his person is a serious, but completely overlooked, question. Similarly, Zizoulas's assertion that the Father is entirely free from givenness, from any necessity whatsoever, is directly countered by his own, seemingly absolute, assertion that there is no being without communion. That much, apparently, is given, even to the Father.

His historical and philosophical difficulties breed theological problems. His personalist metaphysic requires that creation not only be created and sustained by God's power, but also be involved with God in a personal communion. While this explains the real existence of the world, it does so at expense to the divine unity. By seeking to elevate the personal in God to the practical elimination of the impersonal *ousia*, Zizioulas has radically weakened that element which traditionally serves to unify God. This leaves God as three persons, ontologically unequal, bound together only by a communion which includes the created order.

Such a position must be rejected. Zizioulas deviates significantly from the Cappadocian position which, while not normative, does not raise as many serious questions as Zizioulas's own position does. Zizioulas's attempts to affirm the personal at the expense of the impersonal result in an incoherent causal pattern and contradictory statements about the Father's freedom and obligation. The result is a position which gives little substantive reason for understanding the Father, Son, and Spirit to be one God.

5

Wolfhart Pannenberg and Trinitarian Unity

WOLFHART PANNENBERG'S THEOLOGICAL WORK gained attention early on for its commitment to theology as a public, rather than private, endeavor.[1] Pannenberg believes that for theology to be successful in the world it must be fully rational and submit itself to rational judgment and potential falsification. Theological statements are hypotheses to be tested, not dogmas to be accepted solely on authority.[2] For Pannenberg, theology is truly a rational science.[3] As Don Olive summarizes, "The world of Wolfhart Pannenberg is a rational world. It is a world presided over by a self-conscious, full-fledged commitment to reason. . . . To underestimate this element in Pannenberg is to miss the passion that moves the man and the theologian."[4]

Before the publication of his three volume *Systematic Theology*, however, it was noted that the doctrine of the Trinity seemed to play a small role in Pannenberg's thought.[5] That situation changed dramatically with the publication of his *Systematic Theology*, in which Pannenberg attempted to present all of systematic theology as the unfolding of the trinitarian doctrine of God.[6] Pannenberg notes that Christianity hinges upon

1. Grenz, "Appraisal," in *Theology of Wolfhart Pannenberg*, 19, 21; Gilkey, *Reaping the Whirlwind*, 227; Grenz, "Sympathy and Caution," 274; Grenz, "'Scientific' Theology/ 'Theological' Science," 160–61. Veli-Matti Kärkkäinen's chapter on Pannenberg is subtitled, "Trinity as 'Public Theology'" in *Trinity*, 123–50.

2. Pannenberg, "Theological Statement," 8–9; Pannenberg, *Systematic Theology*, 1:56–58; Pannenberg, *Basic Questions in Theology*, 2:28; Mattes, "Pannenberg's Achievement," 52.

3. Peterson, "Go from Here?" 141; Haugen, "Introduction," in *Beginning with the End*, 1–8. This text will hereafter be abbreviated *BE*.

4. Olive, *Wolfhart Pannenberg*, 13.

5. Feenstra and Plantinga, *Trinity, Incarnation, and Atonement*, 3.

6. Olson, "Pannenberg's Doctrine," 175–76; Grenz, *Reason for Hope*, 12, 45; Pannenberg,

this doctrine, and that therefore it cannot be relegated to a secondary, fideistic level of theology. If God can be understood adequately apart from the Trinity, then the doctrine is superfluous, and therefore irrelevant.[7] He writes that the doctrine of the Trinity "can be defended only on the condition that there is no other appropriate conception of the God of Christian faith than the trinity. In that case we cannot have first a doctrine on the one God and, afterwards, in terms of some additional supernatural mystery, the trinitarian doctrine."[8]

This attempt has garnered wide acclaim. Veli-Matti Kärkkäinen calls Pannenberg "the greatest living ecumenical theologian (Protestant)," and writes, "The most significant program of systematic theology of the latter part of the twentieth century comes from the hand of Wolfhart Pannenberg."[9] Richard Rice pens a similar judgment, writing, "Pannenberg's offering is arguably the most impressive *systematic* theology to emerge during the last quarter century."[10]

Pannenberg's systematic work continues his earlier efforts to present Christian doctrine as the truth, now with the doctrine of the Trinity at its center. He believes that the role of a systematic theology is to demonstrate, rather than presuppose, the truth of Christian doctrine. Thus one of his methodological sections is headed, "The Truth of Christian Doctrine as the Theme of Systematic Theology."[11] Philip Hefner believes that Pannenberg "has produced a research program in theology that surpasses any other current program" because he has exposed his position to criticism from both traditional theology and science.[12]

This chapter will offer a critique of Pannenberg's understanding of trinitarian unity. It will begin by presenting Pannenberg's understanding of that unity, an understanding which contains more elements than any of the positions which have been examined so far. Because Pannenberg's unusual methodology plays a key role in his theology, his understanding

Systematic Theology, 1:59–61, 1:335, 1:447–48.

7. Olson, "Pannenberg's Doctrine," 178–79; Pannenberg, *Systematic Theology*, 1:291–92.

8. Pannenberg, "Christian Vision of God," 53.

9. Kärkkäinen, "Spirit, Church and Christ," 339, 343.

10. Rice, "Pannenberg's Achievement," 55, emphasis original. Cf. Letham, *Holy Trinity*, 312.

11. Pannenberg, *Systematic Theology*, 1:48–61.

12. Hefner, "Role of Science," in *BE*, 111–12.

of the divine unity will be prefaced by a brief description of that methodology. Then, his multi-faceted understanding of the divine unity will be considered under two main headings, the monarchy of God and the Spirit of God. After Pannenberg's position has been presented, its strengths and weaknesses will be examined.

WOLFHART PANNENBERG'S UNDERSTANDING OF DIVINE UNITY

Several elements of Pannenberg's understanding of the divine unity will be recognizable from earlier authors. Pannenberg understands the three persons to be united by love, to share a single divine essence, to share the divine attributes, and to be united in a single monarchy.[13] Yet Pannenberg, even when using these traditional concepts, breaks new ground with his own trinitarian doctrine. This is in part based upon his methodology, which will now be examined.

A Futurist Methodology

Pannenberg's methodology is rooted in his desire, noted above, to demonstrate that Christianity is true. As Andrio König writes, "One could characterise Pannenberg as an apologetic theologian who considers it necessary and possible to show to an unbelieving world that it makes sense to believe in God, and that this does not clash with the basic structure of reality or with our modern view of life."[14] However, Pannenberg believes this task is impossible as long as theology attempts to base itself solely on a radical revelation in Jesus Christ which communicates a wholly other God to men; this leads inevitably to subjectivism.[15] He believes this is the problem with Barth's system, which begins by presupposing God.[16] While Pannenberg acknowledges that God cannot be known unless he chooses to reveal himself, he points to Rom 1:19–20 as an indication that God has chosen to reveal himself to all men.[17]

---

13. Pannenberg, *Systematic Theology*, 1:427, 360, 391, 325. Cf. Erickson, *God in Three Persons*, 221; Tertullian, *Adversus Praxean* 22 (*ANF* 3:618); Gregory of Nyssa, *Contra Eunomius* 2.4 (*NPNF2* 5:104); Dionysius of Rome, *Against the Sabellians* 1 (*ANF* 7:365).

14. König, *Here Am I! A Christian Reflection on God*, 148.

15. Pannenberg, *Idea of God*, 87.

16. Pannenberg, "Theological Questions to Scientists," in *BE*, 56.

17. Pannenberg, *Systematic Theology*, 1:189–90.

Where does this revelation lie? Pannenberg devotes a significant portion of his *Systematic Theology* to develop the idea that the universal religious consciousness of mankind is credible evidence for the existence of God.[18] He concludes that, "Because the reality of God is the presupposition of human worship of God, the knowledge of God is the starting point of religion."[19] He likewise notes that the Bible does not present revelation coming to those who have no prior knowledge of God; the God of whom they already are aware is the God who reveals himself.[20] Thus, mankind can reasonably believe in God not by presupposing him, but by recognizing that the religious nature of man suggests the existence of God.

This, however, is a rather limited source for knowledge about God. To complement it, Pannenberg draws on both philosophy and the Bible to argue that history is the locus of divine revelation and therefore the proper basis for theology.[21] His philosophical argument is based upon the unity and universality of all truth, a unity which he believes requires God as its source. He writes, "But in spite of every other disagreement about the idea of God, the proposition has so far remained unshaken, that at least God is not thought of as God at all if he is not thought of as the unity which unites all that is."[22] Since the history of religion is a history which has settled on monotheism, the only meaningful use of "God" is to refer to "the power that determines everything that exists."[23] The truth of such a being cannot be separated from the truth of the world.[24] Pannenberg writes:

> On the assumption, then, that the word "God" is to be understood as referring to an all-determining reality, substantiation of talk about God requires that everything which exists should be shown to be a trace of the divine reality. This requirement applies,

18. Ibid., 1:119–87; Kaiser, *Doctrine of God*, 119. George Tavard notes the unprecedented use of other religions to positively develop a Christian dogmatic. See Tavard, review of *Systematic Theology*, vol. 1, 389.

19. Pannenberg, *Systematic Theology*, 1:189.

20. Ibid., 1:203–4.

21. Grenz and Olson, *20th Century Theology*, 192; Khiok-Khng, "Christ," 310; Venema, "History, Human Freedom," 54–58; Childs, "Significance of Wolfhart Pannenberg," 66.

22. Pannenberg, *Idea of God*, 130. Cf. Pannenberg, *Basic Questions in Theology*, 2:1; Pannenberg, *Metaphysics*, 17; Pannenberg, *Systematic Theology*, 1:53; Pannenberg, "Theta Phi," 37–38.

23. Pannenberg, *Basic Questions in Theology*, 1:1.

24. Pannenberg, *Systematic Theology*, 1:49–51; Rice, "Pannenberg's Acheivement," 59.

however, not to objects in abstract isolation, but to their unbroken continuity: "all," as used in the concept of an all-determining reality, refers not to each individual thing on its own but to each in its continuity with all others. Theology as the science of God would then mean the study of the totality of the real from the point of view of the reality which ultimately determines it both as a whole and in its parts.[25]

Since the reality of the world is historical, the truth about God must likewise be seen in history, for God provides the truth of history.[26]

In his *Systematic Theology*, Pannenberg supplements his philosophical argument with a survey of the Bible's understanding of how God reveals himself.[27] Pannenberg attempts to demonstrate that the Bible understands God to reveal himself in his historical actions.[28] For example, concerning God's name in Exod 3:14, Pannenberg writes, "He will show himself in his historical acts and will not come under any human influence."[29] When the word of the Lord came to the prophets, this word communicated the content of God's future actions towards his people and nations. In this revelation, it is the active content, not the verbal form, that is stressed. Pannenberg notes, "In seeking to understand reception of the word, we should not stress too much the linguistic form. The Hebrew *dabar* denotes both word and content. The content is at issue in reception."[30] After examining several forms of biblical revelation, including prophetic visions, patriarchal sightings of God, and the reception of the divine name, Pannenberg concludes that "the reduction of the revelation of God to divine speaking hardly does justice to the complex variety of the biblical concept of revelation, particularly to the fact that among OT ideas of revelation the one that is closest to the concept of definitive self-revelation is the indirect self-demonstration of God by historical acts, as in the pro-

25. Pannenberg, *Theology and Science*, 303.

26. Ibid., 2:62–63.

27. Pannenberg acknowledges that the earlier *Offenbarung als Geschichte* left some gaps concerning the relation of the word of God to history. See Pannenberg, *Systematic Theology*, 1:228–29; Pannenberg, ed., *Offenbarung als Geschichte*.

28. Pannenberg, *Systematic Theology*, 1:190–244.

29. Ibid., 1:205.

30. Ibid., 1:202.

phetic word of demonstration."[31] God is therefore revealed to all men, though indirectly, through history.[32]

Both the philosophical and the biblical arguments for history being the locus of God's revelation lead Pannenberg to a final conclusion, that of the ontological priority of the eschatological future. Philosophically, Pannenberg's position is based upon God being the unifying force behind all history who gives history meaning. But because events only acquire meaning in historical context, until history is complete, the final meaning of things, and therefore the final revelation of God, will not have occurred.[33] A meaningful historical process requires an end from which the present can acquire meaning.[34] Properly understanding history requires that one have "an understanding of being as the anticipation of the truth concerning its essence, a truth that is revealed only at the end of its course of development."[35] History, like all reality, can only be fully understood as a whole, and only will be a whole at its end.

Pannenberg believes his biblical examination of revelation yields the same conclusion. Prophetic literature, culminating in apocalyptic writings, both canonical and non-canonical, suggests that the locus of God's total revelation is the end of history, the eschaton.[36] The fact that God is not yet fully revealed in part explains why religious questions remain open and debatable.[37] He writes, "According to the witness of the Bible the deity of God will be definitively and unquestionably manifested only at the end of all time and history."[38] The disclosure of God's name is an example, for "the revelation of the name is characterized as only a provisional self-disclosure of God, for the name will take on its content only

---

31. Ibid., 1:227.

32. Ibid., 1:237, 244.

33. Rice, "Pannenberg's Achievement," 56; Pannenberg, *Systematic Theology*, 54–55; Polk, "All-Determining God," in *Theology of Wolfhart Pannenberg*, 153.

34. Adams, "Eschatology," 290.

35. Pannenberg, *Metaphysics*, 109.

36. Pannenberg, *Systematic Theology*, 1:208–13; Thompson, *Modern Trinitarian Perspectives*, 34; Schwöbel, "Rational Theology," 503; König, *Here Am I!*, 150.

37. Pannenberg, *Systematic Theology*, 1:213–14; Shults, "Constitutive Relationality," 309; Grenz and Olson, *20th Century Theology*, 189.

38. Pannenberg, *Systematic Theology*, 1:54.

from God's future action in history."[39] A God who declares himself to be what he *will* be is a future-oriented God.

Such an understanding of revelation might leave one with no hope of knowing God. However, Pannenberg believes that history and the eschaton have met, and that therefore God has been revealed, in the resurrection of Jesus Christ. Pannenberg understands Jesus' resurrection to be an anticipatory appearing of the eschaton in history, and therefore the eschatological revelation of God.[40] He writes, "Only at the end of all events can God be revealed in his divinity, that is, as the one who works all things, who has power over everything. . . . Only because the end of the world is already present in Jesus' resurrection is God himself revealed in him."[41] Thus Jesus is the starting point of Pannenberg's entire system. He believes that "all parts of Christian teaching are to be seen and developed as an explication of the self-revelation of God in Jesus Christ."[42]

The eschatological relevance of Jesus does not change Pannenberg's focus on public history as the source for theology. He believes that a method which presumes Jesus' divinity immediately fails the task of systematic theology, which is demonstrating, not presuming, Christian doctrine.[43] He therefore investigates Christ "from below." By this Pannenberg means that, rather than presupposing Christ's deity, he seeks to demonstrate it from the historical facts of Jesus' life, especially the resurrection.[44] This exposition leads to the doctrine of the Trinity, which is the basis of all theology. Thus Jesus' message, and his divine vindication in the resurrection, serve as the basis for Pannenberg's theological system.[45] The remainder of this section will examine how Pannenberg develops his understanding of trinitarian unity from the historical Christ.

39. Ibid., 1:207.

40. Pannenberg, *Jesus—God and Man*, 67–69; Grenz, "Appraisal," 31.

41. Pannenberg, *Jesus—God and Man*, 69.

42. Pannenberg, *Systematic Theology*, 1:257.

43. Pannenberg, *Jesus—God and Man*, 34–35; Gunton, *Yesterday & Today*, 19–20.

44. Pannenberg, *Jesus—God and Man*, 35–36; Pannenberg, *Systematic Theology*, 2:282–89; Macleod, "Christology of Wolfhart Pannenberg," 26–27.

45. Pannenberg, *Systematic Theology*, 2:285; 2:363; Pannenberg, "Response," in *Theology of Wolfhart Pannenberg*, 326; Jenson, "Jesus in the Trinity," in *Theology of Wolfhart Pannenberg*, 188–206.

The One Kingdom

Pannenberg believes that any doctrine of the Trinity which begins with the presumption of a single divine being and then moves to explain the three persons is bound to fail. It will either derive two persons of the Trinity from an ontologically prior one, which results in ontological subordinationism, or derive all three members from a prior divine subject, which results in modalism.[46] Instead, a successful trinitarian doctrine must begin with the man Jesus and the Father and Holy Spirit to which he claimed relation.[47]

When such a method is used, the Kingdom of God, the heart of Jesus' message, becomes the first basis for Trinitarian unity. That the Kingdom can serve as a basis for the divine unity is based upon an axiom of Pannenberg's, which he seems to draw from Karl Barth, "The deity of God is his rule."[48] Thus, by participating in the one rule of the Father, Jesus and the Holy Spirit also participate in the deity of the Father. Pannenberg writes:

> Son and Spirit share in the divine essence of the Father not just by being begotten and by proceeding from the Father, but by contributing to the kingdom of the Father that is entrusted to the Son and returned to the Father by himself through the Holy Spirit. It is in this concrete dynamic of perichoresis that the three persons share the same kingdom and the same essence which nevertheless remain to be primarily the kingdom and divine nature of the Father. Thus, the one divine being becomes manifest in the three persons but in different ways, the kingdom and the divine essence being always primarily the Father's but effective through the Son and the Spirit.[49]

The one divine Kingdom, the monarchy of God, forms the first leg of Pannenberg's understanding of the divine unity. As Mattes writes, "God's establishing the monarchy of the divine self in the cosmos as the insepa-

---

46. Pannenberg, *Systematic Theology*, 1:298.

47. Pannenberg, "Christian Vision," 57.

48. Pannenberg, *Theology and the Kingdom*, 121. Cf. Barth, *Church Dogmatics*, vol. 1/1:349: "We may unhesitatingly equate the lordship of God ... with what the vocabulary of the church calls the essence of God, the *deitas* or *divinitas*, the divine οὐσία, *essentia*, *natura*, or *substantia*."

49. Pannenberg, "Christian Vision," 57.

rable, cooperative venture of the three persons is the key to understanding how the three persons are one God."[50]

As the quotation above suggests, Pannenberg sees this Trinitarian unity as an improvement over the unilateral relations of origin seen in some traditional Trinitarian systems.[51] In place of relations of origin, Pannenberg sees the members of the Trinity engaging in historical actions of mutual self-distinction to bring about the one divine monarchy, the one divine essence, in which all participate.[52] While methodologically this self-distinction is first seen in the Son, it begins with the actions of the Father, who risks his very deity by handing it over to the Son (John 3:35, 1 Cor 15:24–28). Contrary to the Orthodox view, in which the Father has deity in himself, Pannenberg asserts that the Father is dependent on the Son and Spirit for his deity.[53] Pannenberg writes:

> In the handing over of lordship from the Father to the Son, and its handing back from the Son to the Father, we see a mutuality in their relationship that we do not see in the begetting. . . . The self-distinction of the Father from the Son is not just that he begets the Son but that he hands over all things to him, so that his kingdom and his own deity are now dependent upon the Son. The rule or kingdom of God is not so external to his deity that he might be God without his kingdom.[54]

While the Kingdom is properly the Father's, by allowing that Kingdom to depend upon the work of the Son and Spirit he is united with them in that Kingdom, and therefore his deity.[55]

The Son, in turn, distinguishes himself from the Father by not claiming to be God. Instead he subjects himself to the Father and proclaims the message of the Father's Kingdom. Exemplifying the proper role of a creature, the Son furthers the Father's Kingdom by directing all attention toward it, rather than himself (John 8:18, 14:24, 14:28, 17:4). Pannenberg

---

50. Mattes, "Pannenberg's Achievement," 54.

51. Pannenberg, "Christian Vision," 57; Pannenberg, *Systematic Theology*, 1:329. For example Anselm, *On the Procession of the Holy Spirit*, 1.

52. For other treatments of this aspect of Pannenberg's thought, see Peters, *GOD as Trinity*, 136–39; Grenz, *Reason for Hope*, 47–53, 71.

53. John Zizioulas would be a current proponent of the Orthodox view. See Zizioulas, *Being As Communion*, 40–43.

54. Pannenberg, *Systematic Theology*, 1:313; cf. 1:320.

55. Ibid., 1:322. Olson, "Pannenberg's Doctrine," 193.

writes, "Precisely by distinguishing himself from the Father, by subject-ing himself to his will as his creature, by thus giving place to the Father's claim to deity as he asked others to do in his proclamation of the divine lordship, he showed himself to be the Son of God and one with the Father who sent him (John 10:30)."[56] This, in fact, is the basis for assertions that the Son is consubstantial with the Father.[57]

Pannenberg notes that the Spirit also distinguishes himself from the Father and Son while working to bring in the one divine Kingdom. He glorifies the Son and the Father, while distinguishing himself from them and not speaking of himself (John 14:6, 16:14, 17:4). He works to bring men to accept the Kingdom, thereby expanding God's rule (John 16:8). Perhaps most importantly, he rescues the Kingdom from near-defeat by resurrecting Christ (Rom 8:11).[58]

Thus, Pannenberg puts forth a system where the divine monarchy is not presupposed, but instead is understood as the result of the interac-tion of the three divine persons. While the Father still has a monarchy, it is a monarchy dependent upon the economic work of the Son and the Spirit.[59] Thus the monarchy of God unifies the three divine persons; it is the "content" of their communion.[60]

Pannenberg believes that the one divine Kingdom is essential to God and to the trinitarian unity. "Thus it is necessary to say that, in a restricted but important sense, God does not yet exist. Since his rule and his being are inseparable, God's being is still in the process of coming to be."[61] Pannenberg's eschatological emphasis is ontological, not just epis-temological.[62] Because God's Kingdom has not yet fully come, and his

---

56. Pannenberg, *Systematic Theology*, 1:310. At times, Pannenberg bases the Son's unity with the Father on his self-distinction from the Father without mentioning the Kingdom, but this quotation shows the assumed warrant for grounding unity in self-distinction. See, for example Pannenberg, *Systematic Theology*, 2:29; Pannenberg, "Christian Vision," 59; Pannenberg, "Theta Phi," 41.

57. Pannenberg, *Basic Questions in Theology*, 2:248–49.

58. Pannenberg, *Systematic Theology*, 1:315, 1:320; Gutenson, "One God," 11.

59. Pannenberg, *Systematic Theology*, 1:324; D. Badcock, *Light of Truth*, 197.

60. Pannenberg, *Systematic Theology*, 1:325.

61. Pannenberg, *Theology and the Kingdom*, 56.

62. Grenz and Olson, *20th Century Theology*, 198. Some question whether Pannenberg means this. See Grenz, "Appraisal," 32; Haugen, "Introduction," 24; Venema, "History, Human Freedom," 75. Gutenson agrees that ontology is at stake in Gutenson, "One God," 15.

Kingdom is his deity, God is, in a sense, not yet. As the Kingdom is the "content" of the unity of Father, Son, and Spirit, the true union of the trinitarian God will not be complete until the eschaton.[63]

Pannenberg does not mean, however, that God is in no way God, or in no way one, at the moment. The ontological priority of the future means that future decisions have present effects. Therefore, the future decision concerning God's deity and unity has retroactive force, so that God is one currently because of what happens in the future. Pannenberg does not mean that God is in process, but that "the eschatological consummation is only the locus of the decision that the trinitarian God is always the true God from eternity to eternity."[64] Normally, past events are understood to determine the present and future, but as W. J. Hill notes, Pannenberg "is doing no less than reversing the direction of time."[65] Rather than the historical acts of the Trinity manifesting a unity based in eternity past, the historical acts of the Trinity bring about a future eternal unity, which decides the unity for the present. Thus, while it is not evident that the three trinitarian persons are one because the Kingdom, in which they find their basic unity, is not yet manifest, they are one in virtue of their future Kingdom, the future reality of which retrospectively determines their present unity.[66]

The Divine Spirit

Discussing the unity of God in terms of historical acts can seem somewhat precarious. Pannenberg himself acknowledges that a unity solely in terms of operations is an insufficient understanding of the unity of the Christian God.[67] But because Pannenberg connects God's historical actions in bringing about the Kingdom with the divine essence, he is able to move from actions to essence. So, while the essential unity of Father, Son, and Spirit "may be found only in their concrete life relations," further consideration

63. Pannenberg, *Systematic Theology*, 1:327, 1:340; Schwöbel, "Rational Theology," 524; Boutwell, "Eschatology," 26.

64. Pannenberg, *Systematic Theology*, 1:331; cf. Pannenberg, *Theology and the Kingdom*, 62; Pannenberg, "Problems of Doctrine," 255.

65. Hill, *Three-Personed God*, 159.

66. This position will be assumed while Pannenberg's understanding of trinitarian unity is developed. Even if it is incorrect, and Pannenberg really means God is not yet one, his central thought regarding the unity of God is not altered.

67. Pannenberg, *Systematic Theology*, 1:283; Gutenson, "One God," 8.

"of the unity is a task for a doctrine of God's nature and attributes."[68] Only a unity in terms of essence can be genuine monotheism.[69]

God as Spirit

Pannenberg's exposition of the divine nature is multiplex. Pannenberg begins his discussion of the divine nature by pointing out the incomprehensibility of God. He writes, "Any intelligent attempt to talk about God—talk that is critically aware of its conditions and limitations—must begin and end with a confession of the inconceivable majesty of God which transcends all our concepts."[70] Drawing from Gregory of Nyssa, Pannenberg states that God is incomprehensible because he is infinite.[71] Yet the very fact that men are able to presuppose the infinity of God provides a basis for discussing the essence of God. God's essence is infinite spirit.[72]

Pannenberg believes that the Bible uses spirit to refer to God's essence. He writes, "'God is Spirit' (John 4:24) is one of the few biblical sayings that explicitly characterize the divine essence as such."[73] Therefore, he believes that, "The life-giving Spirit is the deity of God, his essence."[74] In the Old Testament, the spirit of God is seen primarily as a life-giving force (Gen 2:7), with other functions derived from that basic principle.[75] The spirit is the divine breath, the mighty wind, and a moving source of life.[76] While Pannenberg does not give as detailed an account of New Testament usage, he believes it assumes and adopts the Old Testament understanding. He writes, "Suffice it to say that in the NT, too, the idea of the Spirit as the life force that proceeds from God embraces his functions relative to knowledge, including the knowledge of faith."[77] God's essence is spirit.

68. Pannenberg, *Systematic Theology*, 1:335.

69. Pannenberg, "Problems of Doctrine," 256.

70. Pannenberg, *Systematic Theology*, 1:337.

71. Ibid., 1:342, 347. Pannenberg cites Gregory of Nyssa, *C. Eun.* 3.1, but the argument from infinity to incomprehensibility appears in 3.5 (*NPNF2* 5:146–47).

72. Pannenberg, *Systematic Theology*, 1:359; Grenz, *Reason for Hope*, 56; Pannenberg, "Problems of Doctrine," 256. Pannenberg's translator generally capitalizes all uses of spirit. For clarity, this work will only capitalize spirit when it refers to the divine person, the Holy Spirit.

73. Pannenberg, *Systematic Theology*, 1:395.

74. Ibid., 1:383.

75. Wolfhart Pannenberg, "Doctrine of the Spirit," in *BE*, 65–66.

76. Wolfhart Pannenberg, "God as Spirit," 786.

77. Pannenberg, *Systematic Theology*, 1:373.

Pannenberg develops the Old Testament understanding of spirit in part to refute the equation of God as spirit with God as mind, an equation that entered Christian theology as early as Origen.[78] Not only is this equation not biblical, but it also is Platonic and anthropomorphic.[79] It also makes a doctrine of the Trinity which does justice to the three persons difficult, for one mind would seem to require one person.[80]

It is as the one divine spirit that God bears his attributes.[81] Thus essence appears to serve for Pannenberg this traditional function noted in Chapter 1.[82] Pannenberg recognizes two mentally distinct sets of attributes in God. The first he categorizes as attributes of infinity: holiness, eternity, omnipotence, and omnipresence. While Pannenberg recognizes that infinity is not a biblical word, he believes that these four attributes ascribe to God freedom from definition by anything else, which is infinity.[83] Pannenberg develops the second set of attributes around the theme of love, which will be addressed below.

The essence of God also serves as an impersonal element in God which Pannenberg believes the doctrine of the Trinity needs. Pannenberg explains, "The great Buddhist philosopher Nishitani Keiji from Kyoto charged Christian theology with overemphasizing the personal aspect of the divine reality while underestimating its impersonal aspect.... Now the trinitarian concept of God does in fact include an impersonal element. This is the divine essence as such. This one divine essence that makes for the unity of God is not personal by itself, but personal only as it becomes manifested in each of the three persons."[84] This does not mean that the persons are derived from the essence; Pannenberg vigorously rejects any such derivation. There is nothing behind or logically prior to the persons.[85] What it means is that each divine person is a specific form of the existence

78. Origen, *De principiis* 1.1.4–9 (*ANF* 4:243–45).

79. Pannenberg, *Systematic Theology*, 1:374; Pannenberg, "Theological Appropriation," in *BE*, 428.

80. Pannenberg, "Theological Appropriation," 429.

81. Pannenberg, "Problems of Doctrine," 256; Grenz, *Reason for Hope*, 54; Mattes, "Pannenberg's Achievement," 54.

82. See pp. 28–30 above. This is true even though Pannenberg believes essence is a relational concept. See, for example, Pannenberg, *Systematic Theology*, 2:85.

83. Pannenberg, *Systematic Theology*, 1:397–422.

84. Pannenberg, "Christian Vision," 60.

85. Pannenberg, *Systematic Theology*, 1:298, 335; Pannenberg, "Theta Phi," 38.

of the one divine essence, which they are. Rice notes that in Pannenberg's doctrine, "We never get behind the Trinity to something more basic or original. God's fundamental reality is Father, Son, and Spirit. It is not a single divine essence."[86]

Spirit as Field

Pannenberg attempts to elucidate his understanding of the divine nature as spirit by associating it with the scientific concept of a field. Responding to his own rhetorical question about what is one in God, Pannenberg writes, "We should conceive of the 'spiritual' nature of the one God in Father, Son, and Spirit in terms of a field of power rather than in terms of a single divine subject or person."[87] He believes that Psalm 139:7 suggests, "The Spirit is the force field of God's mighty presence."[88] God as infinite spirit is God as dynamic field.[89]

Pannenberg uses the idea of field to express several things about God as spirit. First, he seeks to suggest how an incorporeal, non-spatial entity can exercise genuine power in the universe. He finds fields to be an ideal vehicle for that thought. Rather than attaching force to material bodies, Pannenberg believes field theory sees fields of force as carriers of force independent of matter, and perhaps able to constitute matter.[90] Pannenberg writes, "No longer seen as a property of bodies, energy is now regarded as a field whose interactions result in singular materializations that are finally understood as the bodies themselves."[91] Hefner states that, by making God "the largest field of all," Pannenberg provides a model for how God can be understood to be the cause of all reality.[92]

Pannenberg also likes the connection between fields and space-time. He notes that fields, while independent of matter, are determined by their relations to space-time.[93] Pannenberg, understanding the divine field

---

86. Rice, "Pannenberg's Achievement," 59. The key word is "fundamental."

87. Pannenberg, "Response to Friends," 327.

88. Pannenberg, *Systematic Theology*, 1:382.

89. Ibid., 2:83; Grenz, *Reason for Hope*, 56.

90. Pannenberg, *Systematic Theology*, 1:382, 2:79–82; Pannenberg, "Doctrine of the Spirit," 72. Pannenberg refers frequently to the work of Max Jammer in this respect, particularly his *Concepts of Force*.

91. Wolfhart Pannenberg, "Spirit and Energy," in *BE*, 83.

92. Hefner, "Role of Science," 102–3.

93. Pannenberg, *Systematic Theology*, 1:382; Pannenberg, "God as Spirit," 788.

to be the infinite field presupposed by every finite field, sees in the field model an indication of God's omnipresence, eternity, as well as his role as the ground of all created reality. God as spirit is not just a field, present within space and time, but the infinite field which transcends space and time while encompassing them.[94]

Some of Pannenberg's statements seem to equate the divine spirit as field with a particular physical field.[95] Hefner, quoted above, sees Pannenberg equating God with a particular field, and writes of the "world as a manifestation of spirit."[96] Both comments have pantheistic overtones. Pannenberg has been repeatedly criticized by John Polkinghorne for misunderstanding or distorting the scientific concept of field when applying it to God.[97] Perhaps in light of such comments, Pannenberg has either clarified or amended his position to make clear its analogical nature. He recognizes that his use of field does not exactly correspond to its use in physics, but notes, "Such a theological use of the field concept does not and need not rely on any specific field theory the physicists have produced."[98]

How does God as field enhance Pannenberg's understanding of divine unity? The divine spirit, as the causal field underlying all reality, serves as the mechanism by which God interacts with the world. Pannenberg conceives of the three persons in God as "singularities" or "concretions" within it who, because of the field's immaterial nature, can conceivably possess all of it simultaneously.[99] Each person is the entire field, of which there is only one. Thus the three persons are one nature, one spirit, one field.[100]

94. Pannenberg, "God as Spirit," 789–91; Pannenberg, "Theological Appropriation," 428–30.

95. For example, Pannenberg, Systematic Theology, 2:83;

96. Hefner, "Role of Science," 146.

97. Polkinghorne, "Pannenberg's Engagement," 153–55; Polkinghorne, "Fields and Theology," 796–97; Polkinghorne, Reason and Reality, 93; Polkinghorne, Belief in God, 82.

98. Pannenberg, "God as Spirit," 790; Pannenberg, "Theological Appropriation," 427–30.

99. Pannenberg, "God as Spirit," 792; Pannenberg, Systematic Theology, 1:430.

100. Buckley, review of Systematic Theology, 366.

Spirit as Person

Spirit is used in the Bible to refer both to the divine essence and to one member of the Trinity. Pannenberg uses both referents of spirit in establishing the divine unity. Stanley Grenz describes Pannenberg's position:

> Pannenberg mines from the field theory insight into the two uses of *Spirit* in the biblical materials—*Spirit* as the divine essence as such and as the third person of the Trinity—both of which are theologically important. If the Spirit were solely the impersonal divine field, he notes, the divine essence, which is Spirit, would be impersonal. In the biblical materials, however, the Spirit is not only the common life of the Father and the Son but also appears as a personal center of activity. . . . Although both the Father and the Son are differentiated from the essence of the Godhead that is Spirit, they are bound together through the Spirit, the third person of the Trinity.[101]

Thus spirit, understood as the shared divine essence uniting the Father and the Son, is also the essence of the Holy Spirit, the person who unites the Father and the Son.

Pannenberg sees the Holy Spirit, as person, uniting the Father and Son in the life of Jesus. Pannenberg writes, "The Son's fellowship with the Father is always mediated by the Spirit."[102] The Spirit works in the incarnation and resurrection, bringing about both (Luke 1:35; Rom 1:4). The Son receives the Spirit in preparation for his Kingdom work. Because the Son is Son by glorifying the Father, and it is the Spirit's work to glorify the Father (John 16:14), the Son is Son by the working of the Spirit in him.[103] The Spirit is understood to mediate God's nearness to his people, and his mediation of the Father-Son communion is no exception.[104] While Pannenberg rejects Augustine's concept of double procession, he agrees that the Holy Spirit is properly understood as the bond of love between the Father and the Son.[105]

Thus spirit unites Father and Son both as essential field and as the person of the Holy Spirit. Pannenberg writes:

101. Grenz, *Reason for Hope*, 61. See also Robertson, "Wolfhart Pannenberg," 35.

102. Pannenberg, *Systematic Theology*, 2:84.

103. Ibid., 1:316–17.

104. Pannenberg, "Theta Phi," 40.

105. Ibid., 1:317. Tavard, review of *Systematic Theology*, 391. Cf. Augustine, *De Trinitate*, 15.17–19 (*NPNF*1 3:215–20).

The essence of the Godhead is indeed Spirit. It is Spirit as a dynamic field, and as its manifestation in the coming forth of the Son shows itself to be the work of the Father, the dynamic of the Spirit radiates from the Father, but in such a way that the Son receives it as gift, and it fills him and radiates back from him to the Father.

The Spirit comes forth as a separate hypostasis as he comes over against the Son and the Father as the divine essence, common to both, which actually unites them and also attests and maintains their unity in face of their distinction.[106]

The Father and Son share this one dynamic field of power, and are therefore united by it. But because this dynamic field is distinguished by distinct personal actions, actions in relation to the Son and Father, which therefore cannot be reduced to Son or Father, the field is the Holy Spirit, a distinct person. As both person and essence, spirit is the source of divine unity.[107]

Spirit as Love

Pannenberg's picture of the divine essence is not yet complete, however. He believes the Bible makes another statement about what the divine essence is: "God is love" (1 John 4:8, 16).[108] He also links spirit and love as the essence of God by a consideration of the divine attributes. God as spirit refers to his infinite nature, to his attributes of holiness, omnipotence, eternity, and omnipresence. Yet for Pannenberg, the infinite cannot transcend the finite by opposing it. That would define the infinite, making it not infinite. Instead, the infinite must transcend the finite by encompassing and including it.[109] God has created and continuously affirms by his omnipotence a finite world of creatures which he transcends by inclusion. This idea, that God omnipotently wills and infinitely includes finite reality, can only be thought of as love.[110] Spirit and love are thus the same. Love and spirit can both be identified as the divine essence, and the person of the Holy Spirit. He writes, "On the one side the Spirit and love

106. Pannenberg, *Systematic Theology*, 1:429.

107. Pannenberg, "Christian Vision," 56.

108. Pannenberg, *Systematic Theology*, 1:297, 396; Pannenberg, "Problems of Doctrine," 256.

109. Pannenberg, *Systematic Theology*, 1:397–400; 2:84–85; Pannenberg, *Meta-physics*, 36.

110. Pannenberg, *Systematic Theology*, 1:422; Grenz, *Reason for Hope*, 56; Jenson, "Jesus in the Trinity," 205. Cf. Pannenberg, *Theology and the Kingdom*, 65–67.

constitute the common essence of deity, on the other they come forth as a separate hypostasis in the Holy Spirit."[111]

Pannenberg's point is not simply to propose love as an alternative to spirit, but to draw out the relational nature of God's essential unity implied by "love" but concealed by "spirit." Essence is a relational concept; the divine unity is a relationally constituted unity.[112] It is the love of the persons of the Trinity that constitutes each one in an I-Thou relationship. Their divine unity is based upon "the power of the love which manifests itself in the most original and complete form in mutual self-giving."[113] Love is "the eternal power and deity which lives in the Father, Son, and Spirit through their relations and which constitutes the unity of the one God in the communion of these three persons."[114]

God's one essence is therefore not something that lies behind any of the three persons, but is itself the shared love of their mutual self-giving. Thus it appears that Pannenberg is proposing a form of the social model of the Trinity.[115] As Jenson states, "According to Pannenberg, it is precisely the fellowship of the divine *persons*, using that concept in the full modern sense, and indeed in an intensified version thereof, which *is* the oneness of God, as that oneness has been named with the traditional concept of 'essence.'"[116] Ted Peters agrees that, "To say 'God is love' is to indicate the comprehensive expression of trinitarian fellowship as Father, Son, and Spirit."[117] The love of Father, Son, and Spirit for one another grounds both their unity in the one divine essence and their divine attributes.[118] Jenson concludes that Pannenberg believes "the inner-triune fellowship *is* the one divine essence, of which the attributes which state the one God's relation to his creation are but the concrete stipulations."[119]

---

111. Pannenberg, *Systematic Theology*, 1:429.

112. Ibid., 2:85; Gutenson, "One God," 12–13.

113. Pannenberg, *Systematic Theology*, 1:427.

114. Ibid., 1:428.

115. Olson, "Pannenberg's Doctrine," 195–96. For a discussion of the origin of the contemporary social model, see pp. 75–76 above.

116. Jenson, "Jesus in the Trinity," 194, emphasis original.

117. Peters, *GOD as Trinity*, 141.

118. Pannenberg, "Problems of Doctrine," 256.

119. Jenson, "Jesus in the Trinity," 205, emphasis original.

This also serves to tie the divine essence as love back to Pannenberg's assertion that the divine essence is God's coming Kingdom. The Kingdom is an opportunity for creation to participate in the work of God, a participation made possible by the reconciling love God has towards creation.[120] It is also, like the trinitarian love, the mutual working of the three divine persons. As such, God as love serves as the decisive statement of the divine unity. Pannenberg concludes, "Finally, the statement that God is love will prove to be the concrete form of the divine essence that is initially described as Spirit and in terms of the concept of the Infinite."[121]

A CRITIQUE OF PANNENBERG'S UNDERSTANDING OF UNITY

Pannenberg's understanding of the divine unity is the most nuanced that this text will examine. Like Karl Rahner, Pannenberg believes the immanent Trinity can only be investigated by means of the economic Trinity, which it in fact is.[122] Also like Rahner, he believes a doctrine of trinitarian unity must be grounded in the one essence of God.[123] Like John Zizioulas and Millard Erickson, Pannenberg believes that the unity of God must be understood as a relational unity conceived of in terms of love.[124] However, while Erickson and Zizioulas minimize the unity of essence in God, Pannenberg, by associating this essence with the concept of a field, suggests that the divine essence is as much a concrete reality as are the three persons. His position hearkens back to the traditionally dominant position shown in Chapter 1, which views the essence of God as a genuine *res* and the fundamental location of the divine unity.[125]

There is much to be commended in Pannenberg's work. His "from below" methodology emphasizes that the doctrine of God cannot be approached as if God were not the Father, Son, and Holy Spirit. Pannenberg's position does full justice to the biblical picture of the divine persons as

120. Pannenberg, *Systematic Theology*, 1:445.

121. Ibid., 1:369.

122. Rahner, *Trinity*, 22; Pannenberg actually believes Rahner failed to fully follow through on his thesis. See Pannenberg, "Problems of Doctrine," 251; Pannenberg, "Christian Vision," 54; Jenson, "Jesus in the Trinity," 197; Pannenberg, *Systematic Theology*, 1:328–31.

123. Rahner, *Trinity*, 70.

124. Erickson, *God in Three Persons*, 221; Zizioulas, *Being As Communion*, 46.

125. See pp. 6–25 above.

distinct centers of action. His integration of biblical and philosophical concepts in developing the doctrine of divine unity commend his work as genuine systematic theology. His conception of the single divine spirit as field serves as an adequate model for how one can conceive of the three divine persons as the single divine creator.[126] While Pannenberg deviates significantly from a traditional understanding of the Trinity, his ubiquitous and thorough discussions of historical theology make clear that he is doing so consciously, and that his efforts are to capture the true content of those traditions, despite his radical conceptual changes.[127]

Despite these positive elements, Pannenberg's positions have drawn considerable criticism, some of which relate to his understanding of the divine unity. This section will present criticisms concerning the logical, theological, and Christological difficulties Pannenberg's understanding of divine unity raises. No historical critique will be offered, not because Pannenberg is rehearsing tradition, but because he himself clearly and unabashedly notes where he deviates from and revises prior thinkers, and because he recognizes that his position is not beholden to any particular tradition.[128]

Logical Difficulties

Pannenberg believes that systematic theology seeks to demonstrate the truth of the Christian faith, rather than presupposing it. As such it is a science, which proposes hypotheses to be verified or falsified by empirical evidence. He believes theology is a public endeavor, and welcomes rational criticism of his system.

This section will point to three flaws in Pannenberg's attempt to develop a rational theology. The first two flaws, his pervasive obscurity and methodological selectivity, do not so much demonstrate the irrationality of Pannenberg's system as inhibit an assessment of its rationality. The third flaw regards his treatment of the divine essence. It appears that Pannenberg maintains conflicting ideas about the divine essence, or that

126. Pannenberg, *Systematic Theology*, 2:76–115.

127. Pannenberg, "Response to Friends," 326.

128. For example, Pannenberg says that, while he is aware of his Lutheran and Protestant roots, "I also feel free to criticize what seems too narrow in both." Wolfhart Pannenberg, "An Autobiographical Sketch," in *Theology of Wolfhart Pannenberg*, 18. For the genuine novelty of Pannenberg's thought, see Blocher, "Immanence and Transcendence," 115–16.

at least his discussion of the divine essence is so unclear that it undercuts any attempt to base the unity of God on that essence. These deficiencies, especially when viewed in light of Pannenberg's stated goals for his theology, call the validity of his understanding of trinitarian unity into question.

Pervasive Obscurity

Perhaps the most enduring criticism lodged against Pannenberg's work is that his thought needs to be clarified. It was mentioned earlier that there is uncertainty and disagreement about whether Pannenberg's eschatological ontology means that God does not yet exist, that God does exist but that men do not know it, or that God does exist even though his existence has not yet been decided and therefore men do not know it.[129] If one considers the following quotation by Pannenberg, the confusion is not surprising:

> For what belongs to the future is not yet existent, and yet it already determines present experience, at least the present experience of beings who—like man—are orientated towards the future and always experience their present and past in the light of a future which they hope for or which they fear. Thus the future is real, although it does not yet exist.[130]

Langdon Gilkey states that Pannenberg's language sometimes makes interpreting his futurist ontology difficult.[131] Christopher Kaiser notes that, regardless of its meaning, "Pannenberg has not given us a clear rationale for this significant departure from traditional theology."[132]

His eschatological ontology is not, however, the only area where Pannenberg's thought is obscure, because that ontology lies at the heart of his methodology. Thus his doctrine of the Trinity is afflicted by obscurity. Roger Olson writes, "His doctrine of the Trinity . . . seems to suffer from the same ambiguity that lies within his entire eschatological ontology."[133] Donald Macleod, after posing several questions regarding Pannenberg's

---

129. Grenz and Olson, *20th Century Theology*, 198; Grenz, "Appraisal," 32; Haugen, "Introduction," 24; Venema, "History, Human Freedom," 75; Gutenson, "One God," 15; Pasquariello, "Pannenberg's Philosophical Foundations," 346.

130. Pannenberg, *Idea of God*, 110.

131. Gilkey, *Reaping the Whirlwind*, 231.

132. Kaiser, *Doctrine of God*, 124.

133. Olson, "Pannenberg's Doctrine," 206.

Christology, states that Pannenberg's position needs to be clarified.[134] David Polk notes that Pannenberg's language regarding God and human freedom makes it unclear whether he is proposing hard or soft determinism.[135] Lewis Ford also questions the clarity of Pannenberg's understanding of the relationship of human freedom to divine determinism.[136]

This criticism is not limited to Pannenberg's opponents. Grenz, a former student of Pannenberg's, writes, "Nevertheless, even some of Pannenberg's supporters suggest that more work will be required before he has provided a fully satisfying understanding of this relationship [between time and eternity]."[137] Rice, after presenting a very favorable review of Pannenberg, states that Pannenberg's understanding of time and eternity is intriguing but undeveloped.[138]

Pannenberg also fails to address certain questions which would help clarify his position. Tavard states that Pannenberg does not discuss whether Jesus' references to God refer to the divine nature or to the Father, nor does he say who spoke as God in the Old Testament.[139] While Pannenberg's doctrine of self-distinction almost certainly means that Jesus referred specifically to the Father when he said "God," the answer to the second question is open. Pannenberg's answer could go far to illuminate exactly what he has in mind when he writes of the preexistence of the Son.[140] Obviously no writing answers every possible question, but illustrations by specific examples are notably lacking in Pannenberg's work.

This pervasive obscurity is objectionable precisely because Pannenberg lays such an emphasis on the rational nature of theology. He frowns upon using incomprehensible and unintelligible statements to develop doctrine.[141] His discussion of theological statements argues that they should be theoretically verifiable and falsifiable like proper scientific statements.[142] Yet how can one test the statement, "Thus the future is real,

---

134. Macleod, "Christology of Wolfhart Pannenberg," 40–41.

135. Polk, "All-determining God," 160–61.

136. Ford, "Nature of the Power," in *Theology of Wolfhart Pannenberg*, 86.

137. Grenz, "Sympathy and Caution," 283.

138. Rice, "Pannenberg's Achievement," 72.

139. Tavard, review of *Systematic Theology*, 390.

140. Pannenberg, "Christian Vision," 55; Pannenberg, *Systematic Theology*, 2:283, 371.

141. Pannenberg, "Doctrine of the Spirit," 69.

142. Pannenberg, "Theological Statement," 9–12.

although it does not yet exist"? What could count as evidence for reality and against existence, or vice versa? The answer is unclear. Pannenberg acknowledges that "there will certainly always remain unresolved difficulties in the subject matter of theology; yet even those difficulties should be susceptible to a systematic description that does not get involved in contradiction."[143] While no contradictions have been shown to this point in Pannenberg's work, the lack of clarity noted in many areas by many authors suggests that his position falls short of "systematic description." Without such a systematic description, it is difficult to offer more than a tentative evaluation of Pannenberg's understanding of trinitarian unity, and even more difficult to heartily endorse it.

Methodological Selectivity

Norman Geisler writes, "Adopt a false methodology and it will lead logically to a wrong theology."[144] Pannenberg is certainly concerned with methodology, and intends to develop one which will allow theology to be viewed as rational science. As noted above, he attempts to avoid presupposing his theology, instead developing it from the revelation of God in history proleptically realized in the resurrection of Christ and attested by the Judeo-Christian tradition, especially as it is recorded in the Bible.

Yet as important as a correct methodology is for theology, a selective application of any methodology tends to invalidate its conclusions. Yet it seems that Pannenberg is quite selective in how he applies his method. For example, Pannenberg refuses to presuppose the deity of Christ, or even the existence of God, in accordance with his method.[145] Yet he makes other theological presuppositions equally important to his system. A particularly important example for his understanding of the unity of God is, "The deity of God is his rule."[146] As shown above, this maxim is vital to Pannenberg's system, showing how the divine Kingdom is the location of God's unity and in part how love can be equated with the divine essence.[147] Yet it appears in Pannenberg's writing with little or no foundation. As Polk notes, "The extent to which Pannenberg endeavors to defend this under-

---

143. Ibid., 11.

144. Geisler, "Beware of Philosophy," 16.

145. Pannenberg, *Jesus—God and Man*, 34–36; Pannenberg, *Systematic Theology*, 1:63.

146. Pannenberg, *Theology and the Kingdom*, 55.

147. Pannenberg, *Systematic Theology*, 1:445.

standing is scanty indeed. For the most part, he tends to regard the matter as self-evident—even, perhaps, tautological."[148] That God must rule may be self-evident to a Christian, but it is a strange thought to a deist. Thus, while Pannneberg proposes a methodology which will not presuppose Christian doctrine, he applies that methodology only selectively.

His treatment of the Bible is likewise selective, both as a source of truth and as a witness to history. At times, Pannenberg accepts biblical statements of theology at face value. John Thompson points out that Pannenberg places immense weight in his understanding of the Father's self-distinction on the single verse, 1 Cor 15:28.[149] Note has already been made of Pannenberg's wholesale appropriation of "God is Spirit" (John 4:24) and "God is love" (1 John 4:8, 16) as definitions of the divine essence.[150] Specific biblical statements ground key elements of Pannenberg's understanding of the divine unity.

Yet Pannenberg dismisses or ignores other statements made by the Bible which could affect his understanding of that unity. Pannenberg rejects wrath as an attribute of God, and makes no mention of Heb 12:29, "For our God is a consuming fire," in his discussion of the divine essence.[151] While it may be true that wrath is not an attribute of God, Pannenberg downplays this aspect of the biblical portrait of God to the point that his description of God's holiness differs little from his description of God's love.[152] Thompson points out that Pannenberg's key presupposition that the rule of God constitutes his being is not biblical either.[153]

Pannenberg seems just as selective in his usage of the Bible as a witness to truth about the historical life of Jesus. On the one hand, Pannenberg zealously affirms the historicity of the resurrection, the fundamental datum for his theology. The sayings of Jesus which distinguish him from the Father and describe the Spirit as a distinct person who glorifies the Father and Son are also essential to Pannenberg's doctrine of trinitarian unity.[154]

---

148. Polk, "All-determining God," 154.

149. Pannenberg, *Systematic Theology*, 1:313, 320. Thompson, *Modern Trinitarian Perspectives*, 36.

150. Pannenberg, *Systematic Theology*, 1:395, 297, 369, 396.

151. Ibid., 1:439.

152. Ibid., 1:399–401, 439–42.

153. Thompson, *Modern Trinitarian Perspectives*, 36.

154. Pannenberg, *Systematic Theology*, 2:283–85, 1:308-310, 315.

On the other hand, Pannenberg rejects the historicity of the virgin birth. He claims that the accounts are "apparently legendary," because "[g]ynecology is not the issue, but Christian pneumatology."[155] While he acknowledges that Jesus took upon himself the exercise of divine prerogatives, Pannenberg denies that Jesus made Messianic claims or called himself by Messianic titles, including Son.[156] This is particularly interesting considering his reliance upon the Gospel and epistles of John in developing his trinitarian doctrine. John consistently presents Jesus as self-consciously Son of man (John 5:15–27, 6:53–55, 8:28) and Son of God (John 5:16–25, 9:35–37, 10:36, 11:4, 25–27), and makes only one mention of the Kingdom (John 3:3–5) outside of assertions that Jesus is and claims to be King (John 1:49, 12:13-15, 18:33–39, 19:3, 12–21). If the historical Jesus is the methodological starting point for the doctrine of the Trinity, why are these assertions minimized while John 4:24 is viewed as a precise theological axiom?

The selectivity of Pannenberg's use of the Bible seems to belie Grenz's assertion that Pannenberg looks at the Bible as a sourcebook for theology.[157] It seems instead that Pannenberg uses the Bible to support conclusions he has already reached by other means. It is in part because of this methodology, which approaches the Bible to find what it presupposes, that Henri Blocher asks if Pannenberg would affirm the truth of "One God, Father, Son, and Holy Spirit, apart from the memory of the church dogma?"[158] If Pannenberg did not have the prior teaching of the church as a control, where would his method actually lead him?

Pannenberg's selective methodology may not be a fatal flaw in his system. But it does cast doubt on the extent to which Pannenberg has actually developed a rational theology based on universally accessible history as it is proleptically realized in Jesus Christ. For an evangelical,

---

155. Ibid., 2:318–19; Bloesch, *Jesus Christ*, 125; Macleod, "Christology of Wolfhart Pannenberg," 21. While Pannenberg cites Dibelius, *Jungfrauensohn und Krippenkind* and Brown, *Birth of the Messiah* for support, it seems he is willing to deny an historical virgin birth primarily because he believes the stories are obviously meant to be legends.

156. Pannenberg, *Systematic Theology*, 1:312, 2:363, 372; Pannenberg, *Jesus—God and Man*, 327, 332; Macleod, "Christology of Wolfhart Pannenberg," 35–36. At one point, Pannenberg, *Systematic Theology*, 1:364, Pannenberg states that Jesus' use of Son "may not be historically authentic," and that the messianic title "Son of God" was one "that Jesus did not claim."

157. Grenz, *Reason for Hope*, 37.

158. Blocher, "Immanence and Transcendence," 116.

the seemingly arbitrary handling of the Scriptures raises further doubts. A position that cannot do justice to the whole of Scripture is for that very reason suspect.

Multiplex Essence

As noted above, Pannenberg seeks to unite a complex of ideas in his discussion of the single divine essence as the unifying factor in the one God. This section will question whether Pannenberg's many descriptions of the divine essence can coherently and meaningfully refer to a single reality. Even if the divine essence is incomprehensible, it is the task of systematic theology to provide a clear, systematic, non-contradictory description.[159]

To begin, it should be noted that Pannenberg provides three distinct general descriptions of the divine nature: Kingdom, spirit, and love. Pannenberg believes that it is the historical actions of the three that fully bring about the Kingdom of God, which is the deity of God and the source of trinitarian unity.[160] He also believes that the three persons are singularities within the infinite divine spirit, the real field presupposed by all physical temporal and spatial fields.[161] Finally, the three are united as a divine society, their essence being a relational essence consisting of their relations to one another.[162] The three persons love one another, making their relations fundamentally love, leading to the identification of love with the divine essence.[163] As Pannenberg writes, "According to 1 John 4:8, 16, love as the power that manifests itself in the mutual relations of the trinitarian persons is identical with the divine essence. It is the materially concrete form of 'Spirit' as the characteristic of God's essence. The two statements 'God is Spirit' and 'God is love' denote the same unity of essence by which Father, Son, and Spirit are united in the fellowship of the one God."[164] This one divine essence is the seat of the divine attributes,

---

159. Pannenberg, "Theological Statement," 11. For an example of a well integrated and clearly presented understanding of the divine essence, see Swinburne, *Christian God*, 1994), 125–69.

160. Pannenberg, *Theology and the Kingdom*, 55; Pannenberg, "Christian Vision," 57; Pannenberg, *Systematic Theology*, 1:313, 320, 322, 327; Grenz, *Reason for Hope*, 53.

161. Pannenberg, "God as Spirit," 792; Pannenberg, *Systematic Theology*, 1:430.

162. Pannenberg, *Systematic Theology*, 1:335–6, 385; Grenz, *Reason for Hope*, 59.

163. Pannenberg, *Systematic Theology*, 1:430–32; Letham, *Holy Trinity*, 320.

164. Pannenberg, *Systematic Theology*, 1:427.

which "may be understood through and through as the attributes of his love."[165] Thus the two sets of attributes, those of infinity and those of love, become one set. As Grenz writes, "All of these attributes, he then concludes, form a unified whole, for the loving God is also the infinite spirit."[166] The being of God is thus Kingdom, spirit, and love.

Despite Pannenberg's efforts to show a connection between these three conceptions of the divine essence, the three terms clearly refer to rather distinct ideas. No one would consider Kingdom, spirit, and love synonyms. This would not be a problem if Pannenberg were describing attributes of God, but he is not. "The deity of God is his rule."[167] "The essence of the Godhead is indeed Spirit. It is Spirit as a dynamic field."[168] "Love is . . . the one and only essence of God."[169] Yet if rule is not love, and it is not, how can there be only one essence?

A more specific examination of these three understandings of the divine essence in terms of the trinitarian relations will clarify the difficulty. When the divine essence is understood as the Kingdom, Pannenberg understands the divine essence to belong primarily to the Father. He writes, "Thus, the one divine being becomes manifest in the three persons but in different ways, the kingdom and the divine essence being always primarily the Father's but effective through the Son and the Spirit."[170] However, when Pannenberg conceives of the divine essence in terms of spirit and love, it seems that the essence belongs primarily to the Spirit. He writes, "On the one side the Spirit and love constitute the common essence of deity, on the other they come forth as a separate hypostasis in the Holy Spirit."[171] If each identification of the divine essence could be primarily associated with a different person, a beautiful symmetry might be implied. As it is, however, the divine essence as Kingdom is primarily the Father's, while the divine essence as spirit and love is primarily the Holy Spirit's. These terms do not appear to refer to the same reality.

165. Ibid., 432.

166. Grenz, *Reason for Hope*, 56.

167. Pannenberg, *Theology and the Kingdom*, 55.

168. Pannenberg, *Systematic Theology*, 1:429.

169. Ibid., 1:428.

170. Pannenberg, "Christian Vision," 57.

171. Pannenberg, *Systematic Theology*, 1:429.

A similar conclusion results when the direction of relations in each identification is examined. Pannenberg's analysis of the Kingdom reveals two similar patterns. In the immanent Trinity, the Father rules the Son, who is the locus of the divine monarchy. In the economic Trinity, the Father rules the Son, and entrusts to the Son and Spirit his rule of all creation.[172] Thus, there is an unequal, bi-directional nature to the essence considered as monarchy. The Father rules the Son, who submits to the Father but does not rule the Father.[173]

Love, however, shows a different relational pattern. The Father loves the Son and the Son reciprocates that love.[174] The Holy Spirit is the love between Father and Son, who therefore loves both though he is not loved by either.[175] Here, the essence of God shows an equal bi-directional movement, for it is the love that flows back and forth between Father and Son which is the Holy Spirit.

God as spirit manifests another relational pattern. Pannenberg writes, "The idea of the divine life as a dynamic field sees the divine Spirit who unites the three persons as proceeding from the Father, received by the Son, and common to both."[176] Here the relation between Father and Son appears to be uni-directional.[177] Also, in this instance the essence, spirit, is not the relation between Father and Son, as love and monarchy are, but something logically distinct imparted in the context of the Father-Son relation. Because it is not a relation within the Trinity, it is hard to see how Pannenberg can view spirit as the essence of God at all, since he believes essences must inherently be relational.[178]

Given this analysis, it does not appear that God's essence can be identified with Kingdom, spirit, and love, because Kingdom, spirit, and love are not identical. As commonly used, they do not approximate conceptual synonyms. According to Pannenberg's own exposition, the terms refer to

172. Ibid., 1:324–26.

173. The Spirit's position in this relation is rather vague.

174. Pannenberg, "Problems of Doctrine," 256.

175. Pannenberg, *Systematic Theology*, 1:426, 429.

176. Ibid., 1:383.

177. Pannenberg believes relations do not inhere in substances. In such a system, it would seem that giving-receiving is only a single relation. See Pannenberg, *Metaphysics*, 73.

178. Pannenberg, *Metaphysics*, 73; Pannenberg, *Systematic Theology*, 2:85.

distinct relational patterns. If Pannenberg is not simply being contradictory, what might he be attempting to convey?

Two options seem available. The first is that Pannenberg is not actually identifying the divine essence, but is describing it. This seems unlikely, however. Pannenberg's identification of God's essence with his monarchy is what leads him to say that God does not yet exist because his existence is determined by his eschatological Kingdom.[179] He comments concerning 1 John 4:8, 16, "The mere thought that God is a subject that loves does not do justice to this saying. Even if we presuppose a plurality of persons in a relationship of love, the persons are related to one another by something else, i.e., love, which is not itself thought of as a third, as the third person."[180] He also identifies love, spirit, and monarchy as the location of the divine unity, and makes clear that the divine unity is a unity of essence.[181]

If, however, Pannenberg is simply being overzealous in his language, using identity statements in place of descriptions, then his entire understanding of divine unity collapses. If God's essence is not love, then the interpersonal communion of the three persons is not the ground of their unity. If God's essence is not monarchy, then the mutual self-distinction of the economic activity which results in the Kingdom does not determine their unity. If God's essence is not spirit, then God is not the divine field which grounds all of space-time by transcendental inclusion.

The other option is that Pannenberg is significantly loosening the meanings of these terms in order to equate them with one another. This seems particularly true of love. Pannenberg notes that love is recognized as the motive of God's act of creation. This, however, is not radical enough. Pannenberg writes, "Love is the only real answer we have to the startling question, Why should there be something rather than nothing? *Love* grants new existence and grants it contingently."[182] For Pannenberg, love is omnipotence, power, and the basis for not just the exercise, but the actuality of all the divine attributes.[183]

While this may be a moving notion, it is doubtful that it could stand up to any sort of critical analysis in terms of subjects, objects, and

179. Pannenberg, *Theology and the Kingdom*, 55–56; Pannenberg, "Theta Phi," 37.
180. Pannenberg, *Systematic Theology*, 1:297.
181. Ibid., 1:325, 327, 335, 341, 427; Pannenberg, "Problems of Doctrine," 256.
182. Pannenberg, *Theology and the Kingdom*, 65, emphasis original.
183. Pannenberg, *Systematic Theology*, 1:422, 427, 445.

mechanisms. In this context, Pannenberg's assertion, "Persons do not have power over love,"[184] raises the question of how the divine persons can freely exercise their attributes if they have no power over the love which is their essence. Equating love with the divine essence and attributes also raises the question of the relation of Christian love to divine love, and of human abilities to human love. Generally speaking, humans do not consider their strength, for example, to be love, or love to be the source of their physical strength.

If, however, the meanings of monarchy, spirit, and love could be so loosened as to allow them to be equated, Pannenberg's system would be at best unclear, and at worst meaningless. Identifying the divine essence as love only has meaning if "love" refers to a specific set of concepts and excludes all others. The larger the set of concepts is, the less meaningful the word "love" is. The same holds true for spirit and rule. Also, if Pannenberg is not using these words in their normal sense, the fact that he has failed to provide a clear set of rules for understanding their meaning in his text makes it difficult to determine their meaning.[185]

Pannenberg's understanding of the divine essence, the ground of the divine unity, appears to be fatally flawed.[186] Because love, spirit, and rule are clearly different realities, actually identifying the divine essence with all three is impossible. If the identification is understood as predication, then God is not one in the manners which Pannenberg has suggested. If Pannenberg is using love, spirit, and rule loosely, then all his statements about the divine unity run the risk of becoming meaningless.

Theological Difficulties

Because he presents a social model of the Trinity, it is inevitable that Pannenberg would be charged with tritheistic leanings. Because he understands God's essence to be intimately linked with history, it appears that Pannenberg may be compromising God's transcendent aseity. Both these charges will be examined in this section. While Pannenberg makes

184. Ibid., 1:426.
185. For a fuller discussion of criteria for meaningful words and statements, see Swinburne, *Coherence of Theism*, 31–38.
186. Pannenberg's understanding of the divine essence raises at least one other question. How can the Holy Spirit as person be identified with a relationality that constitutes persons? However, the difficulty of identifying rule, spirit, and love with the divine essence is the clearest example of Pannenberg's weakness in this area.

moves to defend his position against both, it will be concluded that his position adequately protects monotheism, but that it fails to fully protect the independence of God.

Tritheism

As noted in Chapter 2, many theologians state that any understanding of God which allows for the Father, Son, and Holy Spirit to be distinct centers of action and consciousness is tritheism.[187] However, that position begs the question of what is an adequate understanding of trinitarian unity. As long as a social model of the Trinity posits another strong ground for divine unity, it deserves due consideration.

Recently, Robert Letham and Roger Olson have considered the extent to which Pannenberg's position tends towards tritheism. Letham begins by raising the usual concern about social models of the Trinity. He writes, "Pannenberg's idea of mutual reciprocity between the persons drives him in the direction of tritheism, as all social doctrines of the Trinity in some way must."[188] He notes that Pannenberg does more to cement the unity of the Trinity than just this mutual interaction by emphasizing the functional unity of the three persons in establishing the monarchy of the Father. While he concludes that this is an improvement over Moltmann, Letham still believes that Pannenberg shows a "clearly tritheistic tendency" that "flows from Pannenberg's social Trinity with its mutual relations, its intermeshing of God and creation, and its loose identification of the divine essence with love."[189]

Olson raises similar concerns. He begins by noting that, while Pannenberg is aware of the charge of tritheism social models invite, Pannenberg is fully committed to a monotheistic view of God.[190] While Olson notes the strength of Pannenberg's understanding of the divine interdependence, Olson agrees with Letham that "the charge of tritheism

---

187. For example, Gresham, "Social Model," 330, 342; Rahner, *Trinity*, 43; Hill, *Three-Personed God*, 254. Pannenberg, however, believes that the "most widespread heresy in modern Christian thought is that God is one person, one personal God." See Pannenberg, "Theta Phi," 38. Before the publication of his *Systematic Theology*, W. J. Hill denied that Pannenberg allowed three genuine persons. Hill, *Three-Personed God*, 165–66.

188. Letham, *Holy Trinity*, 316.

189. Ibid., 320.

190. Olson, "Pannenberg's Doctrine," 191, 195.

has yet to be overcome."[191] This is in part because Pannenberg leaves open the question of whether the one God is the Father, or the three together, or can refer to both. Olson concludes that those uncomfortable with a social model, or social trinitarians uncomfortable with the reservation of God's perfect unity until the final future, will consider Pannenberg's system unacceptably close to tritheism.[192]

Both these authors seem to ignore what could be the strongest element in Pannenberg's understanding of the divine unity: his understanding of God as the divine field. If the essence of God actually is an infinite immaterial reality over which the three persons, and only the persons, exercise control, then there is only one God. Pannenberg at least allows that the one essence of God is the one God, writing that "the Son reveals the one God, the essence of God, by revealing the Father."[193] Isolated from Pannenberg's other expositions of the divine essence, understanding God's essence to be spirit seems to overcome Blocher's objection that "assigning to the Three a generic or corporative unity equals tritheism, it *is* tritheism!"[194]

As has already been acknowledged, Pannenberg does blur the line between relational and non-relational unity in his equation of rule, love, and spirit. The eventual ascendence of love over spirit as the source of divine unity strongly suggests that relational or corporative unity is what Pannenberg really has in mind.[195] Nevertheless, as long as Pannenberg affirms the unity of the three persons in the reality of one spirit, he retains a reasonable defense against the charge of tritheism.

Aseity

God and the world are related asymmetrically. While God has created the world, the world is traditionally understood to have no effect on the true being of God.[196] God is self-existent, and has no need for anything else to

---

191. Ibid., 193.

192. Ibid., 202–3. Gutenson, "One God," 18, states that, in personal conversation, Pannenberg denied that his model was social because he does not believe societies are like God. Granting that point, the emphasis on the three persons as distinct centers of action is the criterion here for a social model.

193. Pannenberg, *Systematic Theology*, 1:358.

194. Blocher, "Immanence and Transcendence," 107.

195. Pannenberg, *Systematic Theology*, 1:427, 445.

196. Lewis, "God, Attributes of," in Elwell, *Evangelical Dictionary of Theology*, 453; Thiessen, *Lectures in Systematic Theology*, 78.

promote or establish his reality.[197] He is transcendent, meaning that he is other than the world.[198] So, when Pannenberg makes statements such as, "The rule or kingdom of God is not so external to his deity that he might be God without his kingdom," and, "Now, once a world is given, the Godhood of God as its creator is no longer conceivable without the creatures giving praise to him, thanking him for their existence, and thereby, honoring him as their creator,"[199] he is certain to be criticized for weakening the traditional understanding of God's self-existence and transcendence.

This has certainly happened. Grenz and Olson suggest that Pannenberg flirts with pantheism, because he has blurred the line between God and humanity.[200] Blocher criticizes Pannenberg for associating God's holiness with infinity, a non-biblical theme, rather than transcendence and otherness. The result, he claims, could be seen as an abandonment of the distinction between creator and creature.[201] Pannenberg makes the reality of the immanent Trinity dependent upon the historical action of the economic Trinity. Paul Molnar notes the consequences of this move when he writes, "God is dependent on history to become who he will be."[202]

Pannenberg provides a mixed response to these criticisms. On the one hand, he clearly rests in his affirmation of the infinite divine nature to refute the accusation of pantheism. He writes, "Against pantheism, theology always insists on the specific nature of the divine as distinct from all finite reality."[203] He also affirms that creation is a free act of God, and that therefore creation is not, in itself, necessary for God's existence.[204] However, in choosing to create, God has bound his essence to the history of the world. God existed freely before the world, but now

197. Aquinas, *Summa Theologiae* 1a.3.4 (BF 2:31–35).

198. Blocher, "Immanence and Transcendence," 108–9.

199. Pannenberg, *Systematic Theology*, 1:313; Pannenberg, "Problems of Doctrine," 255.

200. Grenz and Olson, *20th Century Theology*, 254. Cf. Letham, *Holy Trinity*, 320.

201. Blocher, "Immanence and Transcendence," 108–9, 115. Kärkkäinen rightly notes the irony of this, since transcendence is no more a biblical term than infinity. Kärkkäinen, *Trinity*, 147.

202. Molnar, "Toward Contemporary Doctrine," 328, cf. Hill, *The Three-Personed God*, 166.

203. Pannenberg, "Theological Appropriation," 430.

204. Pannenberg, *Systematic Theology*, 1:313.

that he has created, his existence is tied to the establishment of his kingdom in the world.[205]

Does this adequately guard God's aseity and distinction from the world? It does not appear that it does. First, discussions of aseity always presuppose the creation of the world, because those who discuss aseity are creatures. Saying that God is not self-existent once he creates means that he is not self-existent. Second, Pannenberg's futurist ontology seems to make his suggestion of pre-existence absurd. Pannenberg writes:

> Only in the future of his Kingdom come will the statement "God exists" prove to be definitely true. But then it will be clear that the statement was always true. In this impending power the coming God was already the future of the remotest past. He was the future also of that "nothing" which preceded Creation.[206]

Because God's existence is always based upon his future Kingdom, even his existence before creation is determined by the future historical Kingdom. There seems to be no reasonable way to speak about the existence of God before creation apart from creation's future. Pannenberg writes, "We cannot separate the eternal reality of God and the status of the reality of God in our world."[207]

It is therefore hard to give much credence to Pannenberg's distinction between God's self-existence before creation and his historical dependence upon creation. Hill seems to correctly conclude that "Pannenberg has reduced the being of God to that of a divine historical process vis-à-vis the world."[208] Tied to history as he is, Pannenberg's God seems limited, finite, and essentially dependent upon creation.[209] Such a God falls short of theological adequacy.

---

205. Pannenberg, "Problems of Doctrine," 254–55; Polk, "All-Determining God," 165.

206. Pannenberg, *Theology and the Kingdom*, 62. That this is still his view is clear from Pannenberg, *Systematic Theology*, 1:331, "But the eschatological consummation is only the locus of the decision that the trinitarian God is always the true God from eternity to eternity."

207. Pannenberg, "Theta Phi," 37–38.

208. Hill, "The Historicity of God," 323.

209. Kaiser, *Doctrine of God*, 124; Badcock, *Light and Fire*, 197; Olson, "Pannenberg's Doctrine," 177; Molnar, "Toward Contemporary Doctrine," 341.

Christological Difficulty

A final area in which Pannenberg's system will be critiqued is in terms of his Christology. As noted earlier, Christology is for Pannenberg the methodological starting point for his understanding of the Trinity, and therefore trinitarian unity.[210] Pannenberg's system manifests the close relationship between Christology and trinitarianism suggested in Chapter 1.

Pannenberg's Christology will now be examined to determine its Chalcedonian adequacy. This examination will involve three steps. First, it will show that Pannenberg seems to properly identify the person of Christ as the eternal Son of God. Second, it will show that Pannenberg argues for the deity of Christ in two ways. Third, it will show that, despite this superficial adherence to the basic doctrine of Chalcedon, Pannenberg's Christology neither consistently identifies the person of Jesus with God the Son nor consistently affirms his full deity.

Who is the Christ?

Pannenberg's methodology does not presuppose the existence of an eternal Son of God, but instead begins with the ministry of Jesus. To establish the existence of God the Son, Pannenberg does not draw upon biblical references to Jesus as Son of God, and in fact is skeptical that Jesus ever referred to himself as Son, much less Son of God.[211]

Instead, Pannenberg notes that Jesus consistently speaks of God as his Father. Jesus lived in complete subordination to, dependence upon, and sacrifice to his Father.[212] When that style of life was affirmed by the resurrection, Jesus was demonstrated to be the Son of God.[213] God, however, is eternal. If Jesus is demonstrated to be in a filial relation with an eternal Father, that filial relation must also be eternal. Thus, there must be an eternal Son of the eternal Father. Pannenberg explains:

> God is from all eternity the One whom Jesus proclaimed him to be. . . . But if the Father is from all eternity the One he is shown historically to be in relation to Jesus his Son, and through him, then we cannot think of the Father apart from the Son. This means on the one hand that the risen Lord is exalted to eternal fellowship

210. Pannenberg, *Systematic Theology*, 1:257.

211. Ibid., 1:312, 2:363, 372; Pannenberg, *Jesus—God and Man*, 327, 332.

212. Pannenberg, *Jesus—God and Man*, 339; Pannenberg, *Systematic Theology*, 2:363.

213. Pannenberg, *Jesus—God and Man*, 335; Pannenberg, *Systematic Theology*, 2:283–85.

with the Father. His relationship to the eternal Father as the Son, however, means on the other hand that the Son was linked to the Father before the beginning of the earthly existence of Jesus.[214]

The resurrection as a demonstration of Jesus as the Son of God was also a demonstration of God's eternal fatherhood, and therefore an eternal or preexistent Son.

In the event of the incarnation Jesus of Nazareth is the person God the Son. As persons who stand in the same filial relation to the Father, Jesus and the Son must in fact be the same person.[215] Pannenberg writes:

> The person of Jesus Christ is identical with the eternal Son. But this does not mean that the human reality of Jesus lacks personality. Precisely in his human history Jesus has his personal identity solely in being the Son of his heavenly Father. This fact integrates all the features of his earthly existence into a unity. The man Jesus has no other identity than this . . . his human existence never had its personal identity in itself but always only in relation to the Father, and therefore in his being the Son of this Father.[216]

This identity is bi-directional, so that "we may not think of this Son in isolation from the historical filial relation of Jesus to the Father if the affirmation of his preexistence is grounded on this alone."[217] This means that "the one person with whom Christology is concerned is certainly the same as that about whom statements must be made in the doctrine of the Trinity."[218] Thus the person of God the Son is the man, Jesus Christ.

How is he God?

Pannenberg presents two major understandings of how it is that Jesus is God. Certainly it cannot be because he is the preexistent Son; the reality of the preexistent Son is a deduction from Jesus' relation to the Father. Instead, Pannenberg cites revelatory presence and self-distinction as the grounds for Jesus' deity.

214. Pannenberg, *Systematic Theology*, 2:367.

215. Pannenberg, *Jesus—God and Man*, 339.

216. Pannenberg, *Systematic Theology*, 2:389.

217. Ibid., 2:368. As will be seen, Pannenberg occasionally makes statements at odds with this statement. However, this statement is the only one consistent with Pannenberg's "from below" methodology. Placing an understanding of the eternal Son, whose existence is only evident in Jesus, over against Jesus, is not consistent.

218. Pannenberg, *Jesus—God and Man*, 343.

Pannenberg's discussion of revelatory presence appears in his earlier work *Jesus—God and Man*. In that work, he surveys several understandings of the presence of God in Christ. He concludes that the proper understanding is that of revelatory presence. Because Christ is God's self-revelation, he is in fact God. Therefore, in the case of Christ, revelatory presence is not set against, but actually includes, the idea of genuine deity.[219] Pannenberg writes that revelatory presence "indicates a presence as appearance that is not—as is presence as *mere* appearance—set in contrast to the identity of essence, but rather includes the idea of substantial presence, of an essential identity of Jesus with God."[220]

Of course, not all those who bring revelation are God. Pannenberg therefore proposes "three steps that lead materially from the concept of revelation to the knowledge of Jesus' divinity."[221] The first is that God proleptically reveals his being, his kingdom, in its final glory through Christ's resurrection. The second is that this revelation, because it is ultimate, must also be unique. The final step is that "the concept of God's self-revelation contains the idea that the Revealer and what is revealed are identical."[222] As the historical man that fully reveals God, Jesus is God the Son.[223]

In his systematic theology, however, Pannenberg says little about the revelatory presence of God in Christ as constituting Christ's unity with God. Instead, he focuses on Christ's self-distinction from the Father as the ground of his unity with the Father examined in the section above on the one monarchy. As noted above, this seems to assume the divine monarchy as an intermediate step. Christ distinguishes himself from the Father to establish the monarchy, which is the deity, of the Father, and thereby participates in that monarchy and deity.[224]

Pannenberg asserts two means of establishing the deity of Christ. Because revelation is self-revelation, Jesus as God's ultimate revelation must be truly God. Because God's being is his monarchy, Jesus' participation in that monarchy is participation in that being. While the presuppositions that lay behind these two assertions of the Son's deity may be

219. Ibid., 116–33.

220. Ibid., 127, emphasis original.

221. Ibid., 129.

222. Ibid.

223. Ibid., 323.

224. Pannenberg, *Systematic Theology*, 1:310; Pannenberg, "Christian Vision," 58–59; Pannenberg, *Jesus—God and Man*, 370.

questionable, Pannenberg clearly affirms the deity of Christ, who is God the Son.

Presented in this way, Pannenberg's Christology seems to adhere to the basic understanding of Chalcedon recognized in Chapter 1.[225] The person Jesus Christ is the person God the Son. Jesus Christ is a genuine man and truly God.

Is this Position Adequate?

Unfortunately, Pannenberg's Christology does not consistently affirm either that the person in Jesus is God the Son, or that Jesus fully possesses the divine nature. In *Jesus—God and Man*, Pannenberg recognizes that a "from below" methodology can only speak of God the Son based upon Jesus. He writes, "How the divine Logos, the Second Person of the Trinity, would be thought of apart from the incarnation and thus apart from the man Jesus completely escapes our imagination."[226] This makes sense in light of his methodology. Since the existence of the eternal Son is deduced from Christ's relation to the eternal Father, it does not add to what is known, it only clarifies it.

However, in the second volume of Pannenberg's *Systematic Theology*, he violates that methodology and begins with Jesus separate from the divine Logos. Jesus' identity with the Son becomes mediated by self-distinction, so that Jesus, as the man who distinguishes himself from God, becomes fully identified with the Son only when his self-distinction is complete. Because Christ's self-distinction is only complete after his death and resurrection, it is only then that Jesus is the person of the Son.[227] Jesus is not the person of the Son, but becomes the person of the Son as his life of self-distinction comes to perfectly match the life of eternal self-distinction lived by the Son.

Pannenberg also seems to fall back from a full assertion of the deity of Christ. Bloesch notes that Pannenberg "tends to deny or radically qualify the two-nature doctrine" of Chalcedon.[228] Even before the incarnation, Pannenberg writes that "the eternal Son in the humility of his self-distinction from the Father moves out of the unity of the deity

---

225. See pp. 30–33 above.

226. Pannenberg, *Jesus—God and Man*, 35.

227. Ibid., 2:387–89.

228. Bloesch, *Jesus Christ*, 68; Pannenberg, *Jesus—God and Man*, 337–42; Pannenberg, *Systematic Theology*, 1:311, 2:386–87.

by letting the Father alone be God" in the act of creation.[229] How can the Son be God if he moves out of the deity, leaving the Father alone as God?[230]

At other places, Pannenberg seems to grant full possession of deity to the Son, but argues that, since Jesus is not identical with the Son, he does not possess the divine nature. Instead, the "human nature of Jesus Christ shares, then, in the deity of the Logos, but only through the mediation of self-distinction from God."[231] Because Christ's self-distinction was only complete after his death and resurrection, it is only then that Jesus fully participates in the deity of the Son. While on earth, and even at the crucifixion, Jesus was not fully divine.[232]

Pannenberg also seems vague on what the preexistence of the Son means, even though preexistence is necessary for genuine incarnation.[233] At times it refers to the prior unity of Jesus with God. In *Theology and the Kingdom of God*, Pannenberg writes, "Jesus' unity with God, insofar as it belongs to God's eternal essence, precedes, however, the time of Jesus' earthly life."[234] At other times it appears to be a suggestion of a genuine person in the Trinity upon whom the human Jesus is based, as when Pannenberg writes, "Hence the eternal Son is the ontic basis of the human existence of Jesus in his relation to God as Father."[235] Still other references to the preexistent Son, now called the Logos, appear to be no more than shorthand for a principle of self-distinction within God.[236] At one point Pannenberg states that statements of preexistence simply mean that the "origin of the divine sonship of Jesus can lie, then, only in the eternity of God himself."[237] This last statement says very little indeed. Molnar suggests that "Pannenberg's belief that Jesus' human self-distinction from

229. Pannenberg, *Systematic Theology*, 2:22; cf. 2:30.

230. Of course, if the deity is the mutually constituting love of Father and Son, as Pannenberg suggests, how can he move out of that at all and remain Son?

231. Pannenberg, *Systematic Theology*, 2:388.

232. Ibid., 2:388–89.

233. Ibid., 2:368.

234. Pannenber, *Theology and the Kingdom*, 150.

235. Pannenberg, *Systematic Theology*, 2:23.

236. Ibid., 2:29–30.

237. Ibid., 2:371.

the Father is the ground of his divine Sonship virtually eliminates any genuine pre-existent Sonship."[238]

It must be admitted that Pannenberg's Christology is too confusing and obscure to allow any positive conclusions regarding its orthodoxy. However, some have seen heretical movements within it. Colin Gunton, writing before the publication of Pannenberg's *Systematic Theology*, states that, "Despite all his careful safeguards and detailed conversation with tradition, it is difficult to see how Pannenberg can avoid an outcome similar to that of degree Christology, of making Jesus into a divinized man."[239] Pannenberg's description of the process by which Jesus comes to be fully identified with the Son, and therefore fully share in the divine nature, will do little to quiet that concern. In fact Bloesch, writing more recently, has also raised it, and Macleod has suggested that Pannenberg's system could suffer from similar problems of Nestorianism or adoptionism.[240]

Macleod also questions how self-distinction can actually ground the Son's deity. If the Father is God as the one who claims and exercises deity, how can the Son be God by rejecting and denying deity? He asks, "Is this simply God being God in two different ways? Or is it a pointer to two incompatible deities?"[241] Of course, it makes sense for Jesus to completely distinguish himself from God if he is, in fact, divine in the fact that he is a creature. His humanity is his deity. If that is the case, Pannenberg sees Jesus fulfilling the ideal of humanity and completely submitting himself to God.[242] And Pannenberg does seem vulnerable to this interpretation. He writes that "in the event of the incarnation, in the relation of Jesus of Nazareth to his heavenly Father, the Son moved out of the unity of the Godhead. In his awareness of being a mere human, a creature, in his self-distinction from the Father, Jesus recognized the Father as the one God over against himself."[243] If the incarnation consists of the Son leaving his deity and becoming solely human, it is only right that he distinguish himself from the Father.

---

238. Molnar, "Toward Contemporary Doctrine," 342.

239. Gunton, *Yesterday & Today*, 23.

240. Bloesch, *Jesus Christ*, 70; Macleod, "Christology of Wolfhart Pannenberg," 22.

241. Macleod, "Christology of Wolfhart Pannenberg," 36.

242. Ibid., 37–38.

243. Pannenberg, *Systematic Theology*, 2:29.

Macleod also sees Jesus' ignorance of his own divine personage as a mark against his deity.[244] Macleod points out that Pannenberg criticizes kenotic theories that postulate the Son laying aside his attributes, including omniscience, in the incarnation. He then asks, "Could there have been any greater eclipsing of divine omniscience than the spectacle of the Son of God moving about the streets of Jerusalem not knowing who he was?"[245] Either Jesus was not omniscient, and therefore not God, or Jesus was not actually the Son, and therefore not God. Macleod therefore denies that Pannenberg actually believes in an incarnation, and requests that he be clearer.[246]

Greater clarity is certainly needed. At present, it seems that Pannenberg's Christology contains no single understanding of who the person of Christ is, no clear affirmation of his genuine, full deity, and no coherent account of his preexistence as the eternal Son. As such, it fails to measure up to Chalcedonian orthodoxy, and serves as a mark against Pannenberg's understanding of trinitarian unity.

CONCLUSION

As a whole, Pannenberg's understanding of the divine unity must be considered inadequate. His positions, while provocative, often lack the clarity required for an enthusiastic endorsement. His Christology clearly manifests this problem, for it fails to meet the standards of orthodoxy not because Chalcedonian elements are absent, but because they are so mixed with other thoughts that a coherent picture does not emerge. His understanding of the divine essence also suffers from his tendency to mix concepts, not so much because it is unclear, but because the concepts of love, rule, and spirit seem impossible to identify with one reality. Finally, Pannenberg's move to make the unity of the triune God a result of the historical process makes God himself dependent upon history.

Despite these drawbacks, two clearly positive elements are visible in Pannenberg's understanding of the divine unity. Perhaps the most promising is his equation of the divine essence, the seat of the divine unity, with an infinite spiritual field. This seems to allow for three divine persons, robustly understood, to exercise one set of divine attributes and to be united in one

244. Ibid., 2:389.
245. Macleod, "Christology of Wolfhart Pannenberg," 40.
246. Ibid., 37, 40–41.

essence without the drawbacks of a grossly material analogy. Also helpful is Pannenberg's insistence that the divine essence serve as an impersonal element in God. As was suggested in the critique of Zizioulas, a purely personal ontology is simply not possible. In the next chapter, an attempt will be made to combine these positive elements in Pannenberg with the positive contributions of the other authors.

6

A Successful Evangelical Understanding
of Trinitarian Unity

To this point, four contemporary understandings of the unity of the triune God have been critically examined. The purpose has not been criticism for criticism's sake, but to reveal what elements should be included in a correct evangelical understanding of trinitarian unity. This chapter will seek to draw this study to a close. It will begin by reviewing Karl Rahner's, Millard Erickson's, John Zizioulas's, and Wolfhart Pannenberg's views of the oneness of God. These reviews will include summaries of the positive and negative aspects of each position. It will then present several suggestions for the construction of an evangelical doctrine of the Trinity. These suggestions will be followed by a doctrine of trinitarian unity which seeks to capitalize on them.

A BRIEF REVIEW OF FOUR POSITIONS[1]

Karl Rahner, a prominent Roman Catholic theologian, develops his understanding of the triune unity in accordance with a rule that identifies the economic and immanent Trinity. In his system, the self-expression of the Father is essentially identical with the Father. The Son and the Holy Spirit, as the two aspects of the Father's divine self-communication and self-acceptance within the Godhead, are essentially one with him. Their roles in the economy mirror their roles in the Godhead. In this system, the Father becomes conceptually identical with the transcendent Godhead, who reveals himself through the Son and Holy Spirit, "persons" virtually distinct from himself.

Two positive elements of Rahner's system were complimented. One was his strong view of God's unity. Practically everything about God is

1. For a full discussion of these issues, see chapters 2–5.

one, save the virtual distinctions of Son and Holy Spirit. Another was his keen awareness of the heresies that surround any construction of the doctrine of the Trinity. One must avoid "mere" monotheism, tritheism, Sabellianism, and a false quaternity which makes "God" something other than or more than the three persons.

It was concluded, however, that Rahner's system is inadequate. While he avoids the charge of Sabellianism by defining this heresy as a failure to recognize eternal distinctions in God, his denial of distinct personality to the Son and Holy Spirit results in a non-Chalcedonian Christology. For Rahner, Jesus is a human person united to that aspect of God called the Son. While Rahner successfully defends his relative Trinitarian position against the charge of logical contradiction, the fact that he identifies only the Father with the One God leaves the Son and Spirit as virtual distinctions within him, not persons relationally opposed to him. Finally, Rahner's mono-personal God is unable to overcome the objection to a lonely God of love, making the world a necessary creation for the fulfillment of God's nature.

Millard Erickson stands on the opposite end of the spectrum concerning the unity of God. While Rahner emphasized that God is one "person," in the modern sense of the word, Erickson believes that each of the three persons of God is a distinct center of action with his own attributes. Each is fully divine, and the three are united together in mutually dependent loving fellowship. Following the work of Leonard Hodgson, Erickson presents God as three divine persons indistinguishable outside of the divine economy and united by love as a divine society.

This description of God, in which God is a single divine society united by love, is appealing to those who note the biblical emphasis on love. Erickson also presents a position in which the full personhood of each of the persons of the Trinity corresponds with the New Testament presentation of Father, Son, and Holy Spirit. Erickson has worked to fill a gap in American evangelical theology by presenting two significant monographs on the subject of the Trinity.

Unfortunately, Erickson's position encounters numerous difficulties. His radically egalitarian understanding of the three persons in God provides no mechanism for resolving conflict or making decisions, offers no clear account of how the three in God can actually be interdependent, and provides no means of distinguishing the three in God apart from creation, making creation necessary. Unlike John of Damascus, Erickson does not found his understanding of the divine *perichoresis* on a prior divine unity of essence. Because of this, his position has little to ensure a significant unity of the Father, Son, and Holy Spirit, especially in the act of creation. This position seems too close to tritheism.

Zizioulas presents a view of divine unity that, like Erickson's, emphasizes love as a unitive force in the Godhead. The divine being is the divine communion. However, for Zizioulas the divine communion is not primarily from the mutual interaction of three indistinguishable divine persons, but is caused by the Father, who as a free person constitutes his own being as the trinitarian relationships among Father, Son, and Holy Spirit. Because being is essentially being-in-communion, the three require their shared communion for their existence, and therefore cannot be separated.

By focusing on the monarchy of the Father, Zizioulas adds to Erickson's understanding of the divine unity by demonstrating that it is in the context of specific relations that the persons of the Trinity are interdependent. By asserting the full personality of Son and Spirit, Zizioulas improves on Rahner's mono-personal understanding of God. Because the Son, according to Zizioulas, is fully personal, he can serve as the center of action in the man Jesus Christ. Because the Father, Son, and Spirit can love one another as distinct persons, God's love is genuine apart from the creation.

Zizioulas's understanding of God's unity still faces insuperable difficulties. Despite his claims to continuity with the Cappadocians, his position eliminates the unity of essence which was so central to the Cappadocian counter to the charge of tritheism. Zizioulas invites that charge not only by abandoning the unity of essence, but also by blurring the line between creator and creation, by redefining person so as to place the Son and Spirit at a lower level ontologically than the Father, and by locating the attributes of God in the distinct persons. All of these moves slide Zizioulas's understanding of God uncomfortably close to tritheism. In addition, Zizioulas introduces cause into the Godhead, moving the concept of person and relation from one of inherent simultaneity to circular causation, an impossibility.

Wolfhart Pannenberg understands God to be one according to a novel ontology, in which the future has priority over the present. Because God will be determined to be one in the culmination of history, the divine Kingdom, he is one now. This oneness is based upon identifying the divine essence with God's Kingdom, which is brought about by the mutual work of the three divine persons, and the divine love, the personal interaction of Father, Son, and Spirit with one another. Thus Pannenberg's understanding of divine unity includes unity of essence, conceived of in terms of relational communion. To this he also adds an impersonal element, that of spirit. The three members of the Godhead are conceived of as personal singularities within the infinite divine field against which all of space-time is set. Thus Pannenberg attempts to mix the relational and monadic understandings of the divine unity.

On the positive side, Pannenberg's understanding of God as spirit presents an image of the divine essence as a *res* which unifies the three in God. The concept of three persons possessing as their own an infinite immaterial field has explanatory power. Pannenberg's methodology stresses that any monotheism which is not the monotheism of Jesus, his Father, and the Paraclete is neither biblical nor Christian. Pannenberg reveals a willingness to engage in the extensive interaction with philosophical and historical theology essential to an adequate systematic theology.

However, several negative elements prevent a full endorsement of Pannenberg's position. For one thing, his consistent obscurity makes his position difficult to evaluate. While his methodology is interesting, its inconsistent application, especially with regard to how Pannenberg handles Scripture, makes it suspect to evangelical eyes. His identification of the divine essence with love, rule, and spirit appears to be either meaningless or contradictory. While Pannenberg's position has sufficient strength, by his exposition of the concept of God as spirit, to resist accusations of tritheism, it involves an inherent connection between God and the world, compromising God's aseity and contradicting Pannenberg's own assertions. Finally, while Pannenberg's Christology is rather confused, it seems to deny not only the full deity of Jesus but also that the person of Jesus Christ is none other than the eternal Son of God.

It must therefore be concluded that none of the positions examined adequately expresses the unity of the triune God. The task ahead is to draw from the successes and failures of these four theologians' suggestions for an evangelical doctrine of trinitarian unity. The next section is devoted to that task.

ELEMENTS OF AN EVANGELICAL DOCTRINE
OF TRINITARIAN UNITY

Despite the wide variance of the positions surveyed, there were several difficulties or warning signs seen in multiple positions. For example, historical precedents were cited, and historical language used, without the content of the precedent or language being retained. In other cases, the difference between two positions revealed that one option had greater potential for developing a doctrine of trinitarian unity. This section will attempt to compile lessons learned both negatively and positively into four specific suggestions for an evangelical doctrine of trinitarian unity.

Be Clear

Clarity is not just a boon to those who read theology. The ability to write clearly depends upon a clearly conceived idea. On the other hand, the inability to express an element of the doctrine of trinitarian unity in a clear and consistent fashion suggests that an underlying idea is faulty. Rahner, for instance, oscillates between descriptions of revelation as having two or three aspects. This was shown to reveal an undesired conclusion of his thought that reduces the Son and Spirit to a binity within the Father, rather than connecting the three as Trinity. Similarly, Zizioulas writes of the Father constituting his being as Trinity, which is a confusing mixture of person and relation within his system. Pannenberg's obscurity has been noted and criticized by several theologians, and his odd equation of love, rule, and spirit via the divine essence was shown to be incoherent. A lack of clarity in expression suggests a lack of coherence in formulation.

An evangelical doctrine of trinitarian unity must be clear. Important terms must be defined or used with their usual sense. The connections between ideas must be specified. This will serve as not only a help to the reader, but also a check on the author's own thought, to be certain that it is coherent.

Respect History

Norman Geisler warns biblical scholars, "We must reject the temptation to believe 'New is true.' It is far more likely that 'Old is gold.' For truth stands the test of time, while recent error has not been around long enough to be tried in the balance and be found wanting."[2] While it would be a mistake to allow theology to simply rest in the words of the Church Fathers, it is an equally grave mistake to ignore the philosophical, biblical, and theological insights these men recorded. While it may be true that the philosophical models by which they contemplated reality differed dramatically from those used today, they contemplated the same universe and the same God. While it may be necessary to deviate from their understanding of the divine unity, such a move should not be made without careful consideration.

The positions of Erickson and Zizioulas both drift uncomfortably towards tritheism in part because they neglect the element of divine unity John of Damascus and the Cappadocians saw underlying the *perichoresis* and personal relations of the three persons, the one divine essence. Rahner overestimates the Greek emphasis on the Father as the one God, a mistake which corresponds to his inability to place the Son and Spirit over against the Father as relations of opposition as he intends. In each case, a deviation from the Patristic doctrine results in a weakness in the contemporary position.

Preserve Essence

One of the conclusions reached in chapter 1 was that the dominant historical understanding of the divine unity understood the one divine essence, the seat of the divine attributes, as a reality which established the unity of the three persons in God. Both of the positions that eschewed this traditional understanding, Erickson's and Zizioulas's, trend dangerously towards tritheism. This is not because affirmation of the unity of the divine essence is an *a priori* test for monotheism. It is because neither position provides adequate grounds for God to be one apart from the one divine essence. Erickson's position attempts to establish interdependence between identical perfect beings without pointing out what such beings might need, and speaks of love as a unifying force without qualitatively distinguishing God's love within the Trinity from God's love for creation. Zizioulas attempts to base his understanding of unity solely on the causal priority of the Father within the Godhead, creating an ontological rift between the Father on one side and the Son and Spirit on the other. Without a single divine essence, both of these positions do not have a mechanism

2. Geisler, "Beware of Philosophy," 16.

to adequately ground the trinitarian unity. This is a mistake that a success-ful evangelical doctrine of the Trinity must avoid.

By essence, an impersonal, non-relational reality is meant. Whether it is conceived of as Pannneberg's spiritual field or not, something about God must bear his capacity to be the single omnipotent creator and ruler of the universe. Attempts to locate God's attributes in the persons of Father, Son, and Spirit seem to lead inevitably to three partial creators, as the examination of Erickson's position suggested. On the other hand, attempts to make the divine essence relational love make it conceptually distinct from spirit as the seat of God's attributes, as the examination of Pannneberg's position demonstrated. In addition, one can conclude from Timothy Bartel's logical argument against relative trinitarianism that the more essence appears to be an extension of personhood, the harder it is to defend a doctrine of three persons and one essence against the charge of logical contradiction.

Retain the Monarchy

Pannenberg's work emphasizes the distinct economic roles of the three divine persons in the economy of salvation, and notes that these distinct actions are described by the Bible as evidences of the unity of God. While it might be an error to fully adopt Rahner's Rule, a successful evangelical doctrine of triune unity should recognize the value of un-derstanding the economic roles of the Father, Son, and Holy Spirit to reflect, to some degree, the eternal relations among them. Erickson's po-sition, which denies this reflection, was shown to face several difficulties because of this denial.

One who understands the Trinity to contain an eternal monarchy has a model for how three ontologically identical persons can make decisions without conflict. If the three persons do not eternally relate to one another as Father, Son, and Spirit, it appears the three collapse into one self-identical, self-relating person without creation. If there is any truth to the assertion that persons are constituted by relation, Father, Son, and Spirit can only be eternally distinct persons if they en-gage in eternally distinct relations. Pannenberg shows that it is possible to present a less one-sided view of the divine relations and still retain the explanatory power of the divine monarchy. While the concept of monarchy does not explain how God is one in essence, it complements that understanding of God's impersonal unity with a description of how the persons in God can be distinct without being chaotic.

What of Rahner's Rule?

Before constructing a position, methodological considerations demand a response to Rahner's Rule. This position will not be based upon Rahner's Rule, at least not if that rule is taken as absolutely as it appears to be intended. There are two reasons for this, both of which involve known necessary corrections to the rule. If the rule has known caveats, proceeding as if no more could exist would be unwise.

The first reason is that the economic Trinity, if that concept is limited to the actions of the Father, Son, and Spirit in the life of Jesus, provides inadequate grounds for unifying the triune God. It is the distinction of the three persons in the one God of the Old Testament which one sees in the life of Jesus. While one sees a unity of operation amongst the persons in the New Testament, if this economic activity is viewed in isolation from the teachings of the Old Testament, it would be hard to see monotheism, including Nicene trinitarian monotheism, in it.

The second reason is that Rahner's Rule provides no criteria for deciding what aspects of the economy must be understood in terms of the Son's true humanity. This true humanity is taken into account when Jesus hungers or thirsts. It seems unwarranted to ignore it when he prays or is baptized. So, rather than being based and strict adherence to Rahner's Rule, this position will be developed with the cautions of Yves Congar in mind. While the economic Trinity is the true Trinity, it is that true Trinity revealed by condescension and veiled somewhat by the mystery of the cross.[3]

A SKETCH OF A POSITION

Before attempting to fill in all the details of the concluding position, a sketch is in order. There exist eternally three divine persons, the Father, the Son, and the Holy Spirit. These three exist as distinct but related centers of consciousness and action each fully possessing the single eternal divine essence. This essential unity is matched by a personal unity amongst Father, Son, and Spirit based upon their shared perfect character and the personal role of the Father as head of the Godhead.

3. Congar, *I Believe*, 15.

These three depend upon one another both personally and essentially. Their reality as persons in realized only in relation to one another. For example, the Father is not the Father without the Son, nor is the Holy Spirit the Holy Spirit unless he is the "Spirit of God" and the "Spirit of Christ" (Rom 8:9, 1 Pet 1:11). At the level of essence, their shared possession of the divine essence means that each person's existence is grounded in something that belongs fully to each of the others.

The three divine persons can be considered three subjects united as one object. Most of the divine attributes, particularly those by which God knows of and acts directly on the world, are aspects of the divine essence.[4] Thus, the omnipotence by which God created the universe is the omnipotence of the one divine essence. Because Father, Son, and Spirit each fully possess this essence, the act of creation is properly attributed to each and all of the persons. On the other hand, not everything about God is one. The divine persons, as divine persons, relate to men individually. Men pray not to the one divine essence, but to Father, Son, and/or Spirit. When God speaks as an "I" it is the Father, the Son, or the Spirit speaking. This view of divine unity allows both united action in the world and distinct personal interaction with the world. This position suggests that the ancient understanding of the unity of all *ad extra* operations needs to be revised to recognize that operations employing personal, rather than essential, attributes are actions of the several persons. Only the Son becomes incarnate, and speaks as the man Jesus. Only the Spirit bears witness within men that they are the children of God.

If this position tends towards one of Rahner's heretical categories, it tends towards quaternity. The language of "possession" has been used in an intentional attempt to avoid suggesting property simplicity. This could be read to mean that, because the essence is distinguished from the persons, it is therefore a fourth in God. This is a mistake for two main reasons. First, the divine essence is in no sense the God of the Bible because it does not act. It does not create, save, redeem, or sanctify. It does not hear prayer, smell sacrifices, or receive worship. The divine persons are the only active principles in the Godhead, and therefore the only realities that can conceivably be worshiped as God. Second, the divine essence does not have existence separate from the divine persons. It is the essence

4. Gerald Bray suggests that a distinction should be made between God's communicable personal attributes and the incommunicable attributes of the divine essence. See Bray, *Doctrine of God*, 212–23.

of the Father, the Son, and the Spirit, and cannot be detached from them. To pose a grossly material analogy, the persons possess the divine essence like a human person possesses his body. He can contemplate his body as distinct from his person, but without his person the body is meaningless, impotent, and disintegrating.

This is a brief sketch of a doctrine of trinitarian unity that attempts to be clear, to preserve tradition, to emphasize the one divine essence, and to retain the relational monarchy of the Trinity. None of the words are being used in an unusual sense, which may give a materialistic impression which the plain use of language makes difficult to avoid. Aside from the rejection of property simplicity, which is a considered move, and a revision of the unity of operations, no key element of the trinitarian position has been abandoned. The divine essence as the sole impersonal seat of the impersonal divine attributes is the key element of God's unity, and the key justification of how vast actions, such as creation, can be attributed fully to each of the persons, even when roles are somewhat distinguished. Finally, the divine monarchy, the personal order headed up by the Father, is seen to be a personal reflection of the essential unity of God.

FILLING IN THE DETAILS

The preceding sketch is far from a complete doctrine of the Trinity, and, of course, "the Devil is in the details." This section will develop the preceding sketch. First, it will examine how this doctrine of Trinitarian unity understands the key terms of person and nature and how both the three persons and the one nature establish the unity of the triune God. Second, it will consider what God's essence is, what is one in God. Third, it will examine the personal distinction and interdependence of the divine persons.

Person and Nature

As suggested in the introduction, the concepts of person and essence or nature play a key role in properly understanding the unity of the Trinity. The language, "three persons and one essence," is crucial. However, both an historical overview and a thorough examination of four recent understandings of the Trinity show that these terms mean different things to different authors. Rahner, for example, views the three persons in God as "manners of subsisting," and prefers to equate the modern use of person with the one nature in God.[5] Erickson has a different and seemingly broader meaning for nature than does Rahner, using the term to refer to both the generic deity of the three persons, of which each is an instance, and rather puzzlingly, the necessary character of the three together, writing, "The triune nature of God is essential to his very being."[6] Therefore, before attempting to explain how the concepts of person and essence can be used to elucidate the unity and diversity of God, some guidelines for understanding these terms within the context of this work will be presented.

As shown in chapter 2, Timothy Bartel's problem with relative trinitarianism hinges on the perceived failure of relative trinitarians to adequately distinguish the concepts of person and nature.[7] To begin with, then, it should be noted that person and essence involve two utterly distinct levels of reality. This is not to deny a connection between them, but to state that neither can be understood entirely, or even primarily, in terms of the other. Rahner himself notes one half of this necessity, writing, "personhood must not be reduced to the level of nature."[8] A theologian who recognizes this is free from any compulsion to perform divine math on the formula, "three persons and one essence." This scheme also opens the door to a coherent distinction between essential properties, i.e., properties of God's nature, and personal properties, a distinction suggested by Gerald Bray, who, for example, assigns sovereignty to God's persons, and omnipotence to God's essence.[9]

Within such a system, the clause, "God is essentially triune," is technically false.[10] It confuses the essence of God, which is one, with the entire reality of God, which is triune. If understood univocally, it reduces the persons to developments from, aspects of, or emergent properties of the

5. Rahner, *Trinity*, 113–14, 106.

6. Erickson, *God in Three Persons*, 225, 264.

7. Bartel, "Relative Trinitarian," 146. See p. 60–61 above.

8. Rahner, *Foundations*, 218.

9. Bray, *Doctrine of God*, 219.

10. This does introduce a wrinkle into the notion of essential properties. Ronald Nash presents the usual understanding, writing, "A property is essential to some being if and only if the loss of that property entails that that being ceases to exist." The God of the Bible could not cease to be triune and continue to exist, but triunity is not a property of his essence. Instead, "being eternally possessed by the three divine persons," is a property of God's essence. Nash, *Concept of God*, 16.

nature. God is essentially one, personally three, and eternally, inherently, immutably triune.

This necessary distinction between person and nature also helps to guard against the seemingly common error of depriving the one nature of God of any content beyond the interaction amongst the three persons. When this occurs, one is liable to either lapse into subordinationism, or walk uncomfortably close to tritheism. The first problem is seen in Zizioulas, who, by making the one person of the Father responsible for the interpersonal relations within the Godhead, which he believes to be the divine essence, leaves the Son and Spirit without commensurate roles. The second is seen in Erickson, who, by locating the "essential" attributes of God in each of the several divine persons, finds little else to bind them together. John Polkinghorne also notes this second danger, writing, "The Trinitarian picture of the eternal exchange of love between the divine Persons, whose communion of mutual openness constitutes the divine being . . . requires great subtlety, as theologians seek to avoid making the Trinity so 'social' that it becomes more or less a tritheistic pantheon."[11]

The utter distinction between person and nature inhibits mixing personal and impersonal descriptions of the divine essence. It was shown that Pannenberg, for example, mixes relational and impersonal categories in his presentation of the divine essence, which results in an incoherent picture thereof. Gregory Boyd's process trinitarianism faces a similar difficulty. He attempts to break from classical metaphysics by replacing "the classical ideas of a qualityless, non-relational, unchanging substance" with the idea of "disposition" as the essence of a thing.[12] Later, however, he writes, "God's essential being is an eternal event—the event of the perfect and eternal exercising of God's disposition to be God; the eternal event of God relating to Godself with unsurpassable beauty and love; the event of God eternally becoming triune and celebrating this triunity."[13] In this system, God's essence appears to be both a disposition and an interpersonal event which is a result of that disposition, which is an untenable position.

A recognition that the persons and the nature of God are distinct realities which cannot be understood simply in terms of one another also

---

11. Polkinghorne, *Science and the Trinity*, 103.

12. Boyd, *Trinity and Process*, 114.

13. Ibid., 391.

provides theological grounding for those who would resist the postmodern urge to reduce everything to the personal. While it was a mistake of ancient philosophy to exalt the static at the expense of the dynamic, it is a perhaps more serious error to abandon the acknowledgment of stable realities in the world. Human persons, for example, have natural limits on their choices of behavior. These include both obvious physical limits regarding, for example, the inability to fly unaided, and more subtle spiritual limits. Because the persons in God have a nature which provides options for their behavior, it is reasonable to expect created reality to reflect the reality of both person and nature.

This idea, of nature providing options for personal behavior, introduces the key distinction between person and essence in the discussion of God. Rather than being a generic definition, or an abstract collection of attributes, the essence of God is the single divine reality which bears the faculties by which the Father, Son, and Spirit act as God. It is the location of the infinite potential action of God. The abilities of the divine nature provide the options amongst which the divine persons can act. By contrast, the persons of God are the realities who put this potential to use, who act using this nature, who draw upon the options provided by their shared essence to bring into existence the world that is and to act within this world.

Within this scheme, the unity of God is found at levels of both nature and person. At the level of nature, God is absolutely one. At the level of person, the distinction of the persons allows a real, unifying, eternal interdependence.

Essential Unity

This position understands "the divine nature" or "the divine essence" to refer to a reality which encompasses those aspects of God which are impersonal, those aspects which one might find in lifeless objects or machines. A robot designed to weld automobiles, for example, exists, possesses a certain quantity of knowledge, its programming, possesses certain power, and abides by certain rules which govern its behavior. It does not, however, make choices, contemplate, or relate itself to the world or persons around it. The divine nature can be understood in a distantly analogous fashion.

As noted in chapter 2, Rahner laments those who discuss the one God prior to and separate from God as three. However, this approach seems proper when dealing specifically with the unity of God, if that unity is indeed grounded in the single divine essence. In addition, the ease with which many have adopted this method may lend subtle support to the position presented here, a position which sees the one nature of God as conceptually distinct from the three persons. Treating the divine nature traditionally involves listing the divine attributes,[14] with little regard for the three divine persons.

For example, Ronald Nash's work, *The Concept of God*, examines the contemporary debates and difficulties concerning the attributes of God, God's "essential properties."[15] He is able to do so without direct reference to the three persons, and in this he is exemplary of philosophical theism.[16] Even authors who are systematic and are elsewhere thoroughly concerned with trinitarian concepts can consider the nature and essential attributes of God with little or no reference to the Trinity. Erickson considers the attributes of God and concludes:

> God is a unitary being. . . . He is a living person, a subject. . . . Much of the discussion has been carried on in terms of a substance metaphysic, in which reality is a substance possessing certain attributes. A better way of thinking may be to conceive of reality as fundamentally personal rather than impersonal. Thus, God is a subject, a person—and a very complex person at that. He is what he is, and is unique. If he did not possess the essential attributes we have discussed in this volume, he would not be the person he is. The attributes, then, are not qualities added to this nature. They are facets of his complex and rich nature.[17]

While it has been noted that Erickson believes each divine person separately possesses an instance of the divine nature, he shows how easily the divine nature can be considered with no regard for threeness.

Thus, the unity of God is grounded in the divine essence, which is an absolutely singular reality. It is a reality which is characterized by certain attributes or properties, properties which are essential both in the sense

14. Kärkkäinen, *Doctrine of God*, 57.

15. Nash, *Concept of God*.

16. Similarly, Plantinga, *Does God Have a Nature?* is conducted without any trinitarian concerns.

17. Erickson, *God the Father Almighty*, 231.

that they apply to an essence, and in the sense that the property is necessary for the existence of God. Various lists of these attributes have been presented through the centuries, and no attempt to give them definitive treatment will be made in considering the divine unity.[18] Instead the divine nature will be considered in terms of six broad attributes: omnipotence, omniscience, self-existence, goodness, incorporeality, and immutability. Because the divine nature, in which these properties inhere, is fully possessed by each of the divine persons, each divine person fully possesses the same instance of each of these properties. But it is important to note that they possess them at a distance, so to speak. For example, the fact that the Son possesses an immutable divine essence does not make the Son an immutable person.

Omnipotence

The divine nature is omnipotent. That is, it bears the potency to bring about any logically possible result. Thus it is written, "Behold, I am the LORD, the God of all flesh: is there any thing too hard for me?" and "with God all things are possible."[19] Because each member of the Trinity possesses the divine nature, each is omnipotent in his own right. Though this is not as explicitly indicated in Scripture, Jesus and the Holy Spirit are both shown to have and grant power to do supernatural things. In John 5:19, the Son's miraculous actions are imitations of the Father's. In Rom 15:19, and throughout the book of Acts, miraculous power is attributed to the Spirit. The Father is omnipotent, the Son is omnipotent, and the Holy Spirit is omnipotent.

Yet the saying of Origen remains true, "[T]he omnipotence of Father and Son is one and the same."[20] There is only one omnipotence, that of the one divine nature. Because of this the ancient belief in the unity of all *ad extra* divine actions, what Phillip Cary calls Augustine's Rule, is, for the most part, true.[21] All that God does through the exercise of his om-

---

18. For exemplary treatments, see John of Damascus, *Expositio fidei orthodoxa*, 1.8 (*NPNF2* 9:6); Aquinas, *Summa Theologiae* 1a.3–10 (BF 2:19–157); Berkhof, *Christian Faith*, 111–18; Strong, *Systematic Theology*, 243–303; Erickson, *Christian Theology*, 289–322.

19. Jer 32:27, Matt 19:26.

20. Origen, *De principiis* 1.2.10 (*ANF* 4:250).

21. Cary, "Classical Trinitarianism," 368; Augustine, *De Trinitate* 1.4.7 (*NPNF1* 3:20). For a brief discussion, see pp. 45–47 above. The reason it is not completely true is because not all divine actions are actions of the divine nature.

nipotence is necessarily an action that involves all three members. Thus creation can be, and is, rightly attributed to each member of the Trinity.[22]

While a fuller discussion of the personal distinctions within the Trinity will wait, it should be noted that, because each person can exercise his own conscious role in the actions of the one divine nature, distinctions can be made in the role each plays. The New Testament often sees subtle nuances in how each member of the Trinity is related to divine actions.[23] Bray notes that the Reformers, unwilling to divide the essence amongst the three persons as Creator, Redeemer, and Sanctifier, instead distinguished the three as having roles within every action. The Father initiates, the Son arranges, and the Spirit effects.[24] Whether or not this is an accurate scheme, it indicates that unified action based upon a single nature does not require identical personal involvement in each divine action.

Omniscience

The divine nature is omniscient. That is, it "contains" or provides access to all true propositions.[25] God's knowledge is described in the Bible as all-encompassing; "his understanding is infinite."[26] He knows the thoughts of people, and the future.[27] Because each person of the Trinity possesses the divine nature, each has access to all knowledge. The divine wisdom, which indicates God's perfect ability to act in a manner that brings about his plan over time, is grounded in his perfect knowledge of counterfactuals.

While any understanding of omniscience which is this comprehensive faces philosophical challenges,[28] there is one trinitarian difficulty concerning omniscience which this position addresses: Jesus shows

22. Gen 1:1–2, Ps 104:30, John 1:1–18, Col 1:16, Eph 3:9.

23. While this usually happens across the corpus, it occasionally can be seen in a single verse, as in 1 Cor 8:6 or 1 Pet 1:2.

24. Bray, *Doctrine of God*, 202–203; Lewis and Demarest offer an alternate ordering, Lewis and Demarest, *Integrative Theology*, 1:279.

25. This author believes this includes both statements about the future, and true counterfactual statements, but the specific content of that knowledge is not the issue here. For a discussion of the coherence of divine foreknowledge, including knowledge of true counterfactuals, see Craig, *Only Wise God*.

26. Ps 147:5.

27. Ps 129:33, 139:2, Isa 46:10, 48:3, 66:18.

28. See, for example, Nash, *Concept of God*, 67–72; Swinburne, *Coherence of Theism*, 167–83.

ignorance. His statement in the Olivet discourse, "But of that day and that hour knoweth no man, no, not the angels which are in heaven, neither the Son, but the Father," seems to distinguish between the knowledge of the Son and that of the Father.[29] Several solutions have been offered to this dilemma, the three most promising of which are seen in A. H. Strong. Strong suggests that Christ's statement of ignorance should be understood in light of the limitations of his full humanity, in light of the fact that "the divine nature itself was in some way limited and humbled during our Savior's earthly life," and in light of the fact that "there is an order of office and operation which is consistent with essential oneness and equality, but which permits the Father to be spoken of as first and the Son as second."[30] The first suggestion, which is exemplified by kenotic theories which might attribute this ignorance solely to the full humanity of Christ,[31] faces significant tension with the Chalcedonian declaration that there is no speaker other than the eternal Son present. There must be something about a divine person which makes this ignorance permissible. The second factor, that the divine nature itself was affected by the incarnation, endangers the immutability and self-existence of that nature. The third suggestion, while helpful and correct, fails to explain how this distinction in knowledge can be consistent with essential oneness.

If divine omniscience is located in the divine nature, rather than the divine persons, the distinction made by Jesus can be understood to be one of personal activity, rather than essential difference. The Son, at least at the time he speaks as Jesus, is not required to access all the information regarding the last days which the Father had accessed and determined.[32] Perhaps Jesus could know the hour and day, and in a sense does know them, but he has not chosen to actively examine them. This idea may be supported by the text, which uses forms of *oida* in both instances, a verb which can indicate personal acquaintance rather than colorless factual knowledge. John MacArthur, Gordon Lewis, and Bruce Demarest recognize the possibility that Christ chooses to be ignorant of this information, though they do so in the context of the full humanity of Christ in the

29. Mark 13:32. Cf. Matt 24:36.

30. Strong, *Systematic Theology*, 314.

31. Hagner, *Matthew 14—28*, 715.

32. John MacArthur notes that Jesus does not disavow knowledge after the resurrection. MacArthur, *Matthew 24—28*, 72.

incarnation.[33] But the basic idea, that ignorance can be a choice, fits well with a model in which the persons possess the same pool of knowledge, but that knowledge is appropriated distinctly by each divine person.

This concession, that the Father can actively know something which the Son does not, makes explicit what is implicit in this understanding of three persons. The perfect knowledge the members of the Trinity have of one another is mediated knowledge. Contra Erickson, they do not, as distinct persons, have "direct access, to the consciousness of the others," nor is it true that, "As one thinks or experiences, the others are also directly aware of this. They think the other's thoughts, feel the other's feelings."[34] Instead, their difference as persons requires genuine otherness.[35] The persons of the Trinity have perfect knowledge of one another through the divine essence, which is omniscient, and through the intentional communication amongst the divine persons. Therefore each person is omniscient, there is only one omniscience, and what each person actively knows can differ.

Self-Existence

The divine nature is self-existent. This means that the divine nature requires no other essences to exist for it to exist. This is seen in the divine name of Exod 3:14, "I am who I am," and suggested by God's priority to creation.[36]

Because a property of the divine nature is "being eternally possessed by the three divine persons," the divine nature is not independent of the divine persons. Likewise, because the persons cannot exist without the divine nature, the divine persons are not independent of the divine nature. In short, the essential self-existence, or aseity, of God means that God, as a whole, requires nothing outside himself for his existence.

The dependence of each divine person on their shared nature is a key element of the interdependence of the divine persons. Because the divine essence cannot now exist without being eternally possessed by each of the three, were one of the three to cease to exist, the divine nature would cease to exist. Because none of the three can exist without the divine nature, the loss of one of the members of the Trinity would result in the non-

---

33. MacArthur, *Matthew 24–28*, 72; Lewis and Demarest, *Integrative Theology*, 2:322.

34. Erickson, *God in Three Persons*, 225.

35. This may be one of Zizioulas's most valuable insights, Zizioulas, "Communion and Otherness," 358.

36. Lewis and Demarest, *Integrative Theology*, 1:184–85.

existence of all the members of the Trinity. Thus the shared possession of the single divine nature binds the three persons together in terms of their existence as well as their activity.

Goodness

The divine nature is good. This does not mean that it meets some external standard of "goodness," but that the moral standard of the divine nature defines goodness. The divine persons share one font of moral absolutes and one source of divine desire to act in accordance with those absolutes. Because that source is the divine nature, those absolutes and desires are, by definition, good. It is because of the perfect goodness of their nature that the divine persons "cannot be tempted with evil."[37]

This is the primary sense in which the three divine persons possess a single will. They possess a single font of preponderant desire.[38] The three divine persons share a common interest in, for example, the eternal glory of perfect divine persons, the utmost good of all reality, the reward of those who obey their proper authorities, and the punishment of those who disobey those authorities.

It is this sense of will which appears in the accounts of Jesus in Gethsemane. The Son, in possession of a human nature, possessed a human font of preponderant desire, a human will. His prayer, "O my Father, if it be possible, let this cup pass from me: nevertheless not as I will, but as thou wilt," reflects not a conflict between his personal choice and the Father's, but a conflict between the natural desire of his human nature to not die horribly and the natural desire of the divine nature to provide a means of salvation.[39] What he, as an incarnate divine person chose, was to act in accordance with the will, the desire, of the divine nature.

Assertions about divine goodness are assertions that the nature of God limits the potential behavior of the divine persons along moral lines. The infinite power of the divine nature is not literally "without limits." Just as God says of actually requiring human sacrifice, "I commanded not, nor

---

37. Jas 1:13.

38. William Wainwright notes the distinction between this "will," and "will" as choice or volition, as well as the tendency of Jonathan Edwards to assimilate the two. Wainwright, "Original Sin," 38.

39. Matt 26:39.

spake it, neither came it into my mind," so all their behavior is limited, not by weakness, but by the perfect moral goodness of their divine nature.[40]

Immutability

The divine nature is immutable. It does not, and indeed cannot, change. The Bible attests that with God there is "no variableness, neither shadow of turning," and God says of himself, "I am the Lord, I change not; therefore ye sons of Jacob are not consumed."[41] Traditionally, the fact that God is perfect means that he is necessarily immutable. Any change will either be for the better, meaning God was not perfect, or for the worse, meaning he is no longer perfect. Even seemingly neutral changes mean a perfection has been lost and another added, when it would be better for God to have both.[42] God cannot change.

Many counter that the God of the Bible clearly does, and must, change, because he acts in time, and changes courses of action. Since Hegel, concepts of God have consistently tried to tie God to change.[43] He raises Saul up as king, and then repents, choosing to replace him with David.[44] If nothing else, the incarnation of the divine Word involves genuine change in God. Some limit is therefore necessary on the concept of immutability.

Several limitations on immutability have been suggested. Isaak Dorner, for example, holds that God is immutable not in his essence, but in his ethic. He believes that the Bible requires God to participate in time, ignorance, and vacillation, but to be immutable in his ethic, which is love.[45] Process theism moves divine immutability to an abstract potentiality, which is to say it removes it from reality.

This position offers a more helpful and complete understanding of what is immutable in God. It is God's nature that does not change. As noted above, that nature provides an unchanging standard of absolute values upon which the persons can act. The persons, acting according to that constant nature, may change their behavior, because it is that nature, and not they as persons, who are immutable.

40. Jer 19:5.
41. Jas 1:17, Mal 3:6.
42. Charnock, *Existence and Attributes of God*, 1:319–21, 333.
43. Langdon Gilkey, "God," in *New Handbook of Christian Theology*, 207–8.
44. 1 Sam 15:35—16:1.
45. Dorner, *Divine Immutability*, 165–66.

This position fits well with the supreme example of divine change, the incarnation. In the incarnation, a divine person, not the divine nature, changed, and was made flesh. The Fathers took pains to clarify that the divine nature did not undergo any change in the incarnation, in which there are "two natures, unconfusedly, immutably, indivisibly, inseparably [united], and that without the distinction of natures being taken away by such union, but rather the peculiar property of each nature being preserved and being united in one Person and subsistence, not separated or divided into two persons, but one and the same Son."[46] So, while the divine persons cannot be changed, they can engage in diverse actions within the range of good potential actions which their unchanging divine nature provides.

Is God "endangered" if the persons are not immutable? No. While that which changes may be liable to destruction, the destruction of a divine person would entail the destruction of the divine being, which is itself immutable and eternal. Nor are the divine persons rendered unreliable, because the spring of their desires is itself unchanging. The divine nature is immutable, and its immutability provides intense stability to the three divine persons who possess it.

Incorporeality

The divine nature is incorporeal. "God is spirit."[47] This means that it in no sense occupies space, and is in no sense composed of physical matter or energy. It has no parts, and no extension, and is therefore invisible.[48] Pannenberg's concept that the divine nature is the infinite field which transcends space and time while encompassing them may not be entirely accurate, but it is a provocative and helpful model.[49]

Those who would take too univocally the biblical descriptions of divine emotions would do well to consider the implications of divine incorporeality for divine passibility. The divine persons, apart from the Son in the incarnation, lack the physiological components which are central to human emotion. Cyril of Alexandria notes that "the divine cannot suffer

46. *NPNF2* 14:264–65.

47. John 4:24.

48. Job 23:9, John 1:18, Rom 1:20, Col 1:15, 1 Tim 1:17, Heb 11:27.

49. Pannenberg, "God as Spirit," 789–91; Pannenberg, "Theological Appropriation," in *BE*, 428–30.

since it is incorporeal."[50] God the Father has no limbic system, no adrenal glands, no heart, and no blood vessels. What then can it mean to say that he "feels" anger? Certainly the Bible ascribes emotions to God, but to take those less analogously than did Aquinas is too confuse God's incorporeal existence with the corporeal existence of his creatures.

This does not mean that God is anti-emotional. As the creator of humanity, God is responsible for human emotions. Moses is at times seen to act in accordance with God's will as a result of his emotions.[51] Once he possessed human physiology, the Son experienced unabashedly a range of human emotion.[52] But to suggest that the divine persons, or the divine nature, experience emotions without explaining what this means for an incorporeal being is a dangerous confusion of categories.

Interestingly, Clark Pinnock seems to recognize this difficulty when he, after arguing for God's passibility, begins to retreat. He warns that care must be taken in ascribing suffering to God, for he cannot experience physical pain, because he has no body, nor loneliness, because he is triune, nor fear, for he is securely God. In the end, his position is reminiscent of the classical explanation of God's love, when he writes, "Change occurs in the world and affects God when he becomes aware of it. When that change involves innocent suffering, God responds tenderly to it."[53] Similarly, Charles Taliaferro attempts to equate divine displeasure at sin with sorrow, writing, "It still remains impossible to not construe the judgment of profound, concerned disapproval . . . as sorrow."[54] Certainly he is free to write that, but he has simply redefined sorrow, not demonstrated how God might experience something like human sorrow.[55] An incorporeal God lacks any physical parts, and does not experience physical sensations, including emotional ones.

---

50. Cyril of Alexandria, *Letters 1–50*, 4.5.

51. E.g., Exod 32:19–20, Num 16:15–35, 31:13–20. Interestingly, no mention is made of Moses's anger when he kills the Egyptian in Exod 2, or when he strikes the rock in Num 20.

52. E.g., Matt 26:37–38, Mark 3:5, John 11:35.

53. Pinnock, "Systematic Theology," 119.

54. Taliaferro, "The Passibility of God," 221. Cf. Wolterstorff, "Suffering Love," 227.

55. The reader will recognize that, at this moment, he knows many things are occurring of which he disapproves but that he is not necessarily sad because of those events.

Conclusion

In all these respects, God is one. They possess a single omnipotent, omniscient, self-existent, good, immutable, incorporeal nature. Each person fully possesses that nature, which cannot exist without its attributes, or without being possessed by each divine person. Similarly, no divine person cannot exist without the shared divine nature. Thus, the essential unity of God is seen first and foremost in the singular divine nature, which results in essential interdependence, singular purpose, and singular action. Now, the character of the divine persons according to this understanding of trinitarian unity will be addressed.

Personal Distinction

Most of the metaphysical attributes of the Trinity are seen to inhere in their divine nature. The singular divine nature, fully possessed by the three divine persons, strongly grounds the unity of God. It remains to be shown what "three persons" means, and how the distinctiveness of the divine persons serves to strengthen, rather than weaken, the reality of divine unity.

As shown in chapter 3, stating that God is three distinct persons without specifying the manner in which those persons are distinguished results in a weak trinitarian position.[56] In this proposed doctrine of the Trinity, the three persons in God are distinguished by distinct consciousnesses, wills, and identifying relations. It is in these specific areas, which might be termed the personal character of the divine persons, that God is three.

The first aspect of divine distinction, that of consciousness, is notoriously difficult to define. What is intended here is that each person of the Trinity is his own self-aware active thought process. The thoughts of the Son are those immediately only of the Son. While the Father can have perfect knowledge of those thoughts, both through the divine omniscience and through interpersonal communication, they do not arise in him immediately. Throughout eternity, each divine person is aware of himself as a thinking subject, confronted from without his person with the thoughts of other thinking subjects.

As noted earlier, the second aspect of personal character, will, can have two meanings, each of which has two aspects. "Will" can mean ei-

56. See pp. 94–98 above.

ther preponderant desire or volitional choice. In addition, the term can be used either for the faculty which produces that desire or choice, or for the desire or choice produced in a given situation. Thus, "will" can have at least four specific senses. When one says, "That decree is the will of the king," he means by "will" the choice produced in a given situation. On the other hand, when one says, "That is a strong-willed child," "will" refers to the source of preponderant desire. Thus, the statement that each divine person includes a distinct will must be clarified.

Apart from the incarnation, it is in only one of those senses, that of a faculty for volitional choice, that there are three wills in God. As noted in the discussion of nature, God has a single source of preponderant desire, his perfectly good moral nature. While each divine person has an independent faculty for volitional choice, the incarnation certifies that those faculties do not result in divergent divine choices. Throughout his earthly ministry, Jesus chooses to act in line with the Father's choices.[57] Even in the sorrow of Gethsemane, and despite the fact that the Son possesses, as a man, a source of preponderant desire distinct from the Father's, the Son exercises his faculty for choice to go to the cross, which is exactly the choice the Father had made.[58]

This certain unity of choice is connected to the third element of divine personal distinction, that of identifying relations. "Identifying" here does not refer so much to human ability to distinguish the persons, but the ability of each divine person to answer for himself, "Who am I?" What makes the genuine distinction of three self-aware centers of volition possible is the relations amongst them, eternal relations which give each divine person an eternal identity. On this count, Zizioulas seems to be correct, writing:

> Thirdly, and most significantly, otherness is not moral or psychological but *ontological*. We cannot tell what each Person is; we can only say *who* He is. Each Person in the Holy Trinity is different not by way of difference of qualities but by way of simple affirmation of being who He is.
>
> As a result of this, finally, otherness is inconceivable apart from *relationship*. Father, Son and Spirit are all names indicat-

---

57. E.g., John 5:30–36, 6:38–40, 9:4.
58. Isa 53:10, Matt 26:53, Acts 2:23, Phil 2:8, Col 2:14, Heb 12:2.

ing relationship. No Person can be different unless He is related. Communion does not threaten otherness; it generates it.[59]

Each person of the Trinity identifies himself by his relationship to the other two. In eternity, the Father has no identity other than being the Father of the Son. The Son has no identity other than being the Son of the Father. The Spirit knows himself only as the Spirit of the Father and Son.

Because those relations have an eternal hierarchal form, the choices of the divine persons made in the light of each person's identity cannot diverge. The Son knows himself only as the Son of the Father, and knows that, as a Son, he has a certain role in the Godhead. Making choices contrary to that role would not only violate the Father's will, but would violate himself, violate his own identity. Similarly the Spirit, who knows himself as the Spirit of God, the Spirit of Christ, and the Holy Spirit, cannot behave in a manner contrary to who he knows himself to be.

The assertion that God is three persons is nothing other than an attempt to embrace the New Testament picture of God. In the New Testament, the Father, Son, and Holy Spirit are seen to be distinct centers of action capable of relating to persons individually while acting with perfect unity of purpose. This description of the divine persons, which sees each as a volitional center of consciousness identified by distinct relations to the two other divine persons, attempts to account for that New Testament depiction. It also provides further grounds for the unity of God, as the next section will show.

Personal Interdependence

As shown in chapter 3, one essential element of Erickson's understanding of trinitarian unity is the concept of interdependence.[60] He states that the three divine persons "can only exist as part of the Triune God," and that "each is dependent on the others for life, and for what he is."[61] While it was shown that Erickson's thoroughly egalitarian understanding of the divine persons cannot provide a reasonable ground for these assertions, personal interdependence complements essential unity in a full understanding of trinitarian unity.

---

59. Zizioulas, "Communion and Otherness," 353.

60. See pp. 81–82 above.

61. Erickson, *Making Sense of the Trinity*, 61; Erickson, *God in Three Persons*, 264.

Traditionally, and as thoroughly developed by Pannenberg, the personal interdependence within the Trinity has been connected to the economic names and roles of the divine persons.[62] While Rahner's Rule may not demand full acceptance, one must take seriously the economic realities of Father, Son, and Holy Spirit if one is to have any chance of understanding the eternal personal relations within the godhead. If God is not, in himself, Father, Son, and Holy Spirit, then there is no means by which man can know who God really is.

This understanding of trinitarian unity will suggest that the persons of the Godhead share asymmetrical relations of personal dependence in terms of both existence and identity. The Father depends upon the Son for his personal identity. The Son depends upon the Father for his personal existence and his personal identity. The Spirit depends upon the Father for his personal existence, and the Father and the Son for his personal identity, while both Father and Son depend on him for their respective identities.

The Father

From the benign subordinationism of Tertullian and Justin, to the exaggeration of Rahner, to the carefully formulated positions of the Cappadocians and Pannenberg, there is a clear tradition of assigning the Father a pride of place within the Godhead. As Erickson acknowledges, this tradition has *prima facie* biblical support.[63] The Father sends the Son and Spirit, is head of the Son, is imitated by the Son, is the source of all good gifts, gives the Holy Spirit, and has his Redeemer and his Spirit.[64] While the New Testament clearly recognizes at least an economic dependence of the Son and Spirit on the Father, and an hierarchal ordering according to that dependence, no text indicates an inverted ordering of dependence or authority.[65]

---

62. For example, Tertullian, *Adversus Praxean* 10 (*ANF* 3:604–5); Origen, *Princ.* 1.2.3 (*ANF* 4:246);Dionysius of Alexandria, *Fragment* 2.8 (*ANF* 6:93); Athanasius, *Orationes contra Arianos* 1.5.14 (*NPNF2* 4:314). For a full discussion of Pannenberg, see chapter 5 above.

63. Erickson, *Making Sense of the Trinity*, 86, 90; Erickson, *God in Three Persons*, 309.

64. Gen 1:2, Isa 44:6, Matt 10:40, Mark 9:37, Luke 11:13, John 9:4, 10:37, 14:26, 1 Cor 11:3, Jas 1:17, 1 John 4:14.

65. Horrell, "Biblical Model," 415.

The person of the Father depends upon noone else for his personal existence. He is therefore, as Gregory Nazianzen puts it, the "Unoriginate Father," who, Athanasius says, "hath His being from Himself."[66] Nevertheless, Athanasius rejects Arian attempts to refer to God the Father as "Unoriginate," both because it is unscriptural, and because the Arians did so to exclude the Son from the Godhead. In the name "Father" his necessary relation to the Son, rather than his accidental relation to the world, is revealed.[67]

This idea, that the term Father implies a necessary relation to the Son, is the basis for the Father's personal interdependence. Yet it is not a dependence of existence; that the Father is does not depend on the Son. It is a dependence of identity; who the Father is depends on the Son. Who the Father is cannot be understood apart from the Son. This may be the truth in Rahner's theology of self-expression. In begetting the Son, the Father is not only known to humanity as Father, but known to himself.[68] His identity as Father is only possible because of the Son.

Thus the Father does not enjoy any logical priority over the Son. If one begins by thinking of the Father as the sole possessor of the divine essence, one is immediately confronted with the fact that he is Father. There can therefore be no "when the Son was not," in either a logical or chronological sense. That the Father's identity is eternally constituted by his relationship to the Son is the basis for understanding the inherent simultaneity of the Father and Son.

The Son

The Son, conversely, depends on the Father for both his personal existence and identity. He is eternally begotten of the Father and eternally Son of the Father. Thus the relation of dependence between the Father and the Son is asymmetrical. While the Father and Son depend upon one another for their respective identities, the Son depends upon the Father for his personal existence as well.

As Jesus, the Son speaks of his dependence upon the Father in terms difficult to restrict to the incarnation. That the Son has life in himself

66. Gregory Nazianzen, *Orations* 33:17 (*NPNF2* 7:334); Athanasius, *Expositio fidei* 1 (*NPNF2* 4:84).

67. Athanasius, *De decretis* 7 (*NPNF2* 4:169–72); Athanasius, *C. Ar.* 1.9 (*NPNF2* 4:324–26).

68. Karl Rahner, *Theological Investigations*, 4:236.

has been given to him by the Father.[69] All things, all authority, and all judgment have been given to the Son by the Father.[70] Finally, the Son is begotten of the Father, a concept which formed the focus of the historical understanding of his asymmetrical dependence.[71]

This understanding is exemplified in the Alexandrian theologians. John Behr recognizes it in Origen, who writes that "the existence of the Son is derived from the Father."[72] Dionysius of Alexandria similarly writes that "the Son has existence not from Himself, but from the Father."[73] The name Son, accompanied by the language of begetting, implies dependency.

This dependency, however, is both ineffable and eternal. Gregory Nazianzen is careful to limit what can be inferred from the language of Sonship:

> In my opinion He is called Son because He is identical with the Father in Essence; and not only for this reason, but also because He is OF Him. And He is called Only-Begotten, not because He is the only Son and of the Father alone, and only a Son; but also because the manner of His Sonship is peculiar to Himself and not shared by bodies.[74]

One can conclude that the Son is from the Father, having the Father's essence, but little more than that. This begetting is not a temporal event, which would give ontological priority to the Father, but an eternal one.[75] The Father eternally begets the Son. He is eternally the ground of the Son's personal existence.

Some might suggest that any understanding of the Son which makes him asymmetrically dependent on the Father amounts to ontological subordination. However, this is not the case. Because the Father possesses the divine nature, rather than "being" the divine nature, the Son is able to have the same relationship to that nature that the Father does, and therefore be just as fully God. On earth, the source of what one possesses does not

---

69. John 5:26.

70. Matt 11:27, 28:18, John 5:22, 13:3.

71. Ps 2:7, Acts 13:33, Heb 1:5–6, 5:5, 1 John 5:1. The occurrences of "only begotten" are omitted due to the controversy surrounding the term.

72. Origen, *Princ.* 1.2.11 (*ANF* 4:251); Behr, *Way to Nicaea*, 187.

73. Dionysius of Alexandria, *Fragment* 4.2 (*ANF* 6:92).

74. Gregory Nazianzen, *Or.* 4.20 (*NPNF2* 7:316). Cf. Basil, *Epistulae* 38.4 (*NPNF2* 8:139).

75. Athanasius, *Exp. fid.* 1 (*NPNF2* 4:84), Williams, *Arius*, 273.

change the extent to which one possesses it. Whether it is earned, innate, or gifted, a possession is possessed.

The Son's identity is also grounded in his relationship to the Father. He is "the brightness of his glory, and the express image of his person." He is ever the Word who is towards God and is God.[76] This eternal identity is manifested in, but in no way depends upon, his actions in history. He is consistently presented as the Father's agent, the one who ever does the will of the Father.[77] If the tradition which views the Angel of the Lord in the Old Testament as the pre-incarnate Christ is correct, this lends further support to the Son's eternal identity as the Son.

Recently, the language of "eternal functional subordination" has been used to describe the relationship of the Son to the Father. This language, while open to correct interpretation, is problematic for several reasons. The first is that many have difficulty distinguishing the term "functional" from the term "economic" when it comes to God. The concept of imma-nent or eternal function seems incoherent to many. To these individu-als, the language of "eternal functional subordination" seems to blur the line between God's self-existence and his relationship to creation, and therefore appears to repeat the failed Logos Doctrine, or even the error of Arianism. The second is that "subordination" suggests activity; either the Father subordinates the son, or the Son subordinates himself to the Father. Yet the Father-Son relationship in God is not an activity in that sense, it is who the Father and Son are. The Father does not tell the Son to obey, and the Son does not swallow his pride and obey. The Son ever is the Son, and when the Father sends him into the world, he delights to do the will of the Father.

The third difficulty is not with the language itself, but with the moti-vation that many assume to be behind it. There are those who seek to base human sex roles on the "eternal functional subordination" they see in the Trinity. This move, however, is both unwarranted and unnecessary. It is unwarranted in that there is no reason to believe that the man-woman relationship is identical to the Father-Son relationship. It is unneces-sary because even if the man-woman relationship is meant to reflect the Father-Son relationship, the economic roles of Father and Son suffice to show how men and women should relate in the economy. The economy,

---

76. Heb 1:3, John 1:1.

77. Gen 1:1, Rom 5:11, 1 Cor 8:6, Heb 1:2, Col 1:16–18.

of course, does not end with the regeneration of individuals. At least until Christ delivers all things back to the Father, the economy persists, and the Son continues to do the will of the Father.[78] Christ has noted a similar time when some aspects of human sexuality will end: the resurrection.[79] Thus, to root the earthly relationships of men and women in the home and the church in the "eternal functional subordination" of the Son appears to be an unnecessary overreaching.

Rather than speaking of the "eternal functional subordination," of the Son, one might prefer to speak of the "eternal filial identity" of the Son. The Son is always Son. It is who he is. It is not a function of what he does, though it does determine his behavior within and without the Godhead. But the Son knows himself as the Son of the Father. His personal decisions and actions are guided by that self-knowledge. The answer to who he was that Jesus most approved was that of Peter: He is the Christ, the Son of the living God.[80] That is who the Son is, and it is no surprise that one who knows himself as the Son of the Father would be sent by the Father, would do the Father's will, and would do all that he could so that the Father might be glorified.

The Spirit

Understanding the Holy Spirit's place within the immanent Trinity has been notoriously difficult. Justin is willing to afford him worship, adoration, and third place with the Father and Son, but says little else.[81] Cyril Richardson sees Augustine as the first to provide a real place for the Holy Spirit within the Trinity, and David Coffey seems to agree, noting that the Cappadocians were content to simply affirm essential unity.[82] Thomas Weinandy believes that churches in both the East and the West have a problem with the role of the Holy Spirit in the Trinity, because both hold to a sequential emanationism.[83] Congar notes that, while discourse regarding the Father and Son can draw from their relational names, "The term 'Spirit', however, has none of these associations. The whole terminology

---

78. 1 Cor 15:24–25.

79. Matt 22:30, Luke 10:34–36.

80. Matt 16:16.

81. Justin Martyr, *First Apology* 6, 11 (*ANF* 1:164, 166).

82. Cyril C. Richardson, *Doctrine of the Trinity*, 44; Augustine, *Trin.* 6.9.10 (*NPNF1* 3:102); Coffey, "Proper Mission," 233–35.

83. Weinandy, *Father's Spirit of Sonship*, 7–10.

used to speak of the third Person is common and absolute."[84] After noting problems with Rahner's treatment of the Holy Spirit, W. J. Hill graciously and accurately acknowledges, "If Rahner's trinitarianism at this point is somewhat less convincing—and it is—it should be remembered that all trinitarian theologies suffer a similar impoverishment when it comes to explaining the Third Person within God."[85]

Nevertheless, any attempt to demonstrate personal interdependence amongst the members of the Trinity must consider the place of the Holy Spirit within the Godhead. However, this will not be so much an attempt to explain the Holy Spirit as an attempt to see how interdependence in terms of personal existence and personal identity might apply to him. Before this attempt is made, some offered understandings of the immanent place of the Spirit, including the *filioque*, will be briefly considered.

The Eastern and Western churches have historically held to different models of the Trinity. The East holds to what Coffey calls "the procession model," in which the Son proceeds from the Father, from whom the Spirit also proceeds, through the Son. There is thus a linear movement out from the Father, which Coffey views as problematic, because it provides no route of return to the Father.[86] Weinandy offers a similar description of the Orthodox position, and believes it should be rejected because it seems to mean little by "through the Son," it cannot distinguish procession from begetting, and it distinguishes the persons to an extent that endangers perichoresis.[87]

In the Western tradition, the Spirit is not at the end of a processional chain. Instead, he exists between the Father and the Son as the mutual love which they bestow upon each other, proceeding from both.[88] It is this idea of "double procession" which is captured in the *filioque*, the addition to the creed that the Spirit proceeds from the Father and the Son. It is important to note, however, that the Roman Catholic tradition sets strict limits on how this procession can be understood as double. As was clarified at the Second Council of Lyons, the Spirit proceeds from both as from a single

84. Congar, *I Believe*, vii.

85. Hill, *Three-Personed God*, 139.

86. Coffey, "Proper Mission," 231–32.

87. Weinandy, *Father's Spirit of Sonship*, 7, 9.

88. Ibid., 6; Coffey, "Proper Mission," 234. See p. 20–21 above for this thought in Augustine.

principle, by a single spiration.[89] Rahner notes that the Spirit ought not be referred to as the "mutual love" of the Father and Son, because that would imply two acts of loving.[90] Understood in this way, the *filioque* is not so much an assertion that the Spirit proceeds from the person of the Father and the person of the Son, but a denial that he proceeds from the person of either. It is an assertion that he proceeds from the one essence of God, which the Father and Son share.

Weinandy has offered an alternative proposal from within the Western tradition. He believes that locating the Spirit between the Father and Son as their mutual love inadequately conveys the activity, and therefore the genuine personhood, of the Spirit. He contends that "The Son, being begotten in the Spirit, simultaneously loves the Father in the same Spirit by which he himself is begotten (is Loved)."[91] The Spirit is not a by-product of a distinct Father-Son relationship, but instead is foundational to that relationship. He writes, "The Spirit proceeds from the Father and the Son and does so by conforming each to be in relation to the other, and so becomes distinct in himself in his mutual relation to them as the love by which they come to be who they are for one another."[92] Weinandy sees similar thoughts in the work of Jürgen Moltmann, who writes, "The Father begets the Son in the power of the eternal Spirit."[93] By placing the Spirit between the Father and the Son as the foundation of their relationship, Weinandy believes he has provided a clear articulation of the Spirit's proper place in the immanent Trinity.

What should be done with these proposals? Can a decision be made between the *per filium* and the *filioque*? What of Weinandy, who, rather than reading the *filioque* as a statement that makes the Spirit third in God, reinterprets it to place the Spirit between the Father and the Son?

It does not appear that these questions can be settled by direct statements from Scripture. While Weinandy correctly notes that New Testament statements associate the possession of the Spirit with sonship, both in the life of Jesus and the life of the believer,[94] it is unclear the extent

89. Denzinger, *Enchiridion Symbolorum*, 275 (Para 850).

90. Rahner, *Trinity*, 106–7.

91. Weinandy, *Father's Spirit of Sonship*, 17.

92. Ibid., 79.

93. Ibid., 19–20; Moltmann, *Spirit of Life*, 71–72.

94. Weinandy, *Father's Spirit of Sonship*, 27–45. Cf. Matt 1:18, 3:16–17, 4:1, Mark 14:36, Luke 1:35, John 3, 14–16, Romans 8, Gal 4:6, 1 John 4:13, etc.

to which those statements can be read back into the eternal begetting of the Son, should be understood to express a causal, rather than correlative, relationship between possession of the Spirit and sonship, and are to be understood in relation to the true humanity of Jesus. If the interpretation of John 15:26 sufficed to settle the question of the *filioque*, it is certain that it would have been settled long ago.

Other considerations, therefore, must drive the answers to these questions. Within the trinitarian system described in this proposal, the *filioque* makes little sense, at least if it is to be understood as the Second Council of Lyons understood it. The person of the Spirit proceeding from the divine essence results in the confusion of categories this proposal believes must be kept distinct; if they are not, the divine essence becomes a fourth active principle within the Godhead. This, "as from a single principle" reading of the *filioque* also results in the seemingly contradictory conclusion that the Spirit proceeds from himself, for the divine essence is his as much as it is the Father's or the Son's. Finally, since this proposal rejects the tenet that the divine persons "are" the divine essence, Anselm's Rule that all must be one except when precluded by relations of opposition is also rejected.[95] This means that there is no real warrant for attributing the procession of the Holy Spirit to the Father and the Son as a single principle.

Weinandy's proposal, that the Son is begotten in the Holy Spirit who therefore serves as the Spirit by which both Father and Son are Father and Son does not face these difficulties. However, it faces subtle problems of its own. The first is that, in making the Spirit the active bond between the Father and the Son, Weinandy has separated the Father from the Son. Consider the following:

> The Holy Spirit does not have a distinct name because he subsists precisely as the one in whom the Father and the Son are named. The Father subsists in relation to the Son (and so is named Father) *only in the Holy Spirit* by whom he begot the Son. The Son subsists in relation to the Father (and so is named Son) *only in the Spirit* who conformed him to be Son.[96]

Weinandy believes that, "The Father and Son experience one another in and through the Holy Spirit."[97] Now, if these statements simply mean that

95. For a discussion of Anselm's Rule, see pp. 45–47 above.
96. Weinandy, *Father's Spirit of Sonship*, 84.
97. Ibid., 105.

the Father and Son are always with the Spirit in their relationship to one another, they seem correct. However, Weinandy's thesis, if it breaks the ground that he says it does, appears to mean more. He appears to understand the Spirit as the mediator between the Son and the Father. While Weinandy draws attention to the biblical texts that support this notion in the life of Jesus, he ignores the preponderance of the evidence, in which Jesus expresses an immediate relationship to the Father as the basis of his work and authority. In John 10, for example, Jesus speaks of the Father's pleasure in him, his obedience to the Father, his Father's care for those in his hand, and his unity with the Father. At no point is the Spirit in view.

While Weinandy refers to John 14–16, he seems to miss the tenor of the passage. In John 14, Jesus speaks of the Spirit as one whom he and the Father would give the disciples. In John 15, when Jesus discusses his unity with the Father, he mentions the Spirit, but not as one who connects him to his Father. In John 16, the Spirit does not bestow what is the Father's on Jesus, but takes from what Jesus has received from the Father and bestows it on the disciples. Clearly, the Spirit is involved in Jesus' relationship to the Father. But it is hard to see him between them.

The second problem is that Weinandy is vulnerable to the same criticism which he levies against the Orthodox. It seems hard to give any content to the statement, "The Father begets the Son in the Spirit," which does not endanger the concept of ineffable begetting by introducing material illustrations. Weinandy falls into this in his text, writing, "The depiction of the Father begetting his Son in the womb of Mary by the Holy Spirit becomes, I believe, a temporal icon of his eternally begetting the Son by the Holy Spirit." Clearly Weinandy does not mean that the Holy Spirit is the means by which the Father begets the Son in some heavenly womb, but it is hard to see what "in the Spirit" adds to the concept of the Father begetting from himself a Son who shares his nature. It either distances the Father from the Son, which is undesirable, implies the Father is unable, of himself, to beget the Son, which is absurd, or makes the Father and the Spirit the parents of the Son, which is a dangerous step towards polytheism.

Does the Greek *per filium* fare any better than these Western positions? One cannot help but note that it is "by the Son" that God created and sustains creation.[98] It is understandable, then, that some believe the

98. 1 Cor 8:6, Col 1:16, Heb 1:2–6.

phrase ascribes an ontological superiority over the Spirit to the Son and the Father. Even if the phrase does not imply ontological subordination, what reason is there for projecting the biblical portrayal of the Son's role in God's dealing with creation into the trinitarian relations? There does not appear to be any. While the Spirit is certainly the Spirit of Christ, there is no reason to read that "of" as "who eternally proceeds from." It suffices that the Spirit belongs to the Son, who has all things that the Father has, for he has received them from the Father.[99]

Rather than opting to follow either the *filioque* or the *per filium*, this position would suggest that neither is correct. There is no relation of origin between the Son and the Spirit. Instead, the Spirit should be understood to eternally proceed from the Father, to eternally depend asymmetrically on the Father alone for his personal existence. The begetting of the Son and the procession of the Spirit can be understood to be parallel acts, the stretching forth of God's two hands.

What of the Weinandy's accusation, that such a position fails to distinguish procession from begetting?[100] This accusation only makes sense in a system where the means of origin determines the character of a divine person. The traditional Roman Catholic system, in which each person is considered a substantive relation within the one Godhead, must distinguish these relations to distinguish the persons. However, it is not the relations of origin which determine the character of the divine persons, but the character of the divine persons which results in the names of the relations of origin. The asymmetrical relationship of the Son to the Father is called begetting because it is a Son who comes from the Father, not vice versa. The Spirit is said to proceed because when the Father brings forth his Spirit it is appropriate to call that procession. Because the Spirit comes forth from the Father he is God; because he and the Father relate as Father and Spirit, he is Spirit.

Like the Son and the Father, the Spirit has an identity determined by his relationship to the other two divine persons. He is the Spirit of God, the Spirit of the Father, the Spirit of the Lord, and the Spirit of Christ.[101] That is his identity, his eternal self-understanding of who he is. He is able

99. John 13:3, 16:15.

100. Weinandy, *Father's Spirit of Sonship*, 9.

101. Matt 3:16, 10:20, Rom 8:9, 1 Cor 2:11, 2 Cor 3:3, 17, et. al.

to distinguish himself from the Father and the Son because they know him as their Spirit, and he knows himself as such.

While it was not mentioned earlier in discussions of the Father and the Son, it should be pointed out that their identities are reciprocally determined by their eternal relationship to the Spirit. On this point, Congar draws attention to the work of Augustine, who noted that the fact that Father and Spirit are not reciprocal terms does not mean they cannot describe a reciprocal relationship.[102] Just as the Spirit is the Spirit of the Father, so the Father is the Father from whom the Spirit proceeds. Just as the Spirit is the Spirit of Christ, so the Son is the Son who has the Spirit who proceeds from the Father. While the Father and Son could have existed had the Spirit not done so, they would not have existed as the Father and Son who they actually are. Their identities, their self-definitions, are tied to their eternal relationship with the Spirit who proceeds from the Father and who is the Spirit of them both.

Thus, despite rejecting his thesis, this position agrees in a sense with Weinandy that, "While the Son and the Holy Spirit come forth from the Father, yet in the coming forth all three persons become who they are, and they do so precisely in reciprocally interacting upon one another, simultaneously fashioning one another to be who they are and so becoming who they are in themselves."[103] While the Son and the Spirit depend upon the Father for their personal existence, it is the interpersonal identifying relationships which eternally and equally unite the three persons while providing order within the Godhead.

Conclusion

God is one. He possesses one nature, one omnipotent, omniscient faculty which defines moral perfection. God is three persons, three centers of consciousness, identity, and volitional choice, who possess that one nature. While that one nature is possessed by three persons, the three persons are not disconnected from one another at the personal level. They depend upon one another, for the Son and the Spirit depend on the Father for their personal existence. All three depend upon one another for their eternal identity, for it is their eternal fellowship which "persons" each member, identifying him not to mankind, but to himself.

102. Congar, *I Believe*, 85; Augustine, *Trin.* 5.12.13 (*NPNF1* 3:93–94).
103. Weinandy, *Father's Spirit of Sonship*, 78–79.

DIVINE ACTION

Augustine thought it prudent to consider which person of the Trinity appeared in various passages of the Old Testament, if only to show that there was no reason to exclude the whole Trinity, united as one God, from those appearances.[104] While it does appear difficult to reach certain conclusions in such an exercise, this section will attempt to suggest what aspects of divine action are united as actions of the divine essence and what aspects can properly be assigned to a specific divine person.

All actions carried out through the omnipotence of the divine essence necessarily involve all three divine persons, for each of them fully possesses that divine essence. Thus, any physical action which God undertakes in the material creation should be understood to be the action of all three divine persons. Their degree of involvement in that action may differ. One divine person may take the lead in initiating a particular action, even to the extent that his is the only active volitional choice for that action, while the other two divine persons simply concur. In these instances, "appropriating" divine action to a specific divine person is permissible. At other times, each divine person may have a distinct volitional role in a particular divine action, as in biblical descriptions of creation.[105] In these descriptions, it appears that the Father is the initiator of creation, the Son the agent and goal of creation, and the Spirit the effector of creation. Yet because creation is an action carried out by means of the divine essence, each person is fully responsible for creation. Miraculous healings and transformations are likewise actions of the entire Trinity, for they are actions involving the omnipotence of the one divine essence.

However, each divine person can undertake distinct divine actions in his own person. The Incarnation is, of course, the clearest example of this. While the miraculous creation of a human being to be the Son's humanity is seen to involve other members of the Trinity,[106] the Son is the only person who is Jesus. The Son alone possesses his humanity, making choices which are carried out with his physical body. Yet the miraculous deeds he performed, because they went beyond the potential of his human nature, necessarily involved all the members of the Trinity, because they involved the exercise of the divine nature.

104. Augustine, *Trin.* 2.8.14–2.18.33 (*NPNF*1 3:43–54).
105. Genesis 1, Col 1:16, Heb 1:1–3, 2:10.
106. Luke 1:35.

The indwelling of the Spirit is likewise a personal action, distinct to the Spirit. It is distinct not in the sense that the Father and Son do not also dwell with the believer,[107] but in the sense that the person of the Spirit relates directly to the person of the believer in a manner distinct from the manner in which the Father and Son relate to the believer. The Spirit guides believers to truth not by miraculously altering their brains so as to provide new information, but by prompting their persons to properly access knowledge already possessed.[108] His guidance does not take the form of omnipotent compulsion, but personal communication, as the Spirit introduces divine thoughts into the human person's thought process. When the inspiration of the Bible occurs in this fashion, it is the action of the Holy Spirit, and not an action of the Trinity that is appropriated to him. Interpersonal communication and relationship are personal, not essential, actions.

It is more difficult to determine whether the manifestations of God to the Patriarchs are actions of a single divine person and, if so, which person. Were the manifestations carried out physically by extant, personal angels, or by ad hoc creations? Were the burning bush, and the pillar of fire which guided Israel manifestations of angelic beings speaking and acting on behalf of God, or persistent creative acts in which God brought light and sound into being by the divine nature? In the former case, it is possible that a divine person communicated the divine message and decision to an angel, and the angel communicated it to man.[109] However, deciding which person communicated the message is nearly impossible. If, on the other hand, these manifestations are immediate creations via the divine nature, they are necessarily the action of all three persons. In either case, it seems reasonable to recognize the Father as the initiator of the message, due to his identity within the Godhead. To the extent that appearances of the Angel of the Lord conform to the filial identity of the Son, it might be best to retain the traditional understanding that the Angel is a personal manifestation of the Son, though the physical reality of the Angel is a creation of the divine nature.

---

107. John 14:23.

108. Clearly, a lengthy discourse on human nature, and the relationship of the mind/person to the brain, is beyond the scope of this work. Suffice it to say that this author works from a model which views the human person as a distinct entity from the human body which nevertheless supervenes over it and fully possesses it.

109. Gal 3:19 and Heb 2:2 both associate the communication of the law with angels.

MEETING THE CRITERIA

After exposing the positions of Rahner, Erickson, Zizioulas, and Pannenberg to rigorous critiques, it would be unconscionable not to do the same to this proposed understanding of the unity of the Trinity. As such, potential difficulties with the historical, theological, and Christological criteria introduced in the first chapter, and others unique to this construction, will now be confronted. However, it must be admitted from the start that human authors tend to have a blind spot where their own constructions are concerned. This is not an unbiased examination of options, but a partisan defense of a position believed to be the best available.

Historical Difficulties?

It was concluded in chapter 1 that the dominant historical understanding of divine unity included two elements. It focused on the divine essence as a genuine *res* which the three persons shared and which each fully was. It also acknowledged that divine unity was a reality which affected everything about the God of the Bible, the Father, Son, and Spirit.

The position proposed here is perfectly in line with these dominant elements. It believes the divine essence is a concrete, not to say material, reality, of which there is only one. This essence is the seat of the essential divine attributes. Because God is one in this sense, all his external actions which involve the exercise of the essential divine attributes are one. This corresponds roughly with, and attempts to clarify, what Phillip Cary calls "Augustine's Rule," that all *ad extra* operations of the Godhead are undivided.[110] It also recognizes that true divine unity must involve the persons of the Godhead as such. By understanding them to be involved in asymmetrical and reciprocal relations of personal dependence and identification, it seeks to express that even in the aspect of persons, in which God is truly three, there is unity in diversity.

However, divine simplicity, at least as it is sometimes understood, is a tenet of trinitarian doctrine which this position rejects. It rejects simplicity as it is understood by Aquinas, that God, as "absolute being" must be "absolutely simple."[111] Part of what Aquinas means by simplicity

---

110. Cary, "Classical Trinitarianism," 372. For a full treatment of this, see pp. 45–47 above.

111. Aquinas, *Summa Theologiae* 1a.3.7.

is that each divine person is identical with the divine essence.[112] This is a problem for several reasons, the most important of which is that it makes person essence, it makes person impersonal. Plantinga has pointed out the difficulty with greater precision:

> If God is identical with each of his properties, then . . . he is a property. . . . This view is subject to a difficulty both obvious and overwhelming. No property could have created the world; no property could be omniscient, or, indeed, know anything at all. If God is a property, then he isn't a person but a mere abstract object . . . So taken, the simplicity doctrine seems an utter mistake.[113]

It is this mistake, of making the persons of God identical with an impersonal reality, which this position attempts to avoid. The persons of God fully possess their single shared nature. They have no other nature, and no one else possesses the nature which they possess. Yet none of the divine persons is in any sense identical with any of the others, nor is any person identical with the divine essence.

Are there any harmful consequences with rejecting simplicity? Nash denies that there are. He writes, "It would appear that Christian theologians have no good reason to affirm the doctrine of divine simplicity. It seems doubtful that the doctrine adds anything significant to our understanding of God."[114] It is possible to understand God to be genuinely one without erasing all distinctions, actual and conceptual, from that unity.

Theological Difficulties?

The first chapter presented two major theological criteria for an adequate understanding of the divine unity. First, it must embrace the biblical picture of a God who is a single creator with one, unshared glory who nevertheless genuinely manifests himself as Father, Son, and Holy Spirit. Second, it must provide some location for the divine attributes which allows each person of the Trinity to have them. Does this position meet these criteria?

112. Ibid., 1a.27 (BF 6:5–24).

113. Plantinga, *Does God Have a Nature?* 47. While Norman Geisler attempts to rebut this attack on Aquinas, he seems to do so at the expense of the heart of Aquinas's position of "absolute simplicity." See Geisler, *Systematic Theology*, 2:51–53. Geisler, for example, compares God's attributes to a stone's which, while several, are properly predicated of a single stone, and emphasizes the analogous nature of Aquinas's language.

114. Nash, *Concept of God*, 95.

It appears to meet both quite well. Because God has one nature, and is therefore one creative power, it is proper to recognize only one creator to the universe, and one who ought to be glorified. Because God is three genuine persons, distinct centers of consciousness and volition, the New Testament picture of God, the Father, Son, and Spirit, and the Old Testament hints of multiplicity in God both accurately present the divine reality. Yet because these three persons have perfect and eternal relationships, in which the Father serves as Father, they are able to speak with a single voice throughout history, though they are in fact three.

There is, however, another theological concern which some might raise. It is the concern of Rahner, that if the persons of God, and particularly the Father, are not identical with the divine nature, the result is a quaternity.[115] Since this position denies that each or any member of the Trinity is identical with the divine nature, it appears to posit four distinct realities in God. While this concern was briefly addressed earlier, it merits further attention here.

It is difficult to rebut the charge of a quaternity in part because there is no clear definition of what must be avoided. There are obviously four elements in the traditional formula, "three persons in one essence." What construals of that formula qualify as heretical?

It may be that rejecting simplicity necessarily makes an understanding of the Trinity a quaternity. If the Father, Son, and Spirit are not identical to their own essence, then their essence is something distinct from them on which they depend. However, it has been shown that simplicity, if it erases the distinction between the Father and his nature, must be rejected. The Father is a person and his nature is not. The nature of God cannot be the same thing as the person of the Father, the person of the Son, or the person of the Spirit. It is, necessarily, a fourth in God.

This does not make it, however, another God, or the source of the Trinity. The Father eternally possesses his nature in a relationship of eternal simultaneity. When he eternally begets and spirates the Son and Spirit, he bequeaths to them full possession of the divine nature. The divine nature begets nothing, produces nothing, and chooses nothing. It is the faculty eternally possessed by each divine person by which they act as one God. It is their nature, a given which is beyond their ability to alter and which grounds their personal existence.

---

115. Rahner, *Trinity*, 70. See pp. 49–50 above.

While some may suggest that this limits God, it does so in a biblical fashion. There are things God cannot do. He cannot be tempted with evil, cannot lie, and cannot deny himself.[116] Certainly, these assertions would be meaningless if God could change what they are. In addition, as the examination of Zizoiulas showed, suggesting that God's nature is somehow created or chosen by one of the divine persons presents insuperable difficulties.[117] So, the only option which appears to remain is the one presented, that the nature of God is an impersonal reality conceptually distinct from the divine persons which grounds their personal existence and by which they possess the divine attributes. If someone should worship this nature, or call it God, he implicitly is worshiping the persons who possess it, and calling them, individually and collectively, God.

Christological Difficulties?

If there is a standard for Christological orthodoxy, it is the defined by the Council of Chalcedon. The findings of that council, interpreted in light of the writings of Cyril of Alexandria and *The Tome of Leo*, indicate that a proper Christology must allow for God the Son to be the only person in Christ, the person who, in Christ, takes unto himself the fulness of a human nature which nevertheless is not mixed or fused with his divine nature.[118]

This understanding of the unity of the Trinity and the ontological distinction it contains between person and nature both support a Chalcedonian understanding of Jesus Christ. Because the person of the Son is a genuine center of consciousness distinct from the Father and the Spirit, he is able to be Jesus, to make decisions, to choose obedience, and to interact personally with the Father and the Spirit. Because that person is not identical with the divine essence, but instead possesses it "at a distance," he is able to fully possess a human nature without the human and divine natures being merged, fused, or damaged. Because person is not nature, or an aspect of nature, one can see the Son as the only person in Christ without lapsing into Apollinarianism. The Son takes on a complete human nature, but that is not, and does not include, a distinct human person. Because the attributes of God are faculties that he has, rather than

116. James 1:13, Tit 1:2, 2 Tim 2:13.

117. See pp. 119, 121–27 above.

118. For more discussion, pp. 30–33 above.

properties that define who he is, Jesus can experience weariness, hunger, and even ignorance without ceasing to be God. This understanding of the Trinity provides considerable resources for those who seek to defend a Chalcedonian understanding of Christ.

Conclusion

The proposed position, that God is one in both the shared possession of the one divine essence by the three divine persons and the interpersonal relations of dependence and identification, meets the criteria originally proposed for a successful evangelical doctrine of the Trinity. It is consonant with history, recognizing the importance of both the singular divine essence and the monarchy of the Father to a proper understanding of trinitarian unity. It accords with a theology that is biblical, a theology which recognizes the core of monotheism running through both Testaments while embracing the trinitarian diversity clear in the New Testament. Finally, it provides no obstacles for a proper understanding of the Incarnation.

CONCLUDING THOUGHTS

I must admit that I feel a compulsion after presuming to criticize my theological betters, to clarify and adjust tradition, and to speak boldly regarding the eternal reality of the Almighty God, a compulsion to appeal to mystery, to step back from or minimize the declarations I have made. The compulsion is not external; the days are long past when a heretic might seek to save himself from the flames by recanting. Yet the Trinity, as Rahner is clear to point out, is a mystery, and to speak confidently regarding the mystery is a precarious undertaking.

However, upon reflection, that compulsion fades. It fades because God is real, and is truly Trinity. It fades because God has made me in his image, as his child, to know him. These truths force me to reject the position that true knowledge of the Trinity is impossible, or that it must be severely limited. This is not to suggest that what is contained in this text is the entire truth about the Trinity. Instead, one might view this like Newtonian Physics; it is true enough for the time being.

God is three divine persons, three centers of choice and consciousness who eternally and perfectly love and fellowship with one another. These three persons possess a numerically singular essence, which provides a basis for their personal reality and divine attributes. While one person is the source of the other two, and while all three persons are genuinely different, genuinely other, none of them is more important than another, more divine than another, or more of a person than another. Each person possesses the same source of moral attributes, but because each person is different, the moral responsibilities of each person can differ in the economy and eternity.

This social understanding of the Trinity is not modeled on human society, though it could serve as a model for a proper human society. The different identities and divinely ordained relationships amongst human persons have implications for human behavior. Not all human persons are the same, though they have a common human nature. On the other hand, love and relationships are not prevented by significant personal differences.

If divine persons are in a sense limited in what they can do by the capabilities of the divine nature, how much more is that true of humans. Attempts to ignore the essential limitations of human beings are certain to have disastrous consequences. On the other hand, attempts to understand human beings solely in impersonal, mechanistic terms are likewise doomed to failure. Humans, like God, appear to be persons with natures, centers of volition and consciousness with access to certain, given faculties.

To sum up, this understanding of the unity of the Trinity serves both to illumine the doctrine of God and to illumine the facts of human life. It meets criteria posed for a doctrine of the unity of the Trinity, avoids the pitfalls of several recent doctrines of the Trinity, and does justice to the biblical picture of One God who is Father, Son, and Spirit. It is eternal life to know them.

Bibliography

Adams, Nicholas. "Eschatology Sacred and Profane: The Effects of Philosophy on Theology in Pannenberg, Rahner and Moltmann." *International Journal of Systematic Theology* 2 (2000) 283–306.

Albright, Carol Rausch, and Joel Haugen, editors. *Beginning with the End: God, Science, and Wolfhart Pannenberg*. Chicago: Open Court, 1997.

Anselm. *Anselm of Canterbury: The Major Works*. Edited and introduced by Brian Davies and G. R. Evans. Oxford: Oxford University Press, 1998.

The Ante-Nicene Fathers. Edited by Alexander Roberts and James Donaldson. 10 vols. 1885–1887. Reprint, Peabody, MA: Hendrickson, 1994.

Aquinas, Thomas. *St. Thomas Aquinas: Philosophical Texts*. Translated by Thomas Gilby. Durham, NC: Labyrinth, 1982.

———. *Summa Theologiae*. 60 vols. Blackfriars. New York: McGraw Hill, 1964–1966.

Aristotle. *The Complete Works of Aristotle: The Revised Oxford Translation*. Edited by Jonathan Barnes. 2 vols. Bollingen Series 71. Princeton: Princeton University Press, 1984.

Badcock, Gary D. *Light of Truth and Fire of Love*. Grand Rapids: Eerdmans, 1997.

Barnard, Leslie W. *Justin Martyr: His Life and Thought*. London: Cambridge University Press, 1967.

Bartel, Timothy W. "The Plight of the Relative Trinitarian." *Religious Studies* 24 (1988) 129–55.

Barth, Karl. *Church Dogmatics*. Vol. 1/1, *The Doctrine of the Word of God*. Translated by G. W. Bromiley. Edinburgh: T. & T. Clark, 1975.

Bauckham, Richard. *God Crucified: Monotheism and Christology in the New Testament*. Grand Rapids: Eerdmans, 1998.

Behr, John. *The Formation of Christian Theology*. Vol. 1, *The Way to Nicaea*. Crestwood: St. Vladimir's Seminary Press, 2001.

Berkhof, Hendrikus. *Christian Faith: An Introduction to the Study of the Faith*. Translated by Sierd Woudstra. Grand Rapids: Eerdmans, 1979.

Bettenson, Henry, editor. *Documents of the Christian Church*. 2nd ed. New York: Oxford University Press, 1963.

Bilezikian, Gilbert. "Hermeneutical Bungee-Jumping: Subordination in the Godhead." *Journal of the Evangelical Theological Society* 40 (1997) 57–68.

Bloesch, Donald G. *Essentials of Evangelical Theology*. 2 vols. San Francisco: Harper & Row, 1978.

———. *Jesus Christ: Savior & Lord*. Christian Foundations. Downers Grove, IL: InterVarsity, 1997.

Bocheński, I. M. *A History of Formal Logic*. Translated and edited by Ivo Thomas. Notre Dame, IN: University of Notre Dame Press, 1961.

Boff, Leonardo. *Trinity and Society*. Translated by Paul Burns. Theology and Liberation Series. Reprint, Eugene, OR: Wipf & Stock, 2005.

Boutwell, W. Stacy. "The Eschatology of Wolfhart Pannenberg." *Southwestern Journal of Theology* 36.2 (1994) 25–26.

Boyd, Gregory A. *Trinity and Process: A Critical Evaluation and Reconstruction of Hartshorne's Di-polar Theism towards a Trinitarian Metaphysics*. American University Studies. Series 7, Theology and Religion 119. New York: Lang, 1992.

Braaten, Carl E. "The Trinity Today." *Dialog* 26 (1987) 245–49.

———. "The Triune God: The Source and Model of Christian Unity and Mission." *Missiology* 18 (1990) 415–27.

Braaten, Carl E., and Philip Clayton, editors. *The Theology of Wolfhart Pannenberg: Twelve American Critiques, with an Autobiographical Essay and Response*. Minneapolis, MN: Augsburg, 1988.

Bracken, Joseph A. "The Holy Trinity as a Community of Divine Persons, I." *The Heythrop Journal* 15 (1974) 166–82.

———. "The Holy Trinity as a Community of Divine Persons, II." *The Heythrop Journal* 15 (1974) 257–70.

———. *What Are They Saying About the Trinity?* New York: Paulist, 1979.

Brändle, Werner. "Immanente Trinität—Ein 'Denkmal der Kirchengeschichte': Überlegungen zu Karl Rahners Trinitätslehre." *Kerygma und Dogma* 38 (1992) 185–98.

Bray, Gerald. *The Doctrine of God*. Contours of Christian Theology. Downers Grove, IL: InterVarsity, 1993.

Bromiley, Geoffrey W. *Historical Theology: An Introduction*. 1978. Reprint, Edinburgh: T. & T. Clark, 1994.

Brown, Colin. "Trinity and Incarnation: In Search of Contemporary Orthodoxy." *Ex Auditu* 7 (1991) 83–100.

Brown, Raymond E. *The Birth of the Messiah: A Commentary on the Infancy Narratives in Matthew and Luke*. Garden City, NY: Doubleday, 1977.

Buckley, James J. Review of *Systematic Theology*, vol. 2, by Wolfhart Pannenberg. *Pro Ecclesia* 4 (1995) 364–69.

Burhenn, Herbert. "Pannenberg's Doctrine of God." *Scottish Journal of Theology* 28 (1975) 535–49.

Cary, Phillip. "On Behalf of Classical Trinitarianism: A Critique of Rahner on the Trinity." *The Thomist* 56 (1992) 365–405.

Case, Jonathan P. Review of *God in Three Persons: A Contemporary Interpretation of the Doctrine of the Trinity*, by Millard J. Erickson. *Dialog* 35 (1996) 234–37.

Calvin, John. *Institutes of the Christian Religion*. Edited by John T. McNeill. Translated by Ford Lewis Battles. Library of Christian Classics 20–21. Louisville: Westminster John Knox, 1960.

Chadwick, Henry. *Early Christian Thought and the Classical Tradition: Studies in Justin, Clement, and Origen*. New York: Oxford University Press, 1984.

Charnock, Stephen. *The Existence and Attributes of God*. Grand Rapids: Baker, 1996.

Childs, James M., Jr. "The Significance of Wolfhart Pannenberg for Contemporary Theology." *Trinity Seminary Review* 13.2 (1991) 61–68.

Clark, Gordon H. *The Trinity*. 2nd ed. Jefferson, MD: Trinity Foundation, 1990.

Cobb, John B., Jr. "Reply to Jürgen Moltmann's 'The Unity of the Triune God.'" *St. Vladimir's Theological Quarterly* 28.3 (1984) 173–77.

Bibliography

Coffey, David. "The 'Incarnation' of the Holy Spirit in Christ." *Theological Studies* 45 (1984) 466–80.

———. "A Proper Mission of the Holy Spirit." *Theological Studies* 47 (1992) 227–50.

Collins, Paul M. *Trinitarian Theology: West and East: Karl Barth, the Cappadocian Fathers, and John Zizioulas.* Oxford: Oxford University Press, 2001.

Congar, Yves. *I Believe in the Holy Spirit.* Translated by David Smith. New York: Crossroad, 1997.

Craig, William Lane. *The Only Wise God: The Compatibility of Divine Foreknowledge and Human Freedom.* Eugene, OR: Wipf & Stock, 1999.

Crouzel, Henri. *Origen.* Translated by A. S. Worrell. San Francisco: Harper & Row, 1989.

Cyril of Alexandria. *Letters 1–50.* Translated by John I. McEnerny. Washington, DC: Catholic University of America Press, 1987.

de Letter, Prudent. "The Theology of God's Self-gift." *Theological Studies* 24 (1963) 402–22.

Denzinger Heinrich, editor and translator. *Enchiridion Symbolorum Definitionum et Declarationum de Rebus Fidei et Morum.* 34th ed. Freiburg: Herder, 1988.

Dibelius, Martin. *Jungfrauensohn und Krippenkind: Untersuchungen zur Geburts-geschichte Jesu im Lukas-evangelium.* Heidelberg: Winter, 1932.

Douglas, J. D., editor. *Let the Earth Hear His Voice.* Minneapolis: World Wide, 1975.

Dorner, Isaak August. *Divine Immutability: A Critical Reconsideration,* translator Robert R. Williams and Claude Welch. Minneapolis: Fortress, 1994.

Doud, Robert E. "Rahner's Christology: A Whiteheadian Critique." *Journal of Religion* 57 (1977) 144–55.

Elwell, Walter A., editor. *Evangelical Dictionary of Theology.* Grand Rapids: Baker, 1984.

Erickson, Millard J. *Christian Theology.* 2nd ed. Grand Rapids: Baker, 2000.

———. "Evangelical Christology and Soteriology Today." *Interpretation* 49 (1995) 255–66.

———. *The Evangelical Left: Encountering Postconservative Evangelical Theology.* Grand Rapids: Baker, 1997.

———. *The Evangelical Mind and Heart: Perspectives on Theological and Practical Issues.* Grand Rapids: Baker, 1993.

———. *God in Three Persons: A Contemporary Interpretation of the Trinity.* Grand Rapids: Baker, 1995.

———. *God the Father Almighty: A Contemporary Exploration of the Divine Attributes.* Grand Rapids: Baker, 1998.

———. *Making Sense of the Trinity: Three Crucial Questions.* Grand Rapids: Baker, 2000.

———. *The New Evangelical Theology.* Westwood, NJ: Revell, 1968.

———. *Postmodernizing the Faith: Evangelical Responses to the Challenge of Postmodernism.* Grand Rapids: Baker, 1998.

———. *The Word Became Flesh: A Contemporary Incarnational Christology.* Grand Rapids: Baker, 1995.

Feenstra, Ronald J., and Cornelius Plantinga, Jr., editors. *Library of Religious Philosophy.* Vol. 1, *Trinity, Incarnation, and Atonement: Philosophical and Theological Essays.* Notre Dame, IN: University of Notre Dame Press, 1989.

Fermer, Richard M. "The Limits of Trinitarian Theology as a Methodological Paradigm: 'Between the Trinity and Hell There Lies No Other Choice.'" *Neue Zeitschrift für Systematische Theologie und Religionsphilosophie* 41 (1999) 158–86.

Fiorenza, Francis Schüssler. Review of *Systematic Theology*, vol. 1, by Wolfhart Pannenberg. *Pro Ecclesia* 2 (1993) 231–39.

Fox, Patricia A. *God as Communion: John Zizioulas, Elizabeth Johnson, and the Retrieval of the Symbol of the Triune God*. Collegeville, MN: Liturgical, 2001.

Garrett, James Leo, Jr. Review of *God in Three Persons: A Contemporary Interpretation of the Doctrine of the Trinity*, by Millard J. Erickson. *Southwestern Journal of Theology* 40.3 (1998) 78–80.

Geach, Peter Thomas. *Reference and Generality: Some Medieval and Modern Theories*. Emended ed. Ithaca: Cornell University Press, 1970.

Geisler, Norman L. "Beware of Philosophy: A Warning to Biblical Scholars." *Journal of the Evangelical Theological Society* 42 (1999) 3–19.

———. *Systematic Theology*. 4 vols. Minneapolis: Bethany, 2003.

Gelpi, Donald L. *Life and Light: A Guide to the Theology of Karl Rahner*. New York: Sheed & Ward, 1966.

Gilkey, Langdon. *Reaping the Whirlwind: A Christian Interpretation of History*. New York: Seabury, 1976.

González, Justo L., *The Story of Christianity*. Vol. 1, *The Early Church to the Dawn of the Reformation*. San Francisco: HarperCollins, 1984.

Grenz, Stanley J. "Pannenberg and Evangelical Theology: Sympathy and Caution." *Christian Scholar's Review* 20 (1990) 272–85.

———. *Reason for Hope: The Systematic Theology of Wolfhart Pannenberg*. New York: Oxford University Press, 1990.

———. "'Scientific' Theology/'Theological' Science: Pannenberg and the Dialogue Between Theology and Science." *Zygon* 34 (1999) 159–66.

Grenz, Stanley J., and Roger E. Olson. *20th Century Theology: God & the World in a Transitional Age*. Downers Grove, IL: InterVarsity, 1992.

Gresham, John L., Jr. "The Social Model of the Trinity and Its Critics." *Scottish Journal of Theology* 46 (1993) 325–43.

Grillmeier, Aloys. *Christ in Christian Tradition*. Vol. 1, *From the Apostolic Age to Chalcedon (451)*. 2nd ed. Translated by John Bowden. Atlanta: John Knox, 1975.

Gunton, Colin E. "Augustine, The Trinity and the Theological Crisis of the West." *Scottish Journal of Theology* 43 (1990) 33–58.

———. *The Promise of Trinitarian Theology*, 2nd ed. Edinburgh: T. & T. Clark, 1997.

———. *Yesterday & Today: A Study of Continuities in Christology*. Grand Rapids: Eerdmans, 1983.

Gutenson, Chuck. "Father, Son and Holy Spirit—The One God: An Exploration of the Trinitarian Doctrine of Wolfhart Pannenberg." *Asbury Theological Journal* 49 (1994) 5–21.

Hagner, Donald A. *Matthew 14–28*. Word Biblical Commentary 33B. Dallas: Word, 1995.

Halsey, Jim S. "History, Language, and Hermeneutic: The Synthesis of Wolfhart Pannenberg." *Westminster Theological Journal* 41 (1979) 269–90.

Hanson, R. P. C. *The Search for the Christian Doctrine of God: The Arian Controversy 318–381*. Edinburgh: T. & T. Clark, 1988.

Harrison, Nonna Verna. "Zizioulas on Communion and Otherness." *Saint Vladimir's Theological Quarterly* 42. 3–4 (1998) 273–300.

Havrilak, Gregory. "Karl Rahner and the Greek Trinity." *St. Vladimir's Theological Quarterly* 34 (1990) 61–77.

Henry, Carl F. H. *God, Revelation and Authority*. 6 vols. Waco: Word, 1982.

Bibliography

Hill, William J. "The Historicity of God." *Theological Studies* 45 (1984) 320–33.

—————. *The Three-Personed God: The Trinity as the Mystery of Salvation.* Washington, DC: Catholic University of America Press, 1982.

—————. "Uncreated Grace—A Critique of Karl Rahner." *Thomist* 27 (1963) 333–56.

Hodgson, Leonard. *The Doctrine of the Trinity: Croall Lectures 1942–1943.* 1943. Reprint, London: Nisbet, 1951.

—————. *Towards a Christian Philosophy.* London: Nisbet, 1946.

Hopko, Thomas. "The Trinity in the Cappadocians." In *Christian Spirituality: Origins to the Twelfth Century.* New York: Crossroad, 1985.

Horrell, J. Scott. "Toward a Biblical Model of the Social Trinity: Avoiding Equivocation of Nature and Order." *Journal of the Evangelical Society* 47 (2004) 399–421.

Hume, David. *A Treatise of Human Nature.* Edited by L. A. Selby-Bigge. 1888. Reprint, Oxford: Clarendon, 1951.

Jammer, Max. *Concepts of Force: A Study in the Foundations of Dynamics.* Cambridge: Harvard University Press, 1957.

Jenson, Robert W. "Three Identities of One Action." *Scottish Journal of Theology* 28 (1975) 1–15.

—————. *The Triune Identity: God According to the Gospel.* Philadelphia: Fortress Press, 1982.

John of Damascus. *St. John of Damascus: Writings.* Vol. 37, *The Fathers of the Church: A New Translation.* Translated by Frederic H. Chase, Jr. New York: Fathers of the Church, 1958.

Kaiser, Christopher B. *The Doctrine of God: An Historical Survey.* Foundations for Faith, ed. Peter Toon. Westchester, IL: Crossway, 1982.

Kannengiesser, Charles. *Arius and Athanasius: Two Alexandrian Theologians.* Hampshire: Variorum, 1991.

Kant, Immanuel. *Critique of Pure Reason.* Translated and edited by Paul Guyer and Allen W. Wood. Cambridge: Cambridge University Press, 2000.

Kärkkäinen, Veli-Matti. *The Doctrine of God: A Global Introduction.* Grand Rapids: Baker, 2004.

—————. "Spirit, Church and Christ: An Ecumenical Inquiry into a Pneumatological Ecclesiology." *One in Christ* 36 (2000) 338–53.

—————. *The Trinity: Global Perspectives.* Louisville: Westminster John Knox, 2007.

Kelly, J. N. D. *Early Christian Doctrines.* 5th ed. London: Adam & Charles Black, 1977.

König, Andrio. *Here Am I! A Christian Reflection on God.* Grand Rapids: Eerdmans, 1982.

Kovach, Stephen D. and Peter R. Schemm, Jr. "A Defense of the Doctrine of the Eternal Subordination of the Son." *Journal of the Evangelical Theological Society* 42 (1999) 461–76.

LaCugna, Catherine Mowry. "Philosophers and Theologians on the Trinity." *Modern Theology* 2 (1986) 169–81.

Laird, John. *Problems of the Self: An Essay Based on the Shaw Lectures Given in the University of Edinburgh, March 1914.* London: Macmillan, 1917.

Leibniz, G. W. *Discourse on Metaphysics, Correspondence with Arnauld, and Monadology.* Translated by George R. Montgomery. With an introduction by Paul Janet. La Salle, IL: Open Court, 1962.

—————. *The Monadology and Other Philosophical Writings.* Translated and introduced by Robert Latta. London: Oxford University Press, 1951.

Leithart, Peter J. "'Framing' Sacramental Theology: Trinity and Symbol." *Westminster Theological Journal* 62.1 (2000) 1–16.

Letham, Roberth. *The Holy Trinity*. Phillipsburg: Presbyterian & Reformed, 2004.

Lewis, Gordon R. and Bruce A. Demarest. *Integrative Theology*. 2 vols. Grand Rapids: Academie, 1987–1990.

Locke, John. *An Essay Concerning Human Understanding*. Edited and introduced by Peter H. Nidditch. New York: Oxford University Press, 1975.

MacArthur, John, Jr. *Matthew 24—28*. The MacArthur New Testament Commentary. Chicago: Moody, 1989.

Macleod, Donald. "The Christology of Wolfhart Pannenberg." *Themelios* 25.2 (2000) 19–41.

Martinich, A. P. "Identity and Trinity." *Journal of Religion* 58 (1978) 169–81.

Mattes, Mark C. "Pannenberg's Achievement: An Analysis and Assessment of His *Systematic Theology*." *Currents in Theology and Mission* 26.1 (1999) 51–60.

McCulloh, Gerald W. "Creation to Consummation: The Theology of Wolfhart Pannenberg." *Anglican Theological Review* 83 (2001) 115–28.

McGrath, Alister E. *Understanding the Trinity*. Grand Rapids: Zondervan, 1988.

Molnar, Paul D. "Toward a Contemporary Doctrine of the Immanent Trinity: Karl Barth and the Present Discussion." *Scottish Journal of Theology* 49 (1996) 311–57.

Moltmann, Jürgen. *History and the Triune God: Contributions to Trinitarian Theology*. Translated by John Bowden. New York: Crossroad, 1992.

———. *The Spirit of Life: A Universal Affirmation*. Translated by Margaret Kohl. Minneapolis: Fortress, 1992.

———. *The Trinity and the Kingdom of God: The Doctrine of God*. Translated by Margaret Kohl. San Francisco: Harper & Row, 1981.

———. "The Unity of the Triune God." *St. Vladimir's Theological Quarterly* 28 (1984) 157–71.

Moreland, J. P. *Scaling the Secular City: A Defense of Christianity*. Grand Rapids: Baker, 1987.

Morris, Thomas V. *Our Idea of God: An Introduction to Philosophical Theology*. Downers Grove, IL: InterVarsity, 1991.

Murdock, William R. "History and Revelation in Jewish Apocalypticism." *Interpretation* 21 (1967) 167–87.

Musser, Donald W., and Joseph L. Price, editors. *A New Handbook of Christian Theology*. Nashville: Abingdon, 1992.

Nash, Ronald H. *The Concept of God*. Grand Rapids: Zondervan, 1983.

The Nicene and Post-Nicene Fathers, Series 1. Edited by Philip Schaff. 14 vols. 1886–1889. Reprint, Peabody, MA: Hendrickson, 1994.

The Nicene and Post-Nicene Fathers, Series 2. Edited by Philip Schaff and Henry Wace. 14 vols. 1890–1898. Reprint, Peabody, MA: Hendrickson, 1999.

Norris, Richard A., translator and editor. *The Christological Controversy*. Sources of Early Christian Thought. Philadelphia: Fortress, 1980.

O'Carroll, Michael. *Trinitas: A Theological Encyclopedia of the Holy Trinity*. Wilmington, DE: Glazier, 1987.

Olive, Don H. *Wolfhart Pannenberg*. Makers of the Modern Theological Mind. Waco: Word, 1975.

Olson, Roger E. "Wolfhart Pannenberg's Doctrine of the Trinity." *Scottish Journal of Theology* 43 (1990) 175–206.

Olson, Roger E., and Christopher Hall. *The Trinity*. Grand Rapids: Eerdmans, 2002.

Patrologia Graecae. Edited by J. P. Migne. 162 vols. Paris, 1857–1886.

Pannenberg, Wolfhart. *Basic Questions in Theology*. 2 vols. Translated by George H. Kehm. Philadelphia: Fortress, 1971.

———. "The Christian Vision of God: The New Discussion of the Trinitarian Doctrine." *Trinity Seminary Review* 13.2 (1991) 53–60.

———. "God as Spirit—and Natural Science." *Zygon* 36 (2001) 783–97.

———. *The Idea of God and Human Freedom*. Translated by R. A. Wilson. Philadelphia: Westminster, 1973.

———. *Jesus—God and Man*. Translated by Lewis L. Wilkins and Duane A. Priebe. Philadelphia: Westminster, 1968.

———. *Metaphysics and the Idea of God*. Translated by Philip Clayton. Grand Rapids: Eerdmans, 1990.

———. "The Nature of a Theological Statement." *Zygon* 7 (1972) 6–19.

———, editor. *Offenbarung als Geschichte*. Göttingen: Vandenhoeck & Ruprecht, 1961.

———. "Problems of a Trinitarian Doctrine of God." Translated by Philip Clayton. *Dialog* 26 (1987) 250–57.

———. *Systematic Theology*. 3 vols. Translated by Geoffrey Bromiley. Grand Rapids: Eerdmans, 1991.

———. *Theology and the Kingdom of God*. Philadelphia: Westminster, 1969.

———. *Theology and the Philosophy of Science*. Translated by Francis McDonagh. Philadelphia: Westminster, 1976.

———. "Theta Phi Talkback Session with Wolfhart Pannenberg." *Asbury Theological Journal* 46.2 (1991) 37–41.

Papanikolaou, Aristotle. "Divine Energies or Divine Personhood: Vladimir Lossky and John Zizioulas on Conceiving the Transcendent and Immanent God." *Modern Theology* 19 (2003) 357–85.

Pasquariello, Ronald D. "Pannenberg's Philosophical Foundations." *Journal of Religion* 56 (1976) 338–47.

Peters, Ted. *God as Trinity: Relationality and Temporality in Divine Life*. Louisville: Westminster John Knox, 1993.

———. "Trinity Talk: Part 1." *Dialog* 26 (1987) 44–48.

Peterson, Gregory R. "Where Do We Go from Here?" *Zygon* 34 (1999) 139–49.

Pinnock, Clark. "Systematic Theology." In *The Openness of God: A Biblical Challenge to the Traditional Understanding of God*. Downers Grove, IL: Intervarsity, 1994.

Plantinga, Alvin. *Does God Have a Nature?* Milwaukee: Marquette University Press, 1980.

Plato. *Plato: Complete Works*. Edited and introduced by John M. Cooper. Indianapolis: Hackett, 1997.

Polkinghorne, John. *Belief in God in an Age of Science*. New Haven: Yale University Press, 1998.

———. *The Faith of a Physicist*. Princeton: Princeton University Press, 1994.

———. "Fields and Theology: A Response to Wolfhart Pannenberg." *Zygon* 36 (2001) 795–97.

———. *Reason and Reality: The Relationship Between Science and Theology*. Philadelphia: Trinity, 1991.

———. *Science and the Trinity: The Christian Encounter with Reality*. New Haven: Yale University Press, 2004.

Bibliography

———. "Wolfhart Pannenberg's Engagement with the Natural Sciences." *Zygon* 34 (1999) 151–58.

Porter, Lawrence B. "On Keeping 'Persons' in the Trinity: A Linguistic Approach to Trinitarian Thought." *Theological Studies* 41 (1980) 530–48.

Prestige, George Leonard. *St. Basil the Great and Apollinaris of Laodicea.* London: SPCK, 1956.

Rahner, Karl. *Faith in a Wintry Season: Conversations and Interviews with Karl Rahner in the Last Years of His Life.* Edited by Paul Imhof and Hubert Biallowons. Translation edited by Harvey D. Egan. New York: Crossroad, 1990.

———. *Foundations of Christian Faith: An Introduction to the Idea of Christianity.* Translated by William V. Dych. New York: Seabury, 1978.

———. *Grace in Freedom.* Translated by Hilda Graef. New York: Herder & Herder, 1969.

———. *Hearers of the Word.* Revised by J. E. Metz. Translated by Michael Richards. New York: Herder & Herder, 1969.

———. *Karl Rahner: Theologian of the Graced Search for Meaning.* The Making of Modern Theology. Edited and introduction by Geffrey B. Kelly. Minneapolis: Fortress, 1992.

———. *Theological Investigations.* 21 vols. Baltimore: Helicon, 1966.

———. *The Trinity.* Translated by Joseph Donceel. With an introduction by Catherine Mowry LaCugna. New York: Crossroad, 1997.

———. "Trinity, Divine." In *Sacramentum Mundi: An Encyclopedia of Theology.* Vol. 6, *Scandal to Zionism,* ed. Karl Rahner et al. New York: Herder & Herder, 1969.

Rahner, Karl, and Karl-Heinz Weger. *Our Christian Faith: Answers for the Future.* Translated by Francis McDonagh. New York: Crossroad, 1981.

Rahner, Karl, and Karl Lehmann. *Kerygma and Dogma.* Edited by Thomas F. O'Meara. Translated by William Glen-Doepel. New York: Herder & Herder, 1969.

Rahner, Karl, and Wilhelm Thüsing. *A New Christology.* New York: Seabury, 1980.

Rice, Richard. "Wolfhart Pannenberg's Crowning Achievement: A Review of His Systematic Theology." *Andrews University Seminary Studies* 37 (1999) 55–72.

Richard of St. Victor. *Richard of St. Victor: The Twelve Patriarchs, The Mystical Ark, Book Three of the Trinity.* Translated by Grover A. Zinn. New York: Paulist, 1979.

Richardson, Cyril C. *The Doctrine of the Trinity.* Nashville: Abingdon, 1958.

Roberts, Louis. *The Achievement of Karl Rahner.* New York: Herder & Herder, 1967.

Robertson, Lindsay. "Wolfhart Pannenberg: Spirit of Life, Spirit of God." *Hill Road* 4 (2001) 35–55.

Sailhamer, John H. *The Pentateuch as Narrative: A Biblical-Theological Commentary.* Grand Rapids: Zondervan, 1992.

Schaff, Philip, editor. *The Creeds of Christendom.* Vol. 1, *The History of Creeds.* Revised by David S. Schaff. 1931. Reprint, Grand Rapids: Baker, 1993.

Scharlemann, Robert P. *The Being of God: Theology and the Experience of Truth.* New York: Seabury, 1981.

Schwöbel, Christoph, editor. *Persons, Divine and Human.* Edinburgh: T. & T. Clark, 1991.

———. "Rational Theology in Trinitarian Perspective: Wolfhart Pannenberg's Systematic Theology." *Journal of Theological Studies* 47 (1996) 498–527.

Shults, F. LeRon. "Constitutive Relationality in Anthropology and Trinity: The Shaping of the *Imago Dei* Doctrine in Barth and Pannenberg." *Neue Zeitschrift für Systematische Theologie und Religionsphilosophie* 39 (1997) 304–22.

Stead, Christopher. *Divine Substance.* Oxford: Clarendon, 1977.

Bibliography

———. *Philosophy in Christian Antiquity.* Cambridge: Cambridge University Press, 1994. Reprint, Cambridge: Cambridge University Press, 1995.

Strong, Augustus Hopkins. *Systematic Theology: A Compendium and Commonplace-Book.* Philadelphia: Judson, 1953.

Swinburne, Richard. *The Christian God.* Oxford: Clarendon, 1994.

———. *The Coherence of Theism.* Rev. ed. Oxford: Clarendon, 1993.

———. "Could There be More Than One God?" *Faith and Philosophy* 5 (1988) 225–41.

Taliaferro, Charles. "The Passibility of God," *Religious Studies* 25 (1989) 217–24.

Tavard, George H. Review of *Systematic Theology,* vol. 1, by Wolfhart Pannenberg. *One in Christ* 28 (1992) 387–92.

Thiessen, Henry C. *Lectures in Systematic Theology.* Grand Rapids: Eerdmans, 1979.

Thompson, John. *Modern Trinitarian Perspectives.* New York: Oxford University Press, 1994.

Toon, Peter. *Our Triune God: A Biblical Portrayal of the Trinity.* Vancouver: Regent College Publishing, 1996.

Vanhoozer, Kevin J., editor. *The Trinity in a Pluralistic Age: Theological Essays on Culture and Religion.* Grand Rapids: Eerdmans, 1997.

van Inwagen, Peter. "And Yet They Are Not Three Gods But One God." In *Philosophy and the Christian Faith,* ed. Thomas V. Morris. Notre Dame: University of Notre Dame Press, 1988.

Venema, Cornelius P. "History, Human Freedom and the Idea of God in the Theology of Wolfhart Pannenberg." *Calvin Theological Journal* 17 (1972) 53–77.

Vorgrimler, Herbert. *Understanding Karl Rahner: An Introduction to His Life and Thought.* Translated by John Bowden. New York: Crossroad, 1986.

Wainwright, William J. "Original Sin." In *Philosophy and the Christian Faith,* ed. Thomas V. Morris. Notre Dame: University of Notre Dame Press, 1988.

Warfield, Benjamin Breckinridge. "The Biblical Doctrine of the Trinity." In *Biblical and Theological Studies,* ed. Samuel G. Craig. Philadelphia: Presbyterian & Reformed, 1952.

Webb, Clement C. J. *God and Personality: Being the Gifford Lectures Delivered in the University of Aberdeen in the Years 1918 & 1919.* Library of Philosophy. New York: Macmillan, 1918.

Weger, Karl-Heinz. *Karl Rahner: An Introduction to His Theology.* Translated by David Smith. New York: Seabury, 1980.

Weinandy, Thomas G. *The Father's Spirit of Sonship: Reconceiving the Trinity.* Edinburgh: T. & T. Clark, 1995.

Welch, Claude. *In This Name: The Doctrine of the Trinity in Contemporary Theology.* New York: Scribners, 1952.

White, James R. *The Forgotten Trinity: Recovering the Heart of Christian Belief.* Minneapolis: Bethany, 1998.

Wiles, Maurice. *The Making of Christian Doctrine.* Cambridge: Cambridge University Press, 1967.

Wilks, John G. F. "The Trinitarian Ontology of John Zizioulas." *Vox Evangelica* 25 (1995) 63–88.

Williams, Rowan. *Arius: Heresy and Tradition.* Rev. ed. Grand Rapids: Eerdmans, 2001.

———. Review of *Being as Communion: Studies in Personhood and the Church,* by John Zizioulas. *Scottish Journal of Theology* 42 (1989) 101–5.

Bibliography

Wolfson, Harry Austryn. *The Philosophy of the Church Fathers.* Vol. 1, *Faith, Trinity, Incarnation.* Cambridge: Harvard University Press, 1970.

Wolterstorff, Nicholas. "Suffering Love." In *Philosophy and the Christian Faith*, ed. Thomas V. Morris. Notre Dame: University of Notre Dame Press, 1988.

Yeo, Khiok-Khng. "Christ the End of History and the Hope of the Suffering: Revelation 5 in the Light of Pannenberg's Christology." *Asia Journal of Theology* 8 (1994) 308–34.

Zizioulas, J. D. "Appendix—The Authority of the Bible, D." *Ecumenical Review* 21 (1969) 160–66.

———. "Apostolic Continuity and Orthodox Theology: Towards a Synthesis of Two Perspectives." *Saint Vladimir's Theological Quarterly* 19 (1975) 75–108.

———. *Being as Communion: Studies in Personhood and the Church.* Contemporary Greek Theologians 4. Crestwood: Saint Vladimir's Seminary Press, 1985.

———. "The Church as Communion." *Saint Vladimir's Theological Quarterly* 38 (1994) 3–16.

———. "Communion and Otherness." *Saint Vladimir's Theological Quarterly* 38 (1994) 347–61.

———. "The Development of Conciliar Structures to the Time of the First Ecumenical Council." In *Councils and the Ecumenical Movement.* World Council of Churches Studies 5. Geneva: World Council of Churches, 1968.

———. "Human Capacity and Human Incapacity: A Theological Exploration of Personhood." *Scottish Journal of Theology* 28 (1975) 401–48.

———. "Informal Groups in the Church: An Orthodox Viewpoint." In *Informal Groups in the Church: Papers of the Second Cerdic Colloquium Strasbourg, May 13–15, 1971.* Pittsburgh Theological Monograph Series 7. Pittsburgh: Pickwick, 1975.

———. "The Mystery of the Church in Orthodox Tradition." *One in Christ* 24 (1988) 294–303.

———. "Orthodox-Protestant Bilateral Conversations: Some Comments." In *The Orthodox Church and the Churches of the Reformation: A Survey of Orthodox-Protestant Dialogues.* Faith and Order Paper 76. Geneva: World Council of Churches, 1975.